The Mo...

"AMAZING GRACE"
The Most Sung but Most Disbelieved Song Ever!

D. G. MILES M^CKEE

"Amazing Grace" The Most Sung but Most Disbelieved Song Ever!

Copyright © 2018 by D. G. Miles McKee. All rights reserved.

Published by Miles McKee Ministries

All scripture references are taken from the King James Version of the Bible. The King James Version is in the public domain.

Cover art by Michael Burns

Typesetting and layout by Jon J. Cardwell

ISBN: 978-1073847013

CONTENTS

Introduction	vii
Chapter 1: A Wretch Like Me	1
Chapter 2: Amazing Grace, How Sweet the Sound	17
Chapter 3: Amazing, Saving Grace! He Died for Us	37
Chapter 4: I Once was Lost but Now I´m Found	65
Chapter 5: Grace will Lead Us Home	81
Conclusion and Summary	95
Appendix 1: What Does the Term "World" Mean in Scripture?	101
Appendix 2: "All?"	105
Questionnaire on Grace	111

Introduction

"My memory is nearly gone, but I remember two things, that I am a great sinner, and that Christ is a great Saviour."

John Newton at age 82, shortly before he died

John Newton, the writer of the magnificent hymn, "Amazing Grace," knew what grace meant. Did you ever hear his story about how he had been a former slave trader? They said of him that he could curse for an hour without repeating any of the same expletives. No one could stand his company for long. He became a slave in Africa and, even then, continued his reprobate living. Eventually, God saved him and made him into a fearless gospel minister. In salvation, Newton was shown that grace was undeserved, unmerited and unearned favour freely given by his sovereign Lord. He was made aware that God owed him nothing. He was forced to face the awfulness of his sin and his wretched nature. He was shown by the Holy Spirit that even though God was not obliged to save and forgive him, he had been saved anyway, by God's divine Grace, and he was amazed. He recognised through many dangers, toils and snares that Grace had caused him to endure. He saw that Grace could not fail, and in this knowledge, he boldly declared that grace would bring him home. To Newton, Grace was amazing!

However, in this day and age, diminishing numbers of professed believers really believe that salvation is by amazing grace. They argue, that salvation has its root in the free will of man. In other words, it's a do it yourself kit! If, however, salvation is a do it yourself kit, how then can we be amazed by grace? Indeed, if a man is by his free will responsible for his salvation, or if he becomes a necessary co-worker with God in redemption, then he is not saved by grace. Mind you, he might still sing "Amazing Grace" with gusto, being ignorant of its meaning. Unfortunately, "Amazing Grace" is the most sung, yet most disbelieved, song ever.

In the following pages, we will examine just how amazing grace really is. May the reader be blessed, challenged and helped to see the magnificence of the Lord Jesus Christ. Indeed, may we all conclude that grace really is an amazing gift of God!

And that's the Gospel Truth!

My thanks go to my good friends Alan and Rebecca Smith for their editing skills and valuable suggestions. Thanks also to the group of partners who fund Miles McKee Ministries. Your prayers and support make it possible for us to continue in this ministry.

Thanks also to my wife Gillian for her endless encouragement.

Thanks to Michael Burns for his cover art.

Thanks to my good friend Pastor Jon Cardwell for getting this book ready for press.

CHAPTER ONE
A Wretch Like Me

Amazing Grace, how sweet the sound,
That saved a wretch like me.
I once was lost but now am found,
Was blind, but now I see.

The first verse of this magnificent hymn is laden with offence to non-gospel lovers.[1] First of all, it tells us that we are wretches! Then it tells us we are lost and must be found. Finally, it informs us that we are blind, thus need to be given the gift of spiritual "sight." Blind, Lost, Wretched! Yes, we can sing heartily about it, but how many of us actually believe this?

Michel de Montaigne, the essayist (1533-1592) said, "There is no man so good, who, were he to submit all his thoughts and actions to the laws, would not deserve hanging ten times in his life." He was entirely wrong! He was much too conservative! Our thoughts and actions deserve hanging 10 times per minute and maybe even per second.

Newton nailed it when he stated that we are, by our nature, blind, lost wretches. But, does the Bible agree with that sentiment? Or does the Bible tell us that, "There is some bad in the best of us, and some good in the worst? Does the Bible encourage us to do the best we can, and depend on God to take care of the rest?

Before we look at the scriptures, let me remark that many people find this idea about having a wretched nature quite offensive. Because of this, many pastors refuse to believe its teachings. They refuse to minister on

---

[1] That is, individuals not grasping the nature of grace.

this subject, choosing rather to offer pleasing little stories about how we are getting better and better all the time. Ministers of the gospel, however, have not been sent here to entertain either sheep or goats, but to declare the full counsel of God, not merely those parts which are popular or acceptable.

Still, let's be fair; perhaps the maxim, "There is some bad in the best of us, and some good in the worst" sometimes applies outside of the spiritual realm. But, what does that matter when it comes to having a right standing with the All Holy God? According to the scriptures, salvation is a matter of grace alone (Ephesians 2:8-9).[2] We are saved by grace alone through faith alone in Christ alone. Anyone who embraces this must immediately see that if salvation is by grace alone, then nothing in anyone can save or recommend them to God. Thus, we have the foundation for the doctrine of the "wretched nature" of man, or as grace theologians call it, the Total Inability of Man.

When Newton wrote about the wretched nature, he did not mean that all people are as bad as they can be. Most people aren't! For example, we have strong restraints placed on us by civil law; as a result, we do not sin with reckless abandon. For instance, if we had no rules of the road, the wretched nature would make its appearance among motorists more often than it does. Human nature needs only an opportunity to declare itself for what it is. As the Irish man prayed, "Lead me not into temptation, for I'll get there myself."

Also, by the wretched nature, we do not mean that all men are equally wicked; some, it would seem, are less sinful than others. When we say all people have a

---

[2] Eph 2:8 *For by grace are ye saved through faith; and that not of yourselves: it is the gift of God: Not of works, lest any man should boast.*

wretched nature, we do not mean that they cannot be useful and upright in society. We do not mean that their actions are always wrong, or that they are incapable of kindness, or love, or loyalty.

What we *do* mean by the wretched nature, is that by nature we are dead in trespasses and sins towards God. To change this state of the mind and produce a heart that loves God takes the gracious work of the omnipotent eternal Holy Spirit. Loving and desiring God is not natural to the human condition. In fact, it is just the opposite! Since we are wretches, we require a supernatural act of God's amazing grace to come to the place where we call out for mercy.

Most Christian churches agree that man is, to some extent, a wretch. But they question as to just how much of a wretch he is? That is, is he a thoroughly, dyed-in-the-wool wretch, or only a partial wretch? Was human nature merely injured, or was it completely ruined when Adam and Eve fell?

The following are three contrasting views concerning the wretched nature:

The first position questions the reality of original sin. The British monk Pelagius (AD 354-418) was the great champion of this point. He taught that Adam's sin ruined Adam, but not the whole human race. This teaching gives the individual, by his free will, the ability to opt for the ways of God, or to live a sinful life, devoid of good works. Had Pelagius heard the song Amazing Grace, he certainly would have refused to add it to his repertoire. According to him, every individual starts with a clean ledger, and could choose whether "good" or "bad" things are recorded on it based on how he lived his life.

The second theory is Arminianism. In the 16th century, Dutch theologian Jacob Arminius taught that human nature had been severely corrupted by the Fall,[3]

---

[3] That is, "fall" from God's favour, as inherited by the fall of

but some small spark of goodness remained in everyone. This spark made it possible to be reconciled to God by His grace, but the individual had to decide to accept this grace. Arminius could have sung Amazing Grace, but only if he didn't look too closely at the words.

The third position is that of the Protestant Reformers. They taught that man is hopelessly endued with a wretched nature; furthermore, his nature is so corrupted by the Fall that self-centred rebellion against God has become his whole motivation in life. That is, man's predilection is neither for God's Glory, nor God's will, but rather to rule his own life without God's interference. Fallen man's theme song is: "All Hail the Power of King Self." In other words, man is such a wretch that only "amazing grace" can rescue him!

We can argue these three points till the cows come home, but rather than do that, let's see what the Scripture actually teaches about the wretched nature. How ruined is man when it comes to spiritual matters?

In Genesis 8:21 we read,

> "And the Lord said in his heart, I will not again curse the ground any more for man's sake; for the imagination of man's heart is evil from his youth."

According to this verse, evil is already present from one's youth. It is of interest to note that God made this declaration immediately after the flood when the only people on this earth were the "Good Guys," (Noah and his family).

A second verse to consider is Psalm 51:5 where David confesses,

> "Behold, I was shaped in iniquity; and in sin did my mother conceive me."

Adam.

Some people tell me David was casting aspersions on his mother's character. Amusing! (But not for David's mother). This verse, rather than casting David's mother in a dim and immoral light, it is a statement about the wretched nature of man. You have probably heard people speak of "innocent" babies, but the Psalmist insisted they were *shaped in iniquity and conceived in sin*. He did not consider himself innocent at birth, but by nature a wretch when he was born. He had inherited the virus of sin from his first parent, Adam.

Furthermore, we read:

> *"The heart of the sons of men is fully set in them to do evil"* (Ecclesiastes 8:11).

Outside of grace, when men see the Judgment hand of God they are emboldened to increase their wickedness instead of repenting.

So, what about the condition of every person's heart? Jeremiah answers when He says, *"The heart is deceitful above all things, and desperately wicked; who can know it?"* (Jeremiah 17:9). This describes you and me on our worst *and* best day! Alas! What can we do then to be saved? Well, we can do nothing in ourselves. Salvation comes by grace and grace alone since we are by nature wretches!

Amazing Grace! Don't sing it if you don't believe it!

We discover more about our wretched nature in Romans 3:10-18 where we read:

> *"As it is written, there is none righteous, no not one: there is none that understands, there is none that seeks after God. They have all gone out of the way, they are together become unprofitable: there is none that does good, no, not one. Their throat is an open sepulchre; with their tongues*

> *they have used deceit; the poison of asps is under their lips; whose mouth is full of cursing and bitterness; their feet are swift to shed blood; destruction and misery are in their ways; and the way of peace have they not known; there is no fear of God before their eyes."*

The same thought is proclaimed later in Romans 7:18 where Paul says:

> *"For I know that in me (that is, In my flesh)dwells no good thing."*

But why is it so important for churches to emphasize of the wretched[4] nature of man? Why indeed? The answer is simple: not emphasizing this truth will eventually cause us to forget the significance of the cross of Christ. Grace will cease to be amazing!

Arthur Pink observed:

> "The first office of the preacher is to stain the pride of all human glory, to bring down the high looks of man, to make him aware of his sinful perversity, to make him feel that he is unworthy of the least of all God's mercies. His business is to strip him of the rags of his self-righteousness and to shatter his self-sufficiency; to make him conscious of his utter dependence on the mere grace of God. Only he who finds himself absolutely helpless will surrender himself to sovereign grace.[5] Only he who feels himself already sinking under the billows of a justly

---

[4] Sometimes referred as the "utter depravity of man."

[5] Sovereign Grace is described thusly: The LORD God Almighty, by his own sovereign will and power, freely gives irresistible, irreversible grace, to those He, who at all times foreknew, elected, and predestined to have eternal life through His Son.

deserved condemnation will cry out, "Lord, save me, I perish." Only he who has been brought to despair will place the crown of glory on the only head entitled to wear it. Though God alone can make a man conscious of his impotence, He is pleased to use the means of the truth— faithfully dispensed, effectually applied by the Spirit— in doing so." (**Arthur Pink**: The Doctrine of Man's Impotence: Chapter 1).

Why is the doctrine of the Wretched Nature of Man rarely or never mentioned in most of today's churches? —because unregenerate man just cannot accept that he is spiritually impotent. Some individuals, rather than admitting to their spiritual paucity, claim a vital spirituality of their own making. Others are willing to accept their spiritual sickness, but unwilling to admit to their spiritual death. Despite these diversions, the Bible still proclaims that unregenerate man is indeed dead in trespasses and sins (see Ephesians 2:1).[6]

Pelagius taught that man was perfectly well. Arminius held that man was sick, but not dead. Do you believe either of these tall tales? Only a person who sees that he had to be raised spiritually from the dead can sing Amazing Grace and mean it!

The Bible tells us that sin brought death (Romans 5:12)![7] It declares the entire world guilty before God (Romans 3:19).[8] Without the intervention of the Holy Spirit, no one would call upon Christ Jesus for mercy!

---

[6] Eph 2:1 *And you hath he quickened, who were dead in trespasses and sins;*

[7] Rom 5:12 *Wherefore, as by one man sin entered into the world, and death by sin; and so death passed upon all men, for that all have sinned:*

[8] Rom 3:19 *Now we know that what things soever the law saith, it saith to them who are under the law: that every mouth may be stopped, and all the world may become guilty before God.*

The wretched nature manifests itself spiritually in man's rejection of God's grace. Man is not forced to refuse God's salvation: He chooses and wants to reject it. When he refuses to be saved, he is merely demonstrating what is really in his heart.

The wretched nature is indeed awful. In Isaiah 45:22 the Lord commands, *'Look unto Me, and be ye saved, all the ends of the earth: for I am God, and there is none else.'* In Isaiah 55:6 the Lord again commands, *'Seek ye the Lord while He may be found, call ye upon Him while He is near.'* But, left to ourselves, we will neither seek nor look unto the Lord! Why? Simply because we have no desire! We have only our wretched nature!

The All-Powerful, Creator God of heaven, declares, *"Seek ye my face."* This is not a mere invitation, it is a command. Yet people show their true colours as they willingly refuse to obey this divine edict.

It commands, *"Look unto me, and be ye saved, all the ends of the earth; for I am God, and there is none else."* But people don't look to Him for salvation. Nevertheless, His words are written large with power and invested with authority: He is the One who works all things after the counsel of His own will (Ephesians 1:11).[9] We are charged to look to Him and no one else for Salvation (Isaiah 45:22).[10] Therefore, all who look elsewhere, to any other being, or to themselves, for salvation are not only guilty of disobedience, but also of idolatry.

God commands, yet people do not call on Him! Why not?

It's because they have no desire to call on Him! We are wretches who need to be rescued. The Reformers saw

---

[9] Eph 1:11 *In whom also we have obtained an inheritance, being predestinated according to the purpose of him who worketh all things after the counsel of his own will:*

[10] Isa 45:22 *Look unto me, and be ye saved, all the ends of the earth: for I am God, and there is none else.*

this taught clearly in the Bible. They knew a man's will was contrary to God's will. Luther and company didn't make this up! They discovered it in the Bible! Here is your proof:

> *"Because the carnal mind is enmity against God: for it is not subject to the law of God, neither indeed can be."* (Romans 8:7)

How can an unsaved man repent of his sin when he loves it? Why would he come to God when he hates God? It is because this doctrine is offensive. We don't want to hear about our vileness. We reject seeing our ugliness in the mirror of the Bible. We'd rather someone just tell us smooth things about an invented god who is just dilly-dallying around his potting shed, delighted with all his little children who are all clenching their collective fists at him and spitting in His face. We'd rather hear about our will being totally within our control, able to turn to God at any time we get good and ready. Is this hopeless? If we don't hear the True Gospel, how will we ever understand that grace is really amazing?

Our sin has made us dead towards God. Some people refuse to believe this regardless of the evidence you put in front of them. I'm reminded of the story of the man who went to the doctor convinced that he was dead. The doctor tried many ways to show him how ridiculous it was to believe such a thing; but, every argument was turned around because the man was totally convinced he was dead. So, the doctor showed him medical books asserting that dead people don't bleed. He then took him to a morgue and cut a cadaver to show him that dead people don't bleed. Finally, the doctor asked the man if he was convinced that dead people don't bleed. He said, "It certainly looks that way." Then the doctor stuck him with a needle and he began to bleed. The man looked at the blood and then said, "My goodness, dead men do indeed bleed!" The point being, unless God intervenes in grace, we will remain spiritually dead to God. We cannot by our intellect turn to God. If this were not true, what do we do with scriptures like, *"Verily, verily, I say unto thee, Except a man be born again* (from above), *he cannot see the kingdom of God"* (John 3:3).

Until a man is born "from above" he remains in his natural, fallen and wretched state, so it is impossible for him to discern or perceive divine things. He cannot see the things of God because, by nature, he is enveloped in total spiritual darkness; he is blind to the light. As Arthur Pink says, "When the Lord of life and light appeared among them, men had no eyes to see His beauty, but despised and rejected Him." The only reason any of us overcome our spiritual darkness is that,

> *"God, who commanded the light to shine out of darkness, has shined in our hearts, to give the light of the knowledge of the glory of God in the face of Jesus* (2 Corinthians 4:6).

Now that's amazing grace!

Notice the gift of light and knowledge of salvation is received exclusively by divine power. The Reformers did not invent this doctrine of man's needing Divine intervention because of spiritual inability; Jesus taught it Himself. Our Master said in John 5:40,

> *"Ye will not come to me, that ye may have life,"*

Jesus proclaimed that man's nature is innately wretched. He taught that men will not of themselves come to Him that they "might have life." But why? Is it because they fail to realize their awful peril? What if they knew they were standing on the brink of the Pit; [11] would they not run from the wrath to come? No! They don't run! Why don't they? Is it because they have no sense of their profound and desperate need? Perhaps if they understood their awful condition: their wickedness, their blindness, their hard-heartedness, their depravity. Would they then run to the great Physician to be healed by Him? No! They still don't run to him. They have no desire to run to him because their carnal mind is enmity against God, and the God-Man, Christ Jesus the Lord and Saviour. They *WILL NOT* come. They have freedom to exercise their will, but their will is set against God in every situation. That's the nature of sin. It has made every child of Adam a wretch by nature. We hate to be compared to the worst of people. And, yes, we cover up what we really are. The Holy Spirit and fear of law enforcement help to restrain our thoughts and actions, but if there were no restraints, we would soon be completely out of control.

Christ further illustrated the wretched nature when He asked, *"Why do you not understand my speech?"* to which He answered, *"Even because you cannot hear my word"* (John 8:43). There is no mistaking His meaning here. Christ is teaching that unregenerate people have no ability to hear his message! Their nature makes it impossible. Man cannot act contrary to his nature any more than a pig would dress up in a three-piece suit and wear cologne. Man is beset by a total inability to hear God's word. Unless the Holy Spirit opens our ears with His life-giving power to hear the gospel, we cannot hear! We need His grace, His amazing grace!

Listen again to Jesus as He further illustrates this truth. John 3:19:

> *"And this is the condemnation, that light is come into the world and men loved darkness rather than light, because*

---

[11] That is, Hell.

their deeds were evil.

What a proof of man's wretched nature! Not only are men in the dark, but they really love the darkness— they prefer ignorance, error and superstition to the light of truth. They love the darkness and hate the light because their deeds are evil. This is how the Lord Jesus taught it. Who are we to argue against God?
Man is utterly unable to come to Christ since his will is set against God. The unsaved man always exercises his free will against God; hence Christ said in His Jerusalem Lament:

> *"O Jerusalem, Jerusalem, thou that kills the prophets, and stones them which are sent unto thee, how often would I have gathered thy children together, even as a hen gathers her chickens under her wings, and ye would not!"* (Matthew 23:37)

Jesus never denied that man, despite his total spiritual inability, is morally free. Man is not a puppet. He not only has a sin nature, he willingly chooses to be a practicing sinner. Notice how Jesus says, unsaved people would not come to Him! This does not mean that anyone who desires the Saviour will be denied Him; it is simply that no man wills to come to Christ unless God, by grace, turns him. People, of their own free will, simply will not come to Christ. Man is free to choose salvation if he wants it (Revelation 22:17),[12] but he doesn't want it.[13] He has a wretched nature. He loves the darkness because his deeds are evil. It's not an appealing sight!

---

[12] Rev 22:17 *And the Spirit and the bride say, Come. And let him that heareth say, Come. And let him that is athirst come. And whosoever will, let him take the water of life freely.*
[13] A grace pastor once said, "The Holy Spirit must give the sinner the 'want to.'"

Dr. Joseph Cook, the great Boston preacher of the latter half of the nineteenth century, gave an illustration of total inability. He said he had in his home an exquisite and valuable clock. It had an exceedingly fine-looking case, a very decent set of works, a nice appearing dial and elegantly smooth hands. It was altogether a good clock to look upon, but it had one fault. It simply would not, or could not, keep time. It had been gone over by many different clockmakers, but no one had been able to correct this fault. As a timepiece, it suffered from total inability! He then asked, "Is not this like man, even at his best, if he has not been born again? There may be much about him that others can admire, but he is positively unable to do the will of the Lord, because his heart is utterly estranged from God. Only the new birth—regeneration by the Word and Spirit of God— can enable him to keep in line with the divine will as laid down in the Holy Scriptures. However righteous he may appear in the eyes of his fellows, because of this fatal defect all his righteousness is as filthy rags in the sight of God."

This is why we must be saved by God's grace and grace alone. Grace alone causes us to will to be saved.

Now read this scathing charge made against all men:

> *Hear now this, O foolish people, and without understanding; which have eyes, and see not; which have ears, and hear not"* (Jeremiah 5:21).

According to this verse, the unregenerate individual is spiritually blind and deaf. This shocking fact was affirmed again and again by our Lord as He addressed hypocritical scribes as:

> *"Blind leaders of the blind,"*
> *"Ye blind guides,"*
> *"Thou blind Pharisee"*
> (Matt. 15:14; 23:24, 26)

Paul takes up this theme and says, *"The god of this world hath blinded the minds of them which believe not"* (2 Corinthians 4:4). From these passages, we learn that the unregenerate mind is incapable of seeing the things of God. We are wretches. We need Amazing Grace!

Worse than that, the unregenerate man is totally blind to his blindness. He hasn't got a clue that his blindness is leading him into, *"the blackness of darkness for ever"* (Jude 13). That is why the majority of the unregenerate live so securely and peacefully. It has always appeared strange to believers why the unsaved can be so indifferent while under sentence of death. They conduct themselves with unbridled flippancy even though the wrath of God in upon them. Why is this? —they are blind! They cannot see their predicament!

So, if we do not have the ability or the inclination to come to Christ, how do we get saved? The answer is found in Psalms 110:3: *"Thy people shall be willing in the day of thy power."* Jesus further explained it when He said,

> *"No man can come to me, except the Father which hath sent me draw him"* (John 6:44).

Furthermore, we read in John 6:65,

> *"Therefore said I unto you, that no man can come unto Me, except it were given unto him of My Father."*

Here, Jesus clearly states that the ability to come to Him is a gift from the Father. There is no ability to come to Christ unless there is divine intervention. This is Amazing Grace! Christ's language is undeniably clear. He doesn't say, "No man will come," but "No man <u>can</u> come" He is teaching that the will of the unsaved man has nothing to do with Salvation because his will is turned against God. John 1:13 expressly declares that the new birth is "*not of the will of the flesh.*"[14]

But will this kind of preaching draw a crowd? It didn't for Jesus. Right after He told them of their inability we read,

> "*From that time many of his disciples went back, and walked no more with him*" (John 6:66).

Again, this is a sad commentary on the human condition!

To summarise:

The Father exercises His sovereign will when He draws us, then we seek Christ. People, if left to themselves, are wretches that love the darkness and hate the light. They, therefore, will not seek God. But, if any do seek Christ, it is because God, in His amazing sovereign grace, has overpowered their resistance caused by their depravity.

Nevertheless, we must face the fact that God does not work this way in everyone. He is under no moral obligation so to do. Why should He make an enemy love Him? Why should His Holy Spirit "draw" to Christ somebody who wants to stay away? That He brings particular individuals to Himself is according to His own eternal counsels and sovereign pleasure. But, try preaching this in your average church and people get mad. I remember well preaching this to a church in Nevada when one man and his wife, long-standing members of the church, stood and screamed at me, calling me all manner of remarkable things. They literally, physically covered their ears and stomped out. If Bible teaching is believed, we find that man is spiritually dead.

---

[14] John 1:13 *Which were born, not of blood, nor of the will of the flesh, nor of the will of man, but of God.*

Not until the Holy Spirit goes to work on him is a man's pride humbled, causing him to realize that without divine intervention and grace he is a spiritual zero! It is only then he can sing Amazing Grace and mean it. Consider these scriptures:

> John 15:5: *"I am the vine, you are the branches: he that abides in me, and I in him, the same brings forth much fruit; for without me you can do nothing."*

> Ephesians 2:1: *"And you has he quickened (made alive), who were dead in trespasses and sin."*

> Ephesians 2:5: *"Even when we were dead in sins, has he quickened us together with Christ; (by grace ye are saved.)"*

> Colossians 2:13: *"And you, being dead in your sins and the uncircumcision of your flesh, has he quickened together with him, having forgiven you all trespasses."*

We ought not to be economical with the truth on this subject. The impression is given by some that a man can come to God anytime he pleases! But how can a dead man turn to God? How can a blind man see his need? How can a deaf man hear? We are ruined by sin and our only hope is the amazing grace of God revealed in Christ Jesus.

And that's the Gospel Truth!

CHAPTER TWO
Amazing Grace, How Sweet the Sound

"Ye have not chosen me, I have chosen you..."
John 15:16

The late S. L. Johnston used to tell a story about an old amazing grace believing woman who lived in Glasgow. Her minister, Dr. Norman McLeod, of The Barony, used to visit her. The poor dear was deaf, and she sported one of those old fashioned ear trumpets that deaf people sometimes used. The old lady used to confront Dr. McLeod and demand, "Gang ore (*go over*) the fundamentals, Doctor, gang ore the fundamentals." The dear sister wanted him to go over the fundamentals of the faith because she so thoroughly enjoyed hearing them.

One of the fundamentals of our faith is the amazing grace of God revealed in the choosing of His family. Every believer holds to the truth that there is a people the scriptures call the Elect or the chosen ones. In the Old Testament it was Israel (Deuteronomy 14:2);[1] in the New Covenant, it's the redeemed (1 Peter 2:9).[2] Yet the subject of election is fiercely debated; however, the argument over election is not over the existence of the Elect, but over how one becomes a member of that group. To elect means to choose. Indeed, all of us are familiar with the word "election" in a secular sense. At election time, we go

---

[1] Deut 14:2 *For thou art an holy people unto the LORD thy God, and the LORD hath chosen thee to be a peculiar people unto himself, above all the nations that are upon the earth.*

[2] 1 Pet 2:9 *But ye are a chosen generation, a royal priesthood, an holy nation, a peculiar people; that ye should shew forth the praises of him who hath called you out of darkness into his marvellous light:*

to the polls and vote for those whom we want to represent us in political office, but with Biblical election we must ask, does God choose his family or does man? That's the question!

We are saved by Amazing Grace; that is, we are saved by something which and someone whom we do not deserve. We should not, therefore, be surprised to read in Ephesians 1:4-5:

> *"God has chosen us in Him before the foundation of the world... having predestinated us into the adoption of children by Jesus Christ to Himself, according to the good pleasure of his will."*

We could end this chapter now. The matter is plainly stated and settled by Scripture. God chose us according to his good pleasure!

But, when did He choose us? He chose us *"before the foundation of the world."* (John 17:24). This means that before there was a moon or sun in the sky, we were elected. Before we were born, we were chosen; before we ever did right or wrong, we were selected. That is amazing grace!

But why did God choose us? Was there something in us that moved Him? Our self-righteousness would like to say yes. But the correct answer is no. The scripture says it was *"according to the good pleasure of His will."* In other words, it was because He wanted to choose that He chose us. This is amazing grace!

John Newton, according to Spurgeon, used to tell the story of an old woman who explained election in this way. She said, "I believe the doctrine of election, because I am quite certain that if God had not chosen me, I should never have chosen Him; and I am sure He chose me before I was born, or else He never would have chosen me afterwards; and He must have elected me for reasons unknown to me, for I never could find any reason in myself why He should have looked upon me with special love."

Good insight!

Before we look at the next scripture, we must ask, did God save us by accident or on purpose? Consider this: if He saved us by accident, then there is no grace, but if He rescued us on purpose, in spite of ourselves, then salvation is all of grace. We read in 2 Timothy 1: 9: *"Who has saved us and called us with a holy calling... according to his own purpose and grace which was given us in Christ Jesus before the world began."*

When did He give us grace? Was it when we asked for it? No, quite the opposite: grace was given to us in Christ before the world began. This is why it is a grace that amazes.

The love of God for us is eternal. It did not begin in time. Because of His infinite love for us, God chose us unto everlasting life and glory. This grace *"is now made manifest by the appearing of our Saviour Jesus Christ, who has abolished death, and has brought life and immortality to light through the gospel:"* (2 Timothy 1:10). We are saved by amazing grace.

Nevertheless, some want to argue that they chose God, and not vice versa. Even when they trip over this truth, they stand up, dust themselves off and continue as though nothing had happened.

But, notice how God's choice was from the beginning (2 Timothy 1:9).[3] The word "chosen" in this verse means to take to oneself. God loved us and took us to Himself at the very beginning. This is amazing grace! God's love and grace towards us are manifest in His choice of us. This fact was confirmed by Jesus when He declared in John 15:16, *"Ye have not chosen me but I have chosen you."* The

---

[3] 2 Tim 1:9 *Who hath saved us, and called us with an holy calling, not according to our works, but according to his own purpose and grace, which was given us in Christ Jesus before the world began.*

scriptures are as clear on this subject! There is no confusion here— salvation is only by amazing grace!

The Father purposed to save His elect in Christ. This is pure grace, amazing grace. It is grace that saves wretches like us. God the Father purposed to choose a bride[4] and give that bride to His Son. In doing so, He gave the bride grace to believe the gospel. As we discovered in the previous chapter, man is such a wretch that he chooses darkness rather than light. People *"will not"* come to the Lord. Their wills are set against God. They cannot enter the Kingdom unless they are born from above. If God, therefore, had not chosen a bride for His Son, no one would ever have accepted Christ. To our unspiritual eyes, there was no beauty in Him that we might desire Him (Isaiah 53:2).[5] We loved our sin and hated the light (John 3:19).[6] Our carnal mind was set against God (Romans 8:7).[7] Left to our own free will, we would have rejected the gospel every time. All men, by

---

[4] Isa 62:4-5 *Thou shalt no more be termed Forsaken; neither shall thy land any more be termed Desolate: but thou shalt be called Hephzibah, and thy land Beulah (married): for the LORD delighteth in thee, and thy land shall be married. For as a young man marrieth a virgin, so shall thy sons marry thee: and as the bridegroom rejoiceth over the bride, so shall thy God rejoice over thee.*

John 3:28-29 *Ye yourselves bear me witness, that I said, I am not the Christ, but that I am sent before him. He that hath the bride is the bridegroom: but the friend of the bridegroom, which standeth and heareth him, rejoiceth greatly because of the bridegroom's voice: this my joy therefore is fulfilled.*

[5] Isa 53:2 *For he shall grow up before him as a tender plant, and as a root out of a dry ground: he hath no form nor comeliness; and when we shall see him, there is no beauty that we should desire him.*

[6] John 3:19 *And this is the condemnation, that light is come into the world, and men loved darkness rather than light, because their deeds were evil.*

[7] Rom 8:7 *Because the carnal mind is enmity against God: for it is not subject to the law of God, neither indeed can be.*

nature, refuse the invitation of the gospel, but God, in the sovereignty of His grace, makes a difference by moving the Elect, by the power of His Spirit, to see their wretched condition. Faith is birthed in them by the Spirit so they can see the mercy and grace of the cross of Christ. That is why we read, *"We love Him because He first loved us"* (1 John 4:19). That is amazing grace!

Why do folks get mad when we talk about the amazing grace of God in election? They read in the Old Testament that God chose some and left others, yet they don't seem to have a problem with that. They don't get mad when the Bible says that God chose Abraham (Genesis 12:1-9), the idol worshipper (Joshua 24:2), and didn't choose Abraham's neighbours. In fact, all of Abraham's neighbours were left to perish, but nary a peep is heard from the opponents of gracious election on this one!

The Bible also tells us that God chose Isaac over Ishmael and chose Jacob over Esau— for no other reason than it was His good pleasure and purpose; again, not a peep (Malachi 1:2-3; Romans 9:10-13).[8] Furthermore, the free-will folk don't seem to mind that in Old Testament times God chose only the Jews! Why didn't He choose the Italians to be His people? Why not the Irish? So, why did He choose Israel? Were they any better? No! All God's choices were made according to the good pleasure and purpose of His will. But that is

---

[8] Mal 1:2 *I have loved you, saith the LORD. Yet ye say, Wherein hast thou loved us? Was not Esau Jacob's brother? saith the LORD: yet I loved Jacob, And I hated Esau, and laid his mountains and his heritage waste for the dragons of the wilderness.*

Rom 9:10 *And not only this; but when Rebecca also had conceived by one, even by our father Isaac; (For the children being not yet born, neither having done any good or evil, that the purpose of God according to election might stand, not of works, but of him that calleth;) It was said unto her, The elder shall serve the younger. As it is written, Jacob have I loved, but Esau have I hated.*

perfectly acceptable with the dear folks who stubbornly hold to free will. They don't get upset that He chose to provide an atonement for Israel exclusively. I've never heard any of them complain about no offering being made for the sins of the Egyptians. Apparently, God sovereignly choose a people in Old Testament times, but He must not do it in the New Testament era! It seems, now that we are in New Covenant times, the free will folks demand that God change His way of operating (even though the Bible proclaims He is unchangeable).

Instead of rejoicing in the amazing grace of God, people object when we say that the elect have nothing to do with how they are elected or chosen. These objectors insist that becoming chosen has to do with our free will. But, isn't it a bit illogical and silly to say that we can choose to be chosen? Besides that, what control does a dead, unregenerate sinner's free will have when it comes to spiritual things? His spiritual understanding is so feeble that He cannot even see the Kingdom of God (John 3:3);[9] yet, nowadays many preachers teach that man can choose his way into God's family by his own free will. There's no amazing grace there!

I, however, concur with Luther when he says,

> *"If any man ascribes anything of salvation, even the very least thing, to the free will of man, he knows nothing of grace, and he has not learned Jesus Christ rightly."* (Martin Luther, quoted by C.H. Spurgeon— New Park Street Pulpit, Sermon 52, Free will - a Slave.)

The Bible plainly teaches that Jesus is the Author and Finisher of Faith (Hebrews 12:2).[10] In other words, He

---

[9] John 3:10 *Jesus answered and said unto him, Art thou a master of Israel, and knowest not these things?*

[10] Heb 12 :2 *Looking unto Jesus the author and finisher of our faith;*

creates faith and *gives eternal life* to His elect. Man certainly cannot create his own faith, since he is dead in trespasses and sins (Ephesians 2:1).[11] Neither can man see with spiritual eyes (2 Corinthians 4:4),[12] nor hear with spiritual ears (Deuteronomy 29:4). Nevertheless, in His great mercy, our Savior chooses to save some! "But that is unfair!" say the well-meaning free-will folks. But why is it unfair? God is under no obligation to save. If we insist that God must save everyone, we deny the guilt and sinnerhood of man and the just nature of God's holy character. If a million guilty people were arrayed before Him and the Father gave mercy to none of them, would He be unjust? No— all gathered before him would be guilty and hell-deserving. He's a just God. If there is to be such a thing as justice, the guilty must be punished. So, when the Lord chooses to save some condemned people, we should not get upset at Him. Why object because He had mercy on some, but not all? No one unjustly goes into The Lake of Fire. All of us justly deserved damnation! As John 3:17-18 says explicitly,

> "God sent not his Son into the world to condemn the world... He who believes not is condemned already."

The unbeliever is already condemned. The unbeliever is not suddenly damned for his refusal of God's salvation. He merely remains under an already existing condemnation. That God should choose to save any is a matter of Amazing Grace.

---

[11] Eph 2:1 *And you hath he quickened, who were dead in trespasses and sins;*

[12] 2 Cor 4:4 *In whom the god of this world hath blinded the minds of them which believe not, lest the light of the glorious gospel of Christ, who is the image of God, should shine unto them.*

On the other hand, when God opens our hearts to the gospel, it seems to us as though we are the ones who did the choosing. But the truth is, the will to embrace Christ was given to us by God. In other words, His will becomes our will. We had neither the ability nor inclination to make such a choice until God stepped in with His amazing grace.

People often get confused about who does the seeking and who does the finding. In John 1:43,[13] for example, we read that Jesus went into Galilee, found Philip and commanded him to follow. Then in verse 45, Philip found Nathanael and said, *"We have found Him of whom Moses and the prophets did write."* Do you see how Philip got it wrong? He said that he had found the Lord, but verse 43 expressly informs us that it was Jesus who did the finding. However, we can excuse Philip. He was young and unschooled in the faith. He would soon grow in grace and the knowledge of the Lord. We should question, those who claim to be mature, but who teach others that it was man who found and chose the Lord. This is a serious error!

It was probably very humbling to the disciples to be told that they had not chosen Christ; nevertheless, what a comfort for them (and us) to know that He is the One who has done the choosing. His choice shows us that His love came first— He loved us even when we were his enemies and dead in sin. We are saved by Amazing Grace!

Some dear people, with an imagination to rival Hans Christian Anderson's, contend that we became believers and then were added to the Elect. But, notice, again that Jesus didn't teach it that way. He said, *"You have not chosen me, but I have chosen you."* In other words, Christ insists that He began this whole matter. Notice again how this truth is illustrated in Acts 18: 4-10. In verses 9-10 we read:

---

[13] John 1:43 *The day following Jesus would go forth into Galilee, and findeth Philip, and saith unto him, Follow me.*

> *"Then spoke the Lord to Paul in the night by a vision, Be not afraid, but speak, and hold not your peace: for I am with you, and no man shall set on you to hurt you; for I have many people in this city."*

Corinth was known as one of the most sinful and wicked cities in the ancient world. Drunkenness, idolatry and rampant immorality filled the place and yet Christ said to Paul; *"I have many people in this city."* They had not chosen Christ; indeed, many of them had not so much as heard of Christ, but the Lord had already chosen them. They had not yet repented, yet Christ called them His people. They had not yet believed, but Christ claimed them as His own. This plainly shows us that Christ Jesus has chosen His own before they even seek him.

On What Basis Does God Choose?

Now, that is an excellent question: why did he choose me? Let's do an experiment. Take a blank piece of paper and write, "God chose me because_____." Now fill in the blank. Whatever your answer, be sure that it is an answer based on scripture.

If you filled in the blank with a "desirable" personal characteristic or some action you have done, you have still not grasped that salvation is by sheer and amazing grace. If, however, there actually was something in you, whether it be some goodness or choice that you made, that caused God to respond to you, then you are not saved by grace. The reason why He chose us was that it was the good pleasure of His will to do so. We see this in Malachi 1:2-3:

> *"I have loved you, saith the LORD; yet you say, Wherein hast thou loved us? Was not Esau Jacob's brother? saith the LORD: yet I loved Jacob, and I hated Esau."*

Why did He love Jacob and hate Esau? The only reason given is this, *"I will have mercy on whom I will have mercy"* (See Romans 9:11-23).

The only reason proclaimed in the Bible, as to why Christ loved us (and if you study till you die, you will not find another) is, *"I will have mercy on whom I will have mercy"* (Romans 9:15).

Is His Choice Based on Foreknowledge?

Grace believers and free will folk alike accept the fact of Election; however, it is not Election that is in question between them, but the basis upon which that Election is established.

Free-will folk hold that Election is based upon foreknowledge. In other words, they teach that God looks out of eternity and sees how man will respond to the gospel. If He sees the sinner responds positively by believing, then God elects him. On the other hand, grace people hold that, if this were the case, then salvation would not be a matter of amazing grace. If a person is chosen based upon what they do, then salvation is of works and not of grace. For this reason, grace believers, hold that the basis of Election is entirely secreted in God. It is undisclosed; it is one of those matters concealed in the private counsels of the Almighty (Deuteronomy 29:29).[14]

The true believer knows that election is not based upon any foreseen worth or quality in the individual; it can only be *"according to his good pleasure"* (Ephesians 1:5). Why it should please God to elect some and pass over others is not ever revealed.

So, according to the free-willers, God must wait on

---

14 Deut 29:29 *The secret things belong unto the LORD our God: but those things which are revealed belong unto us and to our children for ever, that we may do all the words of this law.*

certain information before he decides who the elect will be. But hang on a minute, doesn't the Bible teach that God is Omniscient (Psalm 147:4-5)?[15] That is, He knows everything! But how can that be true if He had to look down through the years to see who would believe of their own free will? Logically, this implies that God is continually increasing His knowledge; however, a god who is increasing his knowledge is not omniscient!

Herein is a beautiful truth: there never was a time when *our* God didn't know everything. He has never had to increase in knowledge. He has known all things eternally. His elect have been chosen from eternity (Acts 15:18; 2 Thessalonians 2:13).[16] He sovereignly, according to his purpose and good pleasure, elects. He does not elect those whom he foresees would believe; He only elects those whom He has purposed to save. Thus, if we are saved, we don't deserve it. That is why, if we are saved, we are the recipients of Amazing Grace.

Let's look further at this matter. Those who insist that Election is based on God's foreknowledge say this is clearly taught in Romans 8:29-30.[17]

These are key verses in their argument and indeed, the only verses which 'seem' to support their presumption. We read as follows:

---

[15] Ps 147:4 *He telleth the number of the stars; he calleth them all by their names. Great is our Lord, and of great power: his understanding is infinite.*

[16] Acts 15:18 *Known unto God are all his works from the beginning of the world.*

2 Thess 2:13 *But we are bound to give thanks alway to God for you, brethren beloved of the Lord, because God hath from the beginning chosen you to salvation through sanctification of the Spirit and belief of the truth:*

[17] Rom 8:29 *For whom he did foreknow, he also did predestinate to be conformed to the image of his Son, that he might be the firstborn among many brethren. Moreover whom he did predestinate, them he also called: and whom he called, them he also justified: and whom he justified, them he also glorified.*

"*²⁹For whom He did foreknow, He also did predestinate to be conformed to the image of his Son, that He might be the first-born among many brethren. ³⁰Moreover whom he did predestinate, them he also called: and whom he called, them he also justified: and whom he justified, them he also glorified.*"

Note, if we look carefully at the sentence in verse 29, we see that it does not say "what" God foreknew, but "whom" he foreknew. Paul is not talking about a well-informed God, but about something which God did. He "foreknew" these people in the same sense that he "called" them and justified them.

Notice the chain of God's saving acts. The very first thing in this passage is "Foreknowledge." Those who think that man has something to do with his salvation latch onto this word.

So, What Does "Foreknowledge" Mean?

Let's first ask, does God predestine and justify all whom He foreknows? or merely some? Evidently, according to the text, He justifies all he foreknows. So, are we to believe that God looks toward the future and sees who will choose him and based on this knowledge, predestines, calls, justifies and glorifies?

Wow! If this is so, all I can say to my free-will friends is, "Well done gentlemen, what a spectacular choice you made! You are to be congratulated! You played as much part in your salvation as did the Lord! Excellent stuff! Now then, take Amazing Grace off the list of songs you sing: evidently you don't believe it!"

Look next at this word 'called', it is important. What does it mean in this verse? Consider this:

There are two types of calling in scripture:

A) The general or external call;
B) The inward call.

Let's look first at the external call. In gospel preaching, all are called by the external calling, but not all get saved. However, by the inward, or effectual calling, God draws, persuades, brings alive by His Spirit and brings us to faith in Christ Jesus.[18] So then, all who are called by the 'inward call' are brought to faith in Christ Jesus. But how did it start? In this context, it started because of foreknowledge. For *whom* He foreknew, (not *what* He foreknew), He predestined, called and justified. The calling comes after foreknowledge.

Those who oppose this gracious message totally change the flawless order of salvation taught in scripture. They begin with the call of the gospel. This is, according to them, the first cause. The person is called, then decides to accept the Gospel. After that, they are chosen because God already has foreknowledge as to how man will respond. The way they now read Romans 8:29-30 is, *"Whom he called and who he knew already would make the right decision, them he foreknew and those he foreknew, them He predestined."*

They totally reverse the order of Romans 8:29-30 by placing Predestination and Foreknowledge after Calling. They make a mockery of grace by adding man's response into a beautiful God-given order of salvation. Yet on a Sunday morning, they stand up and sing Amazing Grace!

Foreloved (or Elected)

To be foreknown is to be 'foreloved' The Bible often uses the word "knew" as a term for intimate love. Adam, for example, "knew" His wife (Genesis 4:25).[19]

---

[18] The is commonly referred to as "Irresistible Grace"
[19] Gen 4:25 *And Adam knew his wife again; and she bare a son, and*

He didn't just know about her existence, he loved her intimately. Furthermore, Jesus says to a group of people in Matthew 7, *"Depart from me I never 'knew' you ye workers of iniquity."* Never knew? He's omniscient, He knows everything! Therefore, it doesn't mean He didn't know of their existence. It means that He never loved them. Many of the modern versions of the Bible, in fact, translate foreknow as forelove, pre-approve and foreordained.

I am not much of a supporter of the modern Bible translations, but I here quote them as many folks put much stock in them. As will be observed by those who know the backgrounds of these translations, they were by no means all produced by evangelicals, much less by men of Sovereign Grace Persuasion.

<u>Romans 8:29</u>:

1. An American Translation: *"For those whom he had marked out from the first he predestinated to be made like his Son."* Smith and Goodspeed, University of Chicago Press, 1923)

2. The Emphasized Bible: *"For whom He fore-approved He also foreappointed to be conformed unto the image of his Son."* (Joseph B. Rotherham, Grand Rapids, Kregel, 1959).

3. Good News for Modern Man: *"For those whom God had already chosen he had also set apart to become like his Son."* (London British and Foreign Bible Society, 1966)

4. The Holy Bible in Modern English: *"For He previously knew them, and appointed them to conformity*

---

called his name Seth: For God, said she, hath appointed me another seed instead of Abel, whom Cain slew.

with the image of his Son." (Ferrer Fenton. London. Black, 1903)

5. The Jerusalem Bible: *"They are the ones he chose specially long ago and intended to become true images of his Son."* (Edited by Alexander Jones, New York, Doubleday and Co., 1966)

6. The New English Bible: *"For God knew his own before ever they were, and also ordained that they should be shaped to the likeness of his Son."* (Oxford University Press and Cambridge, 1970)

7. The New Testament: A New Translation: *"For long ago, before they ever came into being, God both knew them and marked them out to become like the pattern of his Son."* (Vol. 2, William Barclay, London, Collins, 1969)

8. The New Testament: A New Translation: *"For he decreed of old that those whom he predestined should share the likeness of his Son."* (James Moffatt, New York, Hodder and Stoughton, no date)

9. The New Testament: An Expanded Translation: *"Because those whom He foreordained He also marked out beforehand as those who were to be conformed to the derived image of His Son."* (Kenneth S. Wuest; Grand Rapids: Eerdmans, 1961)

10. The Twentieth Century New Testament: *"For those whom God chose from the first he also did predestinate to be conformed to the image of his Son."* (Chicago, Moody Bible Institute, 1967)

11. New Living Translation: *"For God knew his people in advance, and he chose them to become like his Son, so that*

his Son would be the firstborn, with many brothers and sisters. And having chosen them, he called them to come to him. And he gave them right standing with himself, and he promised them his glory." New Living Translation© 1996 Tyndale Charitable Trust

12. The Amplified New Testament: "*For those whom He foreknew (of whom He was aware and loved beforehand) He also did predestinate from the beginning (foreordaining them) to be molded in the image of His Son (and share inwardly His likeness).*" The Amplified New Testament (Grand Rapids, Zondervan, 1958)

The fact that so many modern translations render Romans 8:29 in a way contrary to that which the free-will people have favoured is another very powerful argument against the free-will claims. Without a doubt, many of these translations, even if they do have a bias in other places, would tend toward a non-sovereign grace viewpoint; nevertheless, the translators have not allowed their bias to influence their translation here.

The Bible does not support the idea that Election is the result of God's foreknowing how we will respond to His call. Adherents to this belief say that unless God foresees a willingness for a person to be saved, He does not elect them. This makes salvation dependent upon man's will, not God's will. This is free-will, but certainly is not Amazing Grace!

Why then do some respond to the call and not others? The only answer possible (if the free-will folks are correct) is that those responding to the call must be fundamentally better people. For sure, they may have looked bad outwardly, but inwardly they had enough sense or spiritual light to decide for God. If, however, this were true, the grace of God is nullified." Man's goodness has become the foundation of his salvation, so we might as well throw out the scripture that proclaims, *"Not by works of righteousness that we have done but according to His mercy He saved us."*[20] While we are at it, also throw out the scripture that says, *"Saved by Grace"*[21] God foreseeing that we were willing enough, wise enough, and good enough to respond to Him, so He predestined us— this is not grace! Listen to me, you can't have it both ways. *Either God is sovereign and Election is an expression of God's will or man is sovereign and Election is a result of man's will!*

Free-willism declares that certain persons possess some inherent goodness (or merit) that make them eligible to become one of God's Elect. So, God, by His powers of foreknowledge, makes His plans only for them. He decides what He will do with them after they have decided what they will do with Him. The ultimate decision for the free-willer rests with the individual, not with God. Saying it another way, in the matter of personal salvation, man is sovereign, not God. As Spurgeon said:

> "Free-will doctrine— what does it do? It magnifies man into God. It declares God's purposes null and void, since they cannot be carried out unless men are willing. It makes God's will a waiting servant to the will of man, and the whole covenant of grace dependent on human action. Denying election on the ground of injustice, it holds God to be a debtor to sinners."
> (*C.H. Spurgeon: A Jealous God, Sermon No. 502*)

It is vital that every child of God be continually reminded that neither his faith, his decision, his

---

[20] Titus 3:15 *All that are with me salute thee. Greet them that love us in the faith. Grace be with you all. Amen.*
Eph 2:8 *For by grace are ye saved through faith; and that not of yourselves: it is the gift of God:*

repentance, his yielding, his commitment, his earnestness, his sincerity, his anything brought about his new birth. His new birth was a work of the sovereign grace of God, since everything required for rebirth came from God: his faith, his repentance, his yielding, his everything. Salvation is by amazing grace. It is the gift of God.

The truth is everyone really believes that God is Sovereign in Salvation. Often times they don't know it, but they really are Sovereign Grace believers. Spurgeon illustrates this well. He recounts an incident which I will retell here. He says,

> "I was preaching, not very long ago, at a place in Derbyshire, to a congregation, nearly all of whom were Methodists, and as I preached, they were crying out, "Hallelujah! Glory! Bless the Lord!" They were full of excitement until I went on to say in my sermon, "This brings me to the doctrine of Election." There was no crying out of "Glory!" and "Hallelujah!" then. Instead, there was a great deal of shaking of the head, and a sort of telegraphing round the place, as though something dreadful was coming. Now, I thought, I must have their attention again, so I said, "You all believe in the doctrine of Election?" "No, we don't, lad," said one. "Yes, you do, and I am going to preach it to you, and make you cry 'Hallelujah!' over it." I am certain they mistrusted my power to do that; so, turning a moment from the subject, I said, "Is there any difference between you and the ungodly world?" "Ay! Ay! Ay!" "Is there any difference between you and the drunkard, the harlot, the blasphemer?" "Ay! Ay! Ay!" Ay! There was a difference indeed. "Well, now," I said, "there is a great difference; who made it, then?" for, whoever made the difference, should have the glory of it. "Did you make the

difference?" "No, lad," said one; and the rest all seemed to join in the chorus. "Who made the difference, then? Why, the Lord did it; and did you think it wrong for Him to make a difference between you and other men?" "No, no," they quickly said. "Very well, then; if it was not wrong for God to make the difference, it was not wrong for Him to purpose to make it, and that is the doctrine of Election." Then they cried, "Hallelujah!" as I said they would. (*C H Spurgeon: The Sum and Substance of all Theology; Delivered at Bethesda Chapel, Swansea; On June 25th, 1861. From The Sword and Trowel.*)

In conclusion, the grace of God does not search for men who are willing to accept Him. God, however, chooses unwilling people and makes them willing?

This brings us to the next chapter. Did Christ die for everyone, without exception? or is it possible that He died particularly for those whom the Father had chosen before time? Was Christ invested with power to actually save or did he merely have the power to make it possible to be saved? Did His Atonement actually secure salvation for His people or did it obtain and gain salvation for no one? Did Christ die for a particular group, or did He die for all people generally?

These are questions which must be addressed.

And that's the Gospel Truth!

CHAPTER THREE
Amazing, Saving Grace! He Died for Us

Grace people believe the Bible teaches that Christ Jesus actually saved His people at the cross. That He died 'for us' is the theme of redemption.

This is one of the reasons that grace is so amazing. Consider the following scriptures:

> Galatians 1:4 *"He gave Himself for our sins.*
> Galatians 3:13 *"Being made a curse for us,"*
> 1 Peter 2:24 *"Who his own self bare our sins in his own body on the tree"*
> Isaiah 53:5 *"He was wounded for our transgressions, bruised for our iniquities; the chastisement of our peace was upon Him, and by his stripes we are healed."*
> Romans 4:25 *"He was delivered for our offenses, and raised again for our justification"*
> Titus 2:14 *"He gave Himself for us that He might redeem us from all iniquity and purify unto Himself a peculiar people."*
> Hebrews 1:3 *"When He had by Himself purged our sins."*
> Hebrews 9:12 *"having obtained eternal redemption for us."*
> 1 John 4:9 *"In this was manifest the love of God towards us because God sent his only begotten Son into the world that <u>we</u> might live through Him."*

Notice how in 1 John 4:9, the apostle does not say that God sent his Son into the world that the world might live through Him. No! It says He was sent so that we, not the world, might live through Him and as John records, in the Lord's Prayer in Gethsemane, *"I pray not for the world but for those You gave Me"* (John 17:9).

I want, therefore, to talk to you, in this chapter, about a Saviour who, with certainty, saves. I want to present to you a Redeemer, who really redeems. I want present to you a Christ who purposefully purchased His people at the cross. This gracious doctrine is actually offensive to many people. Those offended approvingly sing "Amazing Grace," but don't actually believe it for they think that they contribute somehow to their salvation.

As mentioned in Chapter One, those who do not believe in the Doctrine of Amazing Grace usually fall into one of two camps:

A) The Pelagians[1]
B) The Arminians

We will refer to these people as the free-will folks. Both groups believe that Christ's redeeming work did nothing more than make it possible for us to be saved if we decide to believe. Redemption, according to their point of view, did not redeem; rather it merely made redemption possible. According to them, no one in particular was purposely saved at the cross.

The free-will folk represent God as willing to receive those who respond "appropriately" to His message. The One True and Living God is not seen as wonderfully sovereign, but rather as being in subjection to the will of sinful men. Accordingly, He is a God who wills for every individual to be saved, but lacks the ability to save without the assistance of unregenerate sinners.

A somewhat moderated view of free-will makes a person's calling dependent upon his responding to God's

---

[1] Pelagianism - the belief that Adam's sin did not condemn man to hell and that mankind's will is still capable of choosing good or evil without divine intervention.

grace. The more extreme view espouses that man has an innate ability to respond to the offer of salvation with no divine help whatsoever. In either case, free-willism carried to its logical conclusion renders God a failure. That is, no matter how hard God tries, a person will not bow to Christ without that person's consent.

Noel Smith, a well-known free-will preacher was candid when he said, "What is hell? It is an infinite negation. And it is more than that. I tell you, and I say it with profound reverence, hell is a ghastly monument to the failure of the triune God to save the multitudes who are there. I say it reverently, I say it with every nerve in my body tense; sinners go to hell because God almighty Himself couldn't save them! He did all he could, he failed!"

At least he was honest, but wrong! Who would worship a god who could be overcome by the will of man?

A God Who Saves!

Going back to the matter at hand: did Christ effectually and actually save, ransom and redeem His people at the cross, or did He save no one in particular at the cross. Rather, did He just make it possible for all to be redeemed by their response to the gospel call? What does the Bible say about this: it says the true God is the One who does the saving and not a god who merely enables man to save himself. Sometimes it seems the free-will folks are reading from a retranslated Bible. For example, some well know versus are retranslated like this:

> Retranslated: *"Fear not for I have made it possible for you to be redeemed; I have potentially called you by my name"* Isaiah 43:1.
> Original verse: *"Fear not: for I have redeemed thee, I have called thee by thy name; thou art mine"* .

Retranslated: *"For I am the Lord thy God, the Holy One of Israel thy potential Saviour"* Isaiah 43:3.
Original version: *"For I am the LORD thy God, the Holy One of Israel, thy Saviour"*

Retranslated: *"I even I am the Lord and beside me there is no Saviour, —except, that is, for those who were spiritual enough to respond to me and thereby save themselves so, just in case you were wondering, I'm not therefore the only Saviour"* Isaiah 43:11.
Original version: *"I, even I, am the LORD; and beside me there is no saviour."*

Retranslated: *"I have declared and have saved... well actually, not really; I have made it possible to be saved"* Isaiah 43:12.
Original version: *"I have declared, and have saved"*

Retranslated: *"I will work and who will let (prevent) it— apart from anyone and everyone who wants to prevent me accomplishing my will"* (Isaiah 43:13).
Original version: *"I will work, and who shall let it?"*

Retranslated: *"They have not known nor understood for He hath shut their eyes that they cannot see; and their hearts, that they cannot understand... Just kidding!"* Isaiah 44:18.
Original version: *"They have not known nor understood: for he hath shut their eyes, that they cannot see; and their hearts, that they cannot understand."*

We could consider many other scriptures which declare God to be the Saviour, (the one who saves), yet I cannot find one scripture which, when taken in its context, says that man is to undertake or partner in his eternal salvation.

Boasting!

Now consider this: if anyone can get to Heaven by the Cross plus their choice of Christ, then they will have substantial grounds for boasting. Mind you, they will feel entirely out of place since the redeemed will be declaring with one accord, *"Thou wast slain and hast redeemed us unto God by thy blood"* (Revelation 5:9). At that point, the free-will folks will think, "What nonsense is this? Christ only made it possible for us to be redeemed. He didn't actually redeem us at the cross. Our redemption was not accomplished until we believed."

Farfetched? Yes indeed, but logical. If you are a dedicated free-willer, maybe some kind saint of God will put a tender hand on your shoulder and point out the relationship in Revelation 5:9 between "slain" and "redeemed."[2] Slaying and actual redeeming happened at same place, at the same time. What spectacular Amazing Grace!

However, the Christ of the free-will folk doesn't actually redeem by the blood which was shed on Calvary. They believe Christ's blood only makes redemption possible. What about you? Do you believe that Christ saved you at the cross or did He merely make it possible for you to be saved?

The Greatest Failure in History

The Christ of the free-will folk accomplished nothing on the cross. By their account, His finished work,[3] finished nothing. A kind of christ who lived and died for

---

[2] Rev. 5:9 *And they sung a new song, saying, Thou art worthy to take the book, and to open the seals thereof: for thou wast slain, and hast redeemed us to God by thy blood out of every kindred, and tongue, and people, and nation*

[3] John 17:4 *I have glorified thee on the earth: I have finished the work which thou gavest me to do.*

"AMAZING GRACE" The Most Sung but Most Disbelieved Song Ever!

sinners to merely make salvation possible is far removed from the Bible teaching. The Sovereign God said that His Word would *not return unto Him void but would accomplish that which He pleased and prosper in the thing whereunto it was sent* (Isaiah 55:11).[4] If Christ's death, as the free-will folk teach, did not accomplish redemption, then Christ Jesus came into the world for no one in particular, and for no particular purpose. Why so? Because, according to the free-will folk, nothing was really accomplished at the cross. Christ only made it possible for redemption to be accomplished. Their theory stands in stark contrast to Isaiah 55:11 where we are presented with the God who accomplishes the things He pleases to achieve. To free-will folk, Jesus was like a boxer going into the ring for the sake of being there, but not for the purpose of winning the fight. Their christ came with no particular purpose to secure anyone. How utterly opposed to Amazing Grace!

The idea is too far-fetched! If it is true, then Luke19:10 should be changed to say, *"I have come perhaps to seek and to try to save that which was lost"* rather than *"I have come to seek and to save that which was lost."* If you are a card-carrying free-will person, you might as well drop, "Amazing Grace" from your selection of Hymns, since you cannot admit to having been so lost that you need to be found. It wasn't grace that saved you at Calvary, but rather your choice of and proper response to that grace.

Best not to sing "Amazing Grace" if you don't believe it!

Double Jeopardy

According to the Law of Double Jeopardy, a person cannot be put on trial twice for the same crime. This is a

---

[4] Isa. 55:11 *So shall my word be that goeth forth out of my mouth: it shall not return unto me void, but it shall accomplish that which I please, and it shall prosper in the thing whereto I sent it.*

principle of justice in every civilized country; however, the free-will folk, by denying that Christ actually died and paid for the sins of His people at the cross, charge God with being unjust. Of course, not one of them will admit to doing that, but they do it all the same. Here's how: they say that Jesus died for the sins of every individual who has ever lived. Yet they freely admit that many of these same people will be charged with and punished for their sins on Judgment Day. That's a violation of the Law of Double Jeopardy. I doubt they can sing Augustus Toplady's old hymn, "From Whence This Fear and Unbelief" as one of its verses says:

> "If Thou hast my discharge procured,
> And freely in my place endured
> The whole of wrath divine,
> Payment God will not twice demand,
> First at my bleeding Surety's hand,
> And then again at mine."

How can the God of Justice demand payment for sins that have already been paid for by Christ Jesus? Did Christ not actually pay enough with His precious blood? Indeed, if the free-will folk are correct, that must be the case. Per their flawed reasoning, God has no understanding of Justice.

Substitution[5]

If the free-will folks are right by saying Christ merely made it possible to be saved, then we must also do away with the glorious doctrine of Substitution. Evidently the free-will folks refuse to accept that Christ was actually judged and punished in our place on the cross. "But no,"

---

[5] 2 Cor. 5:21 *For He hath made Him to be sin for us, who knew no sin; that we might be made the righteousness of God in Him.*

says the free-will exponent, "Christ really was our sin-bearing substitute." Well, He must have been a pretty lousy one, if those for whom he substituted were not actually saved by His dying.

But here's the gospel truth: the God of the Bible is the saving God. He came here in the person of His Son and became His people's substitute. That is, Christ Jesus bled and died on the cross to atone for the sin of His people. The free-will folks say that He became a substitute for all individuals, but admit that multitudes for whom Christ died will be lost. This implies that Christ's substitution was unsuccessful. What's more, His futile work at the cross substituted for no one in particular. However, grace people believe the very opposite. They believe that everyone for whom Christ became a substitute was and will be saved by the almighty Christ. He is an amazing Saviour who saves with outstanding, amazing grace!

Sinners do not save themselves; they contribute absolutely nothing. Salvation, first and last, whole and entire, past, present and future, is of the Lord, to whom be Glory forever and ever.

Alas, the god of the free-will folks, by his puny substitution, only secured the right for the Almighty to make an offer of salvation. Free-will substitution actually guarantees salvation for no one. By their reasoning, Christ's substitutional death merely created an opportunity to exercise saving faith and no more. But this idea is far removed from what is presented in the Bible. Paul says, *"The Son of God loved me and gave himself for me"* (Galatians 2:20). This is no general redemption[6] of which he speaks, but rather he tells of a particular love and mercy; hence, Christ actually saved Paul and all other believers at the cross. He actually became a real (not a potential) substitute. He effected a real (not a potential)

---

[6] That is, "redemption for every person"

reconciliation at the cross. The believer's title to eternal life was actually secured at the cross. *"He entered in once into the holy place having obtained eternal redemption for us"* (Hebrews 9:12). Notice how the scripture plainly states that redemption was most certainly achieved by Christ's saving work. This is amazing grace! Don't sing it if you don't believe it!

The Christ of Calvary saved us when He hung on the Cross. Of course, no free-will person can admit to this! They only pay lip service to the work on the cross. They say, "Without Calvary, I could not have gained my salvation." The genuine grace believer, on the other hand, says, "Christ won and accomplished my salvation at Calvary."

Once more I will digress. If you are a dedicated follower of the free-will doctrine, I hope you also don't sing the hymn: "My Jesus I love Thee, I Know Thou Art Mine" since one of its verses might give you indigestion:

"I love Thee because Thou hast first loved me,
And <u>purchased</u> my pardon when nailed to the tree."

Don't sing it if you don't believe it!

But Where Is Faith in All This?

"But," asks someone, "don't I need faith to get saved?" Yes indeed, faith is crucial. The theologians call it the instrumental cause of salvation. That means it brings us to the salvation that has already been accomplished. However, faith, no matter how pure and vigorous, can never serve as as sin-bearer since it neither removes guilt, nor is able to make an offering that turns away the wrath of God. No matter how intense and sincere our faith, it cannot pay the penalty of our sin. Faith cannot satisfy God's just and righteous demands; it cannot legally remove the guilt of sin. Indeed, faith cannot provide, in itself, the righteousness by which we can stand faultless before the Father. We are not partial sinners, but by our very nature, *ruined* sinners.[7] Therefore, we need Christ Jesus the All-Sufficient One, to be our Rescuer and Saviour.

So where does faith come in? It's an ancient message that is never out of date: faith brings us to Christ and makes the sinner to see Him as perfect offering for his sin,[8] the perfect payment,[9] the complete cleansing,[10] and the required righteousness.[11] But faith, in itself, has no merit and no virtue.

Again it must be stressed that faith is neither Christ nor His substitutionary life and death. Although it is utterly impossible to be saved without faith, faith is neither the blood nor the final sacrifice for sin. Faith is not the mercy-seat. Faith does not work, but accepts the work which was done for us by Christ. Faith does not wash us; instead, it brings us to the fountain which is opened for sin and uncleanness.[12]

Faith always leads us outside ourselves to receive the worthiness found in the Lord Jesus but imputed to us, but faith has no worthiness of its own. Gospel faith is not faith produced by feelings. In fact, relying on feelings is

---

[7]Ephesians 2:1 And you *hath he quickened*, who were dead in trespasses and sins

[8]Rom. 3:25 *Whom God hath set forth to be a propitiation through faith in his blood, to declare his righteousness for the remission of sins that are past, through the forbearance of God*

[9]Acts 20:28 *Take heed therefore unto yourselves, and to all the flock, over the which the Holy Ghost hath made you overseers, to feed the church of God, which he hath purchased with his own blood.*

[10]Rev. 19:8 *And to her was granted that she should be arrayed in fine linen, clean and white: for the fine linen is the righteousness of saints.*

[11]1 Cor. 1:30 *But of him are ye in Christ Jesus, who of God is made unto us wisdom, and righteousness, and sanctification, and redemption*

[12]Zech. 13:1 *In that day there shall be a fountain opened to the house of David and to the inhabitants of Jerusalem for sin and for uncleanness.*

just another way of relying on self. Since feelings are internal actions, relying on them is just another form of salvation by works! Faith, on the other hand, reaches out and knits us to Jesus, our infinitely worthy Saviour (Psalm 18:3; Hebrews 3:3; Revelation 4:11)[13] and in so doing, presents us perfect in the perfection of Christ (Hebrews 5:7).[14]

Since God the Father sees us in the perfection of His Son, the Father will always accept us as being legally perfect. Faith accepts this and sees Christ alone as our hope. Faith receives and rests on the fact that Christ has done everything required of us and has done it perfectly (Deuteronomy 32:4).[15] Faith sees that The Lord Jesus has worked perfectly, prayed perfectly, worshiped perfectly and believed perfectly on our behalf. By faith, we accept this perfection as accomplished on our behalf and we now make a perfect approach to the Father, in the name of Jesus, clothed in Christ alone. Although we are a people zealous for good works (Titus 2:14),[16] we also know that the Father is more pleased with our resting in the doing, dying and rising again of Christ than with all our attempts at personal obedience. (For more

---

[13] Ps 18:3 *I will call upon the LORD, who is worthy to be praised: so shall I be saved from mine enemies.*

Heb 3:3 *For this man was counted worthy of more glory than Moses, inasmuch as he who hath builded the house hath more honour than the house.*

Rev 4:11 *Thou art worthy, O Lord, to receive glory and honour and power: for thou hast created all things, and for thy pleasure they are and were created.*

[14] Heb 5:7 *Who in the days of his flesh, when he had offered up prayers and supplications with strong crying and tears unto him that was able to save him from death, and was heard in that he feared;*

[15] Deut 32:4 *He is the Rock, his work is perfect: for all his ways are judgment: a God of truth and without iniquity, just and right is he.*

[16] Titus 2:14 *Who gave himself for us, that he might redeem us from all iniquity, and purify unto himself a peculiar people, zealous of good works.*

information on this subject see, *The Gospel Truth about Faith* by D. G. Miles McKee*).*

Power Not Impotence

But back to the Atonement: The Bible reveals God's power to save, not His impotence. His salvation is not a theoretical one for imaginary believers. It is a real redemption and an effectual salvation accomplished by the Saviour who actually saved sinners on the cross.

A careful reading of Scriptures shows that Christ not only powerfully and effectually died for sinners but also demonstrates that the people for whom He died were already His people before He died for them. Consider this:

> *'You shall call his name Jesus for He shall save his people from their sins."* (Matthew 1:21). Notice how they were already His people before He saved them.

> *"The good shepherd gives his life for the sheep"* (John 10:11). Again notice that He did not give his life for the goats. The goats will face His awful wrath on the Day of Judgment (Matthew 25:32-46) but the sheep are safe, for He sacrificed Himself for the sheep.

> *"Christ loved the Church and gave Himself for it"* (Ephesians 5:25). Certainly this is abundantly clear— He gave Himself exclusively for His bride.

Fallen man cannot bear to face the fact that he is not master of his destiny and captain of his soul. He cannot bear to face the fact that the God of the Bible saves only those whom He has chosen. He detests the idea that God saves by grace, apart from works, so that no man may boast even slightly. He shuns the fact that salvation comes to him in the person of a perfect Saviour apart from any contribution on his part!

Salvation... A Futile Wish?

Was the salvation of sinners merely a vain wish on God's part? Does salvation depend on man's willingness to believe for it to exist? Not at all - the Bible teaches that Christ actually saved at the cross. The power of the finished work does not depend on faith being added to it. At the cross, Christ secured full salvation for all for whom He died. Grace Believers wholeheartedly, therefore, join with Paul when he says, *"God forbid that I should glory save in the cross of our Lord Jesus Christ"* (Galatians 6:14). We boldly declare that salvation is exclusively by amazing grace.

So far from magnifying the love and grace of God, the free-will position turns redemption into a monumental failure. God is dishonoured, and His purpose transformed into an impotent wish. No free-will person, who understands the logic of their position, could ever say, "Christ died for me." They could not admit that their salvation was secured at the cross apart from any involvement on their part. They could say, however, Christ potentially died for me. For them, their salvation was accomplished when they added the contribution of faith to the equation. Their faith, it seems, was able to do that which Christ found it impossible to do. According to them, their faith secured the salvation that Christ could not secure by His death.

The Almighty?

Since repetition is the price of learning, let's further unpack the reasoning of the free-will position. The free-will believer neglects to face that, if his position is correct, Christ's death accomplished nothing for him since his salvation hinges upon himself and his response to the gospel. However, since he believes his salvation depends on this response, he must be a co-saviour with Jesus. Were he to testify of his co-saviourhood (essentially his self-saviourhood), no Biblically-educated person would believe him. Our free-will friend actually thinks that God Almighty is only willing to save, but not able to save until He gets the nod and wink from him, the fallen, cursed, depraved and spiritually dead son of Adam. This position requires the sinner to empower God first so that He can save the sinner.

How could anyone possibly think that he is a co-saviour with the Almighty.[17] This is preposterous! The fact is, such a person probably does not realize that he is a co-savior, but his position says otherwise.

Once more, anyone who holds to this "saved by free-will" position is bound to stand in silence when the rest of us rise to sing, "Man of Sorrows, What a Name." The third verse will present a problem for you.

> "Guilty, vile and helpless we,
> Spotless Lamb of God was he;
> 'Full Atonement' can it be?
> Hallelujah! What a Saviour!"

Don't sing it if you don't believe it!

No Power in the Blood?

Back to the Atonement! If Christ died for every individual, as the free-will folks say, then every person

---

[17] Incidentally, if the free-will position is correct, we ought to stop referring to God as Almighty since that designation evidently should not apply to one who cannot save without our help.

would be saved, unless Christ's death is insufficient to save. Yet the free-will advocates assert that Christ died for every individual, but that His death did not accomplish salvation for anyone, only the possibility of salvation. This position asserts that Christ's shed blood has no power by itself to redeem. This is an incomplete atonement. Free-will folks limit the atonement's very power.

In his attempt to magnify the saving grace and mercy of God, the free will champion asserts that since Christ died to save every person, it follows that redeeming love extends to every person. Then, to avoid criticism for believing in universalism (the belief that everyone goes to Heaven), he says that nothing Christ has done actually saves the sinner until the faith necessary to believe is acquired by that sinner, presumedly by the intellect.[18] The decisive factor in salvation then becomes our believing. According to this theory, faith becomes our Saviour rather than the means of receiving the salvation which was accomplished on our behalf at Calvary. Yet the free-will folks have no problem singing, Cowper's Hymn,

> "Dear dying Lamb Thy precious blood
> Will never lose its power
> Till all the ransomed church of God
> Be saved to sin no more."

Don't sing it if you don't believe it!

Intended Accomplishments

Our God is the Sovereign God. Indeed, although the

---

[18] This type of faith has to be of the intellect, otherwise, faith would have to be a gift of God; thus only certain individuals would be saved. This precludes "making a decision" to accept Christ as the free-willers believe.

word sovereignty is not used in the Bible, the concept of God's sovereignty is fundamental to understanding His divine majesty.

Here are but a few of the many verses that establish the Sovereignty of God:

> 1 Chronicles 29:11-12 *"Thine, O Lord, is the greatness and the power and the glory and the victory and the majesty, for all that is in the heavens and in the earth is Thine. Thine is the kingdom, O Lord, and you are exalted as head above all. Both riches and honor come from you, and you rule over all. In your hand is power and might, and in your hand it is to make great and to give strength unto all."*

> Psalm 115:3 *But, our God is in the heavens; he hath done whatsoever He has pleased.*

> Proverbs 16:9 *A man's heart devises his way, but the Lord directs his steps.*

> Job 42:2 *I know that you can do everything and that no thought can be withheld from Thee.*

> Isaiah 46:9-10 *Remember the former things of old; for I am God, and there is none else; I am God, and there is none like me, declaring the end from the beginning and from ancient times the things that are not yet done, saying, 'My counsel shall stand, and I will do all my pleasure.*

> Psalm 103:19 *The Lord has prepared His throne in the heavens, and his kingdom rules over all.*

> Proverbs 19:21 *There are many devices (plans) in a man's heart; nevertheless the counsel of the Lord, that shall stand.*

Ephesians 1:11 *"In whom also we have obtained an inheritance, being predestined according to the purpose of him who works all things after the counsel of his own will..."*

Romans 9:2 *"Has the potter no right over the clay, to make out of the same lump one vessel for honorable use and another for dishonorable use?"*

Ephesians 1:11 *"In him we have obtained an inheritance, having been predestined according to the purpose of him who works all things according to the counsel of his will,"*

Romans 9:18 *"So then he has mercy on whomever he wills, and he hardens."*

In the light of these scriptures, when dealing with the death of Christ, we need to know both what the Sovereign God intended by this death and what was accomplished by it.

Jesus announced His particular purpose when He proclaimed, *"For the Son of man is come to seek and to save that which was lost"* (Matthew 18:11). The Apostle Paul also proclaimed this same divine intention for he tells us, *"This is a faithful saying and worthy of all acceptance, that Jesus Christ came into the world to save sinners"* (1Timothy 1:15).

Which sinners are these? They are the ones of whom Jesus spoke in Matthew 20:28, *"The Son of Man came... to give his life a ransom for many."* This "many" is in other places called "us" to distinguish the redeemed from the world (i.e. *the elect* from those not chosen for salvation).

He *"gave himself for our sins that he might deliver us from this present evil world according to the will of God and our Father"* (Galatians1:4).

"Wait a minute," the free-will champion interrupts, "that verse says that he might deliver, it doesn't say that he does deliver." Thank you, I'm glad you brought that up. The Greek word translated "might deliver" is 'exaireō.' It means, "To pluck out, draw out, to choose out (for one's self), select one person from many, to rescue and deliver!" Hey, do you know what? It sounds like God had a purpose after all. He did not, if we were to add our two cents worth, make salvation possible: He actually chose and saved us. But the god of the free-will folk doesn't seem to have the will, purpose or ability to even get to first base. He can't even begin to save without our help. There's no amazing grace in that scheme!

Then we must ask, what did Christ's death accomplish?

Reconciliation

Christ first attained reconciliation (at-one-ment) between God and us. Romans 5:10 reads, *"When we were His enemies we were reconciled to God by the death of his Son."* Again, *"God was in Christ reconciling the world unto Himself not imputing their trespasses unto them"* (2 Corinthians 5:19). Notice, the reconciliation was actual, not potential. (Also, for a more detailed treatment of the meaning of the word 'World' see Appendix 1)

Redemption

Redemption was also obtained, *"He redeemed us from the curse of the law being made a curse for us"* (Galatians 3:13). According to this verse, an actual redemption was obtained, not a potential one! While on the cross our sins were placed on Him and he became accursed in the eyes of the Father. Was there no result from this? Did his being cursed achieve nothing? To the contrary, he actually accomplished a genuine redemption by His sacrifice of Himself in the place of sinners. Nothing but a powerfully effective redemption, could have ever paid for our sins and made satisfaction for them. The number of our sins were like the sand on the seashore. We were lost, but God's grace found us and paid for us apart from any contribution of our own. At Calvary, Christ paid His people's debt and paid it all at once; so, there now remains not one cent of debt owing from Christ's people to their God.

Justification

Also, justification of sinners was accomplished: *"We are justified freely by his grace through the redemption which is in Christ Jesus"* (Romans 3:23). That is, elect sinners were made holy in the eyes of God. The God of the Bible is a God of both love and unbending justice. We were guilty before him but now because of the finished work of Christ Jesus, those elect sinners owe nothing to the unbendable demands of God's justice because a real and effective punishment was meted out at Calvary in times past. Christ paid it all; He suffered the just for the unjust.[19] Now, the believer is entirely free from all guilt. He is justified, (declared not guilty), and set free from all punishment, through that which Jesus has done.

Sanctification

Sanctification was obtained, for we read, *"To sanctify the people with his own blood he suffered outside the gate"* (Hebrews 13:12). The blood set us apart unto the Lord. When did it do that? At the cross. Faith would later be granted so that we could receive it, but our faith did not cause our sanctification. If that were the case, grace would not be amazing.

---

[19] *For Christ also hath once suffered for sins, the just for the unjust, that he might bring us to God, being put to death in the flesh, but quickened by the Spirit* (1 Peter 3:18)

If the free-will position is correct and Christ's died for every individual, then all people must be reconciled, redeemed, justified and sanctified, but we know that is not the case. Only some people are reconciled, redeemed, justified and sanctified. The free-will preacher admits this but explains it away by saying that only those who added their faith to the cross, and chose Christ, enjoy the benefits of all Christ accomplished while of the earth. Again, this belief makes Christ's death only a token death, void of all power, with no particular purpose or design; nothing particular was intended by it and nothing particular was accomplished. Yet the free-will folks still sing Amazing Grace!

Is it not strange to you that we see in the Bible, the Sovereign, Omnipotent ruler of the universe thwarting the purposes of sinful men and yet, today, free-will folks would have us believe that the positions are reversed! Sinful men, according to them, may, at will, thwart and veto the very purpose and intentions of the all-powerful, majestic, and holy God?

Owen's Three Propositions

The Puritan writer, John Owen, came up with three propositions which concisely show for whom Christ died. He said only one of the following three propositions could be true:

> Either,
> 1. Christ died for all the sins of all men,
> 2. Christ died for some of the sins of all men, or
> 3. Christ died for all of the sins of some men.

If Proposition #1 is correct, then no one will go to Hell. We know is not true for Jesus often taught about people ending in the fires of damnation. "Oh," says someone, "He died for everyone's sins, but they refused to believe and that's why they were lost!" But let me ask you this: since when is unbelief not a sin? Since when is the rejection of Christ not an act of wickedness? Unbelief and rejection of Christ are heinous sins. In 1 John 5:10 we are warned, *"he that believeth not God hath made him a liar; because he believeth not the record that God gave of his Son."* But if Jesus died for all the sins of all men, that must mean He died for their unbelief and rejection of Him! It follows then that all will be saved since there is no legal basis for the sinner's condemnation. Nonetheless, no free-will advocate in his right mind will agree with this both obvious and logical conclusion to Proposition #1 even though he strenuously maintains that Proposition #1 is correct!

If Proposition #2 is true, then all men will have certain sins to answer for and no one will be saved. For *"If the Lord should mark iniquities who should stand"* (Psalm130:3)

"Christ died for all of the sins of some men," is the only one of the three propositions which withstand biblical scrutiny.

Why So? First, let us consider Christ in His office of the Mediating High Priest. As you well know, the book of Hebrews makes it clear that Christ's intercession is based upon His finished work for, *"Christ... by His own blood entered once into the holy place, having obtained eternal redemption for us"* (Hebrews 9:11-12). Notice again, that He obtained eternal redemption for us at the cross and then embarked on His High Priestly ministry of mediation for us.

Where did he go with His blood? *"He is not entered into the holy places made with hands, which are the figures of the true; but into heaven itself, now to appear in the presence of God for us"* (Hebrews 9:24). Mark this down, He is the High Priest for everyone for whom He died. He appears in Heaven for all those whom He redeemed.

His very act of death was done as our High Priest ... *but now once in the end of the world He has appeared to put away sin by the sacrifice of Himself"* (Hebrews 9:25-26). If he died for everyone's sins, He would be everyone's High Priest.

In the Old Testament, the High Priest had the names of the twelve tribes of Israel written on his breastplate. This was edicted by God to show that the priest represented these tribes. As their representative, he would make a sacrifice once a year to atone for their sins (Leviticus 16). This atonement was limited to Israel! No atonement was made for the sins of the Philistines, Hittites and Egyptians. This was very significant since this worldly High Priest was a type and picture of Jesus Christ, the believer's High Priest, Who made atonement only for His chosen people.

Furthermore, as our High Priest in Heaven, Christ Jesus intercedes to ensure all the benefits of His death are applied to those for whom He died. This is the purpose of His intercession. This intercession continues until we reach Glory but is in effect even now: *"If any man sin we have an advocate with the Father, Jesus Christ the righteous"* (1 John 2:1).

Scripture clearly teaches that all persons for whom Christ died must have the benefits of His death applied to them, but free-will doctrine proclaims that Christ died for the salvation of every person. Also, Free-willers freely admit that most individuals are not saved. In other words, they believe our heavenly High Priest Christ Jesus is unable to apply all the benefits of His death to all of those for whom He died. Thus, free-will preachers, who praise Christ for His power and mercy from the pulpit unknowingly mock Him as an ineffective high priest! Yet, they can boldly get to their feet and bellow out with gusto about the Amazing Grace that saves wretches and finds the lost.

Does the Father Pay Attention to the Son?

"But," asks someone, "how can we be so sure that Christ's intercession is effectual? How do we know He is an effective High Priest?"

To answer that, we must ask, *"Does the Father pay attention to the Son's prayers?"* Are Christ's prayers heard? Absolutely! For Christ prayed to the Father, *"I know that thou heareth me always"* (John 11:42). Furthermore, we discover, *"He is able to save them to the uttermost that come to God by Him seeing He ever lives to make intercession for them"* (Hebrews 7:25). Well then, we can be assured that His intercession is always successful! That means **everyone for whom He intercedes as High Priest will be saved** and will enjoy all the benefits of Calvary applied to them.

Does Christ intercede for everyone? No indeed! He point-blank refused to pray for the world! *"I pray not for the world but for them thou hast given me"* (John17:9). Are we to believe then that Christ died for men for whom He refuses to pray? I can't get my head round that one! That would make Him only half a High Priest because He, by neglecting to pray for His people, ignores a vital part of His role. If He died for everyone, but does not afterwards intercede for everyone, then the His shed blood must be somewhat ineffectual. How could He pour out His precious blood for a people for whom He will not offer even one moment of intercession?

Indeed, the heavenly high priest of the free-will folk cannot be trusted for he is neglectful of his office; he apparently has no a real will to save. Even though this high priest prays for all for whom He died, and the Father is hears his prayers, many people for whom died go to Hell. So, He is either, (1) not praying hard enough, or (2) the Father is refusing to grant His requests. This cannot be true, since the Father and the Son are one: disagreement between them is impossible. This high priest may not in truth proclaim, *"I kept them in thy name:*

those that thou gave me I have kept, and none of them is lost..." (John 17:12).

How can millions for whom Christ died go to Hell? Could it be the Lord Jesus is praying out of the will of God - that is impossible! Well then, why do millions of people perish if Christ has died for them? This implies two unthinkable conclusions: (1) Christ's intercession is either insincere or ineffectiveness, (2) God lacks power to save all those for whom Christ died! If news of this ever gets out to the Christ haters, they will have a field day!

Alas, the free-will folk reduce the God of sovereign grace to a lackey, yet they stand to their feet belt out 'Amazing Grace' along with the best of them.

Why Do People Perish?

Here's the truth of this matter: people perish because Christ is **not** their High Priest. Christ's victorious death and His priestly mediation are inseparable! To establish this, let's look briefly at some essential aspects of the High Priestly work of Christ.

As a High Priest, he offered Himself as a sacrifice for the sins of particular ("elect") individuals and He successfully intercedes for every one of them before God the Father. It follows then that people who perish, do so because Christ has *not* prayed for them. In other words, if He doesn't pray for them, it's because He did not die for them. The free-willer must ignore this verse to believe otherwise:

> *"Who shall lay anything to the charge of God's elect? It is God that justifies. Who is he that condemns? It is Christ that died, yea rather that is risen again, who is even at the right hand of God who also makes intercession for us"* (Romans 8: 33-34).

If Christ has died for every individual, then every

individual is elected to salvation, so Christ must be praying for them. In fact, if every individual is elected, everyone now living can be confidently assured that Christ is interceding for them and that no one may lay any sin to their charge. But we know that those who perish have all their sins laid to their charge. So, how can we say that Christ died for them? If He died for them, why doesn't He pray for them?

Furthermore, it is the Father's purpose for Christ to bring many sons to glory (Hebrews 2:10)[20] and to this end He prayed, *"Father, I will that those whom thou hast given me be with me where I am"* (John.17:24). In that great chapter of John 17, Christ prays for His own. Who are His own? Those are they who were given to Him by the Father. Who are they who were given to Him? They are the ones for whom Christ died and the same ones for whom He appears in the presence of God with His own shed blood. These are Christ's own! But who are they? Is the Scripture talking about everyone who has ever lived? If it is, then both the Father's gift to the Son and the Son's intercession are ineffectual. Why? Because, since multitudes perish in Hell, the Father's gift and the Son's intercession obviously don't guarantee salvation for anyone.

We should also consider Isaiah 53:11 where we read, *"By His knowledge shall my righteous servant justify many for he shall bear their iniquities."* That His mission to the Cross was to be a success was also prophesied and guaranteed in verse 12 of the same chapter *"...and He was numbered with the transgressors and He bare the sin of many and made intercession for the transgressors."*

In the light of this, we need to ask for which transgressors did He intercede? Was it for every

---

[20] Heb 2:10 *For it became him, for whom are all things, and by whom are all things, in bringing many sons unto glory, to make the captain of their salvation perfect through sufferings.*

transgressor who ever lived? No! The answer is in the text! He interceded only for the ones whose sin he bore ... and they are here called "many." (Notably, not "all").

Lest there be any doubt that the benefits of Christ's death are applied to those for whom He died, Isaiah 53:5 further tells us *"and with His stripes, we are healed."* But, why aren't all healed spiritually if this verse is true? Why do most men perish? Is it because Christ's sacrifice on the cross and intercession are ineffective? No! Such a notion blasphemes God and implies that He is both impotent and purposeless. This belief of limiting the power and purpose of God makes a sham of the Christ's work on the Calvary's cross.

All Things

Romans 8:32 must also be considered. It declares,

> *"He that spared not His own Son but delivered Him up for us all, how shall He not with Him freely give us all things."*

This clearly indicates that all for whom He died will share in the benefits of His substitutionary death.

Here these benefits are called "all things." This again is a declaration of the power of Christ's intercession; however, saying that He died for every individual leaves us with this question: *"Why does He not give every individual the 'all things' of Romans 8:32?"* After all, if the free-will position is correct, God delivered up Christ for the offences of every man, but not every person receives these "all things" since the Lake of Fire will be full. According to the free-will folk, Christ's offering at Calvary was insufficient since it necessarily requires that we wretched rebels, dead in sin, to contribute our two cents worth (that is, our acceptance of the offer) to be saved.

The free-will doctrine reminds me of the ancient fable of Saint Denys. According to the Roman Catholicism, some angry pagans who were infuriated by his preaching, martyred this great man by cutting off his head. Undeterred, the bold Denys stood up, collected his head and walked 500 miles to a place where he stopped and finally admitted he was dead and collapsed. So there, on that very site, they built a church, which I am told stands to this day, to commemorate and perpetuate his noble memory.

Now why do I have a problem believing that story? Do I have difficulty believing he could walk 500 miles with his head under his arm? No, not one bit of me! That's not the problem I have. My problem is believing he could take the first step. The man had had his head cut off; therefore, he was dead. After all, if he could take the first step then 500 miles would be nothing for a man in his condition.

This brings me back to the free-will theory. I just cannot see how a dead man can take the first step and add anything to the saving work of Christ. How can a dead man "make a decision" to follow Christ? How can a dead man make the right choice? And lest there be any confusion, the scripture plainly says we were dead before salvation, *"and you hath He quickened who were dead in trespasses and sins"* (Ephesians 2:1). So how then do dead men contribute anything to their salvation?

Moving back to the central thought of this chapter: *If all individuals are not saved, and Christ died for every individual, Christ is a failed High Priest whose prayers are ineffective.* One would think no individual believing this would bother to pray, since even Christ's prayers are sometimes ineffective. To pray successfully, we must come to the Father in the mighty name of Jesus in full confidence that our High Priest has the ear of His Father and that the Father always hears Him.

For a much fuller treatment of this subject, I would

refer you to, *The Works of John Owen, Vol. 10*, especially the sections "A Display of Arminianism" and "The Death of Death in The Death of Christ."[21]

And that's the Gospel Truth!

---

[21] As one of the leading Puritan theologians, Owen's defence of the Doctrine of "Particular Redemption" has never been refuted. This book can be downloaded at http://www.ccel.org/ccel/owen/deathofdeath.i.html

CHAPTER FOUR
I Once was Lost but Now I'm Found

"Amiable agnostics will talk cheerfully about 'man's search for God.' To me, as I then was, they might as well have talked about the mouse's search for the cat."

C. S. Lewis in *Surprise by Joy*

I like that quote. Man is not, by nature, a seeker after God. In fact, when sin entered the human race, man became a hider from God (Genesis 3:8)¹ [1] and continues to be so to this day (Romans 3:11).[2] It was God who came looking for man in the Garden and not the reverse. God is the seeker and those whom He seeks He always finds. Nothing is haphazard about our salvation. We were lost, now, by grace, we are found! It is sad that many professing Christians sing the words of Amazing Grace with gusto, not realizing that Grace must by necessity find them and not the opposite.[3]

These days, we don't hear much about this gracious "finding ministry" of the Almighty. In much of today's evangelism, it is assumed that man in his wisdom is searching for God. This, however, disagrees with Romans 3:11 which clearly states that no one seeks after God (that

---

[1] Gen 3:8 *And they heard the voice of the LORD God walking in the garden in the cool of the day: and Adam and his wife hid themselves from the presence of the LORD God amongst the trees of the garden.*

[2] Rom 3:11 *And he said, Who told thee that thou wast naked? Hast thou eaten of the tree, whereof I commanded thee that thou shouldest not eat?*

[3] "T'was Grace that taught my heart to fear
And Grace, my fears relieved
How precious did that grace appear
The hour I first believed"

is, the God of the Bible). We are taught that man must earnestly seek after God, but he can at any time exercise his free will to choose Christ for salvation. That is, the truth of total inability is not reckoned with (see Chapter 1). In this scheme, man may be a sinner, but he's not a lifeless spiritual wretch with no prospects outside of grace.

This theory is precisely the opposite Bible teaching. The Bible clearly states that the natural mind is not subject to the law of God; indeed, it cannot be (Romans 8:7).[4] The unsaved man does not receive the things of the Spirit of God, for they are foolishness to him, and he cannot know them, because they are spiritually discerned" (1 Corinthians 2:14).[5] This is specifically what Jesus taught when He said, *"No man can come unto me, except the Father who hath sent me draw him"* (John 6:44); and *"No man can come unto me, except it were given to him of the Father"* (John 6:65).

Is Jesus correct about this? Does He really know? Does He have His facts straight? Ah but, if anyone knows, it is Jesus. He is the God/Man, the one who knows what is in man and who knows the Father as the Father knows Himself.

The truth is, according to the Lord Jesus, a man is saved only by divine intervention— an effectual call (a call that achieves its purpose). God must intervene because man, in his lostness, neither wants salvation nor has the power or ability to get it for himself. For man, salvation is impossible, but with God all things are possible (Matthew 19:25-26).[6] God's grace must intervene

---

[4] Rom 8:7 *Because the carnal mind is enmity against God: for it is not subject to the law of God, neither indeed can be.*
[5] 1 Cor 2:14 *But the natural man receiveth not the things of the Spirit of God: for they are foolishness unto him: neither can he know them, because they are spiritually discerned.*
[6] Mat 19:25-26 *When his disciples heard it, they were exceedingly*

and break us down. It must soften our hard hearts. It must bend our inflexible necks. Grace works on us and takes our away rebelliousness, causing us to cry out, *"God, be merciful to me a sinner"* (Luke 18:13).

In order to clarify this matter of God's "Finding Ministry" we need to once more consider the two calls.

The Two Calls: General and Effectual

When we understand these two calls of God, will help clarify our understanding of the amazing grace which saves us.

1. The *general call*. This comes to everyone who hears the preaching and sharing of the Word. This call can and is resisted, since all who hear the Gospel do not respond favorably to it, so are not converted. Some are actually stirred by Gospel preaching, and still not converted. They may be excited enough to raise their hands at a meeting, walk forward, and join the church. They may be moved enough to make some sort of decision to follow Christ, but are not in any way converted, nor translated into a New Kingdom where they trust Christ alone for righteousness.

2. The second call is the *effectual call*. It is the call which accomplishes God's purposes. We read of it in Isaiah 55:8-11:

> *"For my thoughts are not your thoughts, neither are your ways my ways, saith the LORD. For as the heavens are higher than the earth, so are my*

---

amazed, saying, Who then can be saved? But Jesus beheld them, and said unto them, With men this is impossible; but with God all things are possible.

ways higher than your ways, and my thoughts than your thoughts. For as the rain comes down, and the snow from heaven, and returns not thither, but waters the earth, and makes it bring forth and bud, that it may give seed to the sower, and bread to the eater: So shall my word be that goes forth out of my mouth: it shall not return unto me void, but it shall accomplish that which I please, and it shall prosper in the thing whereto I sent it."

God's word accomplishes what God pleases! That's the effectual call! God takes whosoever won'ts and makes them into whosoever wills.

But much modern evangelism knows little to nothing of the effectual call. Often the gospel is presented as a ballot and man is given a vote concerning salvation; however, three get a vote on this ballot. First, God votes. —He votes "Yes" for your salvation. Secondly, the devil votes —he votes "No." Then there is your vote. Your vote becomes the deciding vote. So, ultimately, whether a person is saved is determined by the person.

But what kind of god is this who, though he votes, must wait for your vote before your salvation is finally determined? This is a god whose word has no power to accomplish what he desires. This surely is not the God of Isaiah 55:8-11![7]

---

[7] Isaiah 55:8-11 *For my thoughts are not your thoughts, neither are your ways my ways, saith the LORD. For as the heavens are higher than the earth, so are my ways higher than your ways, and my thoughts than your thoughts. For as the rain cometh down, and the snow from heaven, and returneth not thither, but watereth the earth, and maketh it bring forth and bud, that it may give seed to the sower, and bread to the eater: So shall my word be that goeth forth out of my mouth: it shall not return unto me void, but it shall accomplish that which I please, and it shall prosper in the thing whereto I sent it.*

So, let's look at some powerful scriptures that teach us about the Amazing Grace of God, demonstrated by His irresistible grace and effectual call!

In the beginning of John's Gospel, we read a beautiful description of believers, *"who were born not of blood nor of the will of the flesh nor of the will of man but of God"* (John 1:13). Let's break that down:

> *Not of blood:* Descent from Abraham, David or any other godly person does not make a person a child of God.
>
> *Nor of the will of the flesh:* The efforts and exertions of our hearts and natures may reform but cannot regenerate.
>
> *Nor of the will of man:* We are not begotten of God by the acts and deeds of our fellow-men, no matter how much they may encourage us to get saved.
>
> *But of God:* The work is all God's. Man does not play a part. Man does not even have a vote. It is not what man does, but what God accomplishes exclusive of all human will.

Why should there be any reluctance to accept the truth of irresistible grace? After all, it is God's intervention to do for us what we cannot do for ourselves. It is God cancelling our hopeless impotence with His Majesty. It is Amazing Grace! It is a display of sovereign mercy. Gospel preachers may faithfully proclaim the true Gospel, but grace manifested by the sovereign power of the Holy Spirit is the only hope for the salvation of lost souls. When someone is brought to Christ, it is truly Amazing Grace!

The writer of Amazing Grace, John Newton said it

like this, "The gospel is a salvation appointed for those who are ready to perish and is not designed to put them in a way to save themselves by their own works. It speaks to us as condemned already and calls upon us to believe in a crucified Saviour, that we may receive redemption through the blood, even the forgiveness of our sins. And the Spirit of God, by the Gospel, first convinces us of unbelief, sin and misery; and then, by revealing the things of Jesus to our minds, enables us, as helpless sinners, to come to Christ, to receive Him, to behold Him, or, in other words, to believe in Him" (John Newton, *The Voice of the Heart*).

Opponents of this truth would say Stephen's speech in Acts 7 teaches a resistible grace of God. But, wait a minute: we have already made the point that the general call can be resisted. However, let us examine that passage. Verse 51 states,

> *"Ye stiff-necked and uncircumcised in heart and ears, ye do always resist the Holy Ghost: as your fathers did, so do you."*

Stephen addresses the Jews who were about to stone him saying, *"You do always resist the Holy Ghost"* (Acts 7:51).[8] Those who do not believe in the effectual call seize on this saying, "You see, you see, God's grace is, after all, resistible?" But remember, Stephen is speaking to the Jews concerning the words of the prophets who were sent to past generations. In resisting the words of these prophets, the Jews had resisted the Holy Ghost.

How did they resist the Holy Spirit? The Holy Spirit revealed God's Word to the ordained prophets and apostles. The Holy Spirit used ministers of the Word to proclaim the Word of God throughout every age: to the

---

[8] Acts 7:51 *Ye stiffnecked and uncircumcised in heart and ears, ye do always resist the Holy Ghost: as your fathers did, so do ye.*

Jew of the Old Testament times, and to every tribe and tongue and language in the New. And what do people who hate the Word do? They resist; they rebel; they show scorn. They kill those whom the Holy Spirit uses to proclaim the Word. This is what Stephen was speaking about. He was not telling them that the Spirit of God was given to all to lead all to repentance, for many resisted. Certainly not! The Spirit was resisted when the messengers whom the Spirit sends to proclaim the Word were resisted. And the truth is, all men inherited from the first man Adam a resistance to the Spirit and Word of God. So, we are natural God-haters and the Gospel exposes us to be such! Unless God intervenes by His Grace and draws us to Himself, we will perish.

Now consider other pertinent passages of Scripture.

John 3:3 "Jesus answered and said unto him, Verily, verily, I say unto thee, except a man be born again, he cannot see the Kingdom of God... Verily, verily, I say unto thee, Except a man be born of water and of the Spirit, he cannot enter into the kingdom of God."

What does this passage teach? First, it presents us with the picture of birth. Every birth is wholly by the will and activity of others. It is the same in the new birth: we don't jump out of bed one day and decide to be born again. It is a sovereign work of the amazing grace of God.

John 3:5 "Except ye be born of water and of the Spirit, ye cannot enter into the kingdom of God."

· Notice man's inability! Since repetition is the price of learning, let's say it again, man left to himself cannot enter the Kingdom of God. Therefore, the irresistible, gracious power of God is required for the new birth. Besides, the term "born again" can also be translated, "born from above." Again, John 3:3 also states that, *"Except a man be born again (or from above) he cannot see the kingdom of God."*

One who cannot see this kingdom is blind to the reality of its existence. This verse clearly teaches that no man can possibly see the Kingdom until he is born from above. For us to see the Kingdom, a divine and gracious intervention must occur.

John 3:6: That which is born of the flesh is flesh, and that which is born of the Spirit is spirit.

Like begets like in all things. It's a principle of nature! A horse has never given birth to a cow, nor has a bird given birth to a fish. Likewise, the unsaved person cannot give birth to a spiritual man. The claim that unregenerate persons contribute to any degree toward their spiritual origin is contrary to the direct statement of the Lord (John 3:6).[9]

1 Corinthians 2:14 reads,

> *"But the natural man receives not the things of the Spirit of God: for they are foolishness to him: neither can he know them, because they are spiritually discerned."*

Accordingly, natural man (unsaved man) is both unwilling and unable to receive spiritual things, so it is certain he is neither willing nor able to receive the Holy Spirit Himself. How is he then to experience the spiritual birth? It is an impossibility unless God graciously steps into the picture with His supernatural power.

John 3:8: *"The wind blows where it listeth (*wants to*), and you hear the sound of it, but cannot tell where it comes from, and*

---

[9] *John 3:6 That which is born of the flesh is flesh; and that which is born of the Spirit is spirit.*

where it goes, so is everyone that is born of the Spirit."

In other words, the wind is sovereign and irresistible in its course. It blows where it wants. No one in their right mind stands outside shouting at the wind declaring, "I'm going to resist you. You do not have my permission to blow." Only the Lord Jesus possesses such power (Mark 4:39).[10]

The wind blows where it wants to blow, and so it is with the Holy Spirit in His work of the new birth. He undertakes the spiritual quickening when and where He pleases, and His efforts have never proven futile.

Further, observe, that there are no exceptions to the rule per John 3:8:

> *For ". . . so is every one that is born of the Spirit."*

Additionally, we read in Ephesians 2:10,

> *"For we are his workmanship, created in Christ Jesus unto good works, which God hath before ordained that we should walk in them."*

To whom does this work of salvation belong? According to the scriptures, we are His workmanship, not the workers. God Himself works and forms His elect people to be what they are. This is confirmed through His prophet. In Isaiah 43:21 we read:

> *"This people have I formed for myself; they shall show forth my praise."*

He, the Master-Planner, formed us for Himself. That

---

[10] Mark 4:39 *And he arose, and rebuked the wind, and said unto the sea, Peace, be still. And the wind ceased, and there was a great calm.*

surely is Amazing Grace! It's the grace that deliberately and irresistibly saves! The power of the Almighty does not wait for poor miserable sinners to accept Christ: it irresistibly forms them to be His people. Accept that and become a worshipper!

Again, we read in John 6:37,

> *"All that the Father giveth me shall come to me; and him that cometh to me I will in no wise cast out."*

In John 6:44 we read, *"No man can come to me, except the Father which hath sent me draw him: and I will raise him up at the last day."*

In John 6:65 Jesus says' *"...Therefore said I unto you, that no man can come to me, except it were given unto him of my Father."*

A man can by no means of himself come unto Christ. The individual must have been given to Christ by the Father and the Holy Spirit assures that all whom the Father gives shall come![11] Indeed, whosoever may come, will come[12] simply because the Father always draws whom He gives. This is the amazing, irresistible grace of God, which takes the dead sinner and brings him to eternal life.

The Greek word for "draw" is "helkuo." It means to draw by inward power, to lead and to impel. In John 12:32, we see the same word used. Jesus said, *"And I, if I*

---

[11] John 17:11 *And now I am no more in the world, but these are in the world, and I come to thee. Holy Father, keep through thine own name those whom thou hast given me, that they may be one, as we are.*

[12] Rev 22:17 *And the Spirit and the bride say, Come. And let him that heareth say, Come. And let him that is athirst come. And whosoever will, let him take the water of life freely.*

am lifted up from the earth, will draw (helkuo— to draw by inward power, lead, impel) all men unto me."

This word *helkuo* is used in many Bible passages. It is used to describe the hauling bricks, towing, or dragging. It is used in Acts 16:19 when Paul was dragged into the marketplace or out of the Temple (Acts 21:30). John uses it in 18:10 in the context of drawing a sword, and in 21:6 and 21:11 in the dragging a net. James 2:6 uses it in the sense of dragging the poor before a judge. Sinners are so spiritually dead that they must be drawn like fish in a net and carried by the Spirit to the foot of the cross.

The grace of God is irresistible, so we cannot push it aside or ignore it. However, this does not mean the drawn ones are ever drawn against their will since once the Spirit intervenes, all resistance disappears

Let's illustrate how God irresistibly calls! Do you remember how Matthew was called?

He sees Matthew sitting at the table at the receipt of custom, and he said to him, "Arise, and follow me," and Matthew did immediately – that is the amazing effectual call (Matthew 9:9)!

Then there's the delightful story of Lydia in Acts 16:14,

> *"And a certain woman named Lydia, a seller of purple, of the city of Thyatira, which worshipped God, heard us: whose heart the Lord opened, that she attended unto the things which were spoken of Paul."*

Lydia's heart was opened by the Lord. This is entirely unlike what is often preached today. We are told to, "Open your heart and let Him come in" and "Christ stands waiting at your heart's door; won't you let Him in before it is too late?"

"But," says someone, "I seem to recall in Revelation 3:20 that Jesus does knock on the door of the heart and it's up to us to open it to get saved." It is true that in

"AMAZING GRACE" The Most Sung but Most Disbelieved Song Ever!

Revelation 3:20 Jesus is presented as knocking at the door. But this is not the door of anyone's heart. He knocks at the door of that corrupt church of Laodicea and He calls them to Himself. But Christ does not whack at any man's heart asking for permission to save blind, dead sinners. Christ does not stand there making pleas for us to open our hearts. The Lord opened Lydia's heart, then she listened and believed. That is the amazing, irresistible power of the grace of our God. He breaks open the closed heart, and the child of God believes.

Again, we read in Acts 13:48, "*...and as many as were ordained to eternal life believed.*" This too emphasizes the idea presented above: God will save those whom He has chosen. The ones He has ordained (or called) to eternal life will believe. How can this be explained? Before the Holy Spirit intervened was there a willingness to believe within those whom He saves? Oh, no! Only the amazing, irresistible grace of God accomplishes that which He has eternally determined to do.

As the Hornet Song says:

> God does not compel us to go, oh, no!
> He never compels us to go.
> God does not compel us to go 'gainst our will,
> But He just makes us willing to go.

> If a nest of live hornets were brought to this room,
> And the creatures allowed to go free,
> You would not need urging to make yourself scarce,
> You'd want to get out, don't you see!

> They would not lay hold and by force of their strength,
> Throw you out of the window, oh, no!

They would not compel you to go against your will,
But they would just make you willing to go.

When Jonah was sent to the work of the Lord,
The outlook was not very bright.
He never had done such a hard thing before,
So he backed down and ran off from the fight.

Now, the Lord sent a great fish to swallow him up,
The story I am sure you all know.
God did not compel him to go against his will,
But He just made him willing to go.

Everything we have, we have by grace. In 1 Corinthians 4:7 we read: *For who makes you differ from another? And what do you have that you did not receive? Now if you did indeed receive it, why do you glory as if you had not received it?*

Salvation is by amazing grace. It's all a gift. Why sing Newton's song if you don't believe it?

Again, consider the following scriptures:

1 Corinthians 1:9: *"God is faithful by whom you were called into the fellowship of His Son."* God called us in faithfulness to His plan and purpose. We are saved by Amazing Grace.

Acts 5:31: *Him God exalted to His right hand to be Prince and Savior, to give repentance to Israel and forgiveness of sins.*
But some would erroneously tell us that this is a gift He can persuade few to take.

Acts 11:18: *"Then God has also granted to the Gentiles*

repentance to life." To those He effectually calls, He grants repentance unto life. This is Amazing Grace.

Acts 14:27; *"(God) had opened the door of faith to the Gentiles.* Notice who opened the door! Salvation is by Amazing Grace!

Acts 18:27: *"(Apollos) greatly helped those who had believed through grace."* They had believed through grace! Yep! That's amazing!

Philippians 1:29: *"For to you it has been granted on behalf of Christ ... to believe in Him."* ... Grace, grace, grace.. Amazing Grace!

Romans 1:6: *"Among whom are you also the called of Jesus Christ."* Thank you Lord for your effectual call. We are saved by Amazing Grace!

The grace of God not only brings His people to Glory, but it also prepares them for Glory. Grace works within them to create a desire to enter the heavenly splendour. Grace is irresistible in the sense that it changes the will of stubborn men.

The Bible says nothing of this imaginary god who must wait for the endorsement and permission of the spiritually dead sinner before he can confer upon him his salvation? Gospel grace is bestowed by the irresistible hand of the One True Omnipotent God! The Apostle Paul knew he was of himself nothing except by the grace of God. Remember what he said in 1 Corinthians 15:10? *"But by the grace of God I am what I am: and his grace which was bestowed upon me was not in vain; but I laboured more abundantly than they all: yet not I, but the grace of God which was with me."*

What a brief statement yet rich with meaning! Paul had persecuted the church; he had imprisoned Christians and participated in killing them. Yet Paul was taken and turned around so radically that he became a follower and apostle of the one he had persecuted. For Paul, grace was amazingly irresistible!

If a sinner is totally depraved, dead in sin, and totally unable to accomplish salvation, then he needs far more than a little assistance. Why give a dead man a crutch to help him on his way! No, he must be made alive again or he will never walk. Likewise, God does not give the spiritually dead sinner some sort of cane and say, "Here is something to assist you; now serve me!" On the contrary, His grace actually takes the dead sinner and makes him alive. Total inability requires the application of the irresistible grace of God to make a dead sinner spiritually alive.

My good friend, Keith Lamb says it like this: "Salvation is a work that man would not do if he could and could not do if he would." Indeed, he is right! If God's grace were merely an influence which could be resisted, then we would remain lost. We would never have willed our salvation. We "would not do if we could and could not do if we would." We were dead and incapable of attaining spiritual life. That is just the nature of the beast!

One old time preacher tells of being in a meeting where an older Christian was giving his testimony. The old gentleman told of how God had sought him, found him, cleansed him, and healed him. He testified mightily to the grace, power, and glory of God. After the meeting, a legalistic Christian criticized his testimony saying, "I appreciated all you said about what God did for you, but you didn't mention anything about your part in it. Salvation is really part us and part God. You should have mentioned something about your part."

"Oh yes," said the old gentleman, "and I apologize for that. I really should have said something about my part. My part was running away, and His part was running after me till He caught me."

"AMAZING GRACE" The Most Sung but Most Disbelieved Song Ever!

When it comes right down to it, only Grace Believers can believingly sing,

> *"Amazing grace, how sweet the sound!*
> *That saved a wretch like me.*
> *I once was lost, but now am found;*
> *Was blind, but now I see.*
>
> *'Twas grace that taught my heart to fear,*
> *And grace my fears relieved;*
> *How precious did that grace appear*
> *The hour I first believed."*

And that's the Gospel Truth!

CHAPTER FIVE
Grace will Lead Us Home

"Through many dangers, toils and snares
I have already come;
'Tis Grace that brought me safe thus far
And Grace will lead me home."

If we are gospel believers, the grace which saved us will also keep us. Grace believers call this the perseverance or preservation of the saints. This gracious truth teaches that those who truly have been brought to saving faith in Christ will, by grace, continue in the faith; however, this doctrine is actually not centred on how we persevere, but how God perseveres in accomplishing our salvation. Said another way, we are saved by grace alone and this saving grace brings with it a desire to continue in the faith. God gives us, by His power alone, the desire to continually press on in Christ, subduing and mortifying the deeds of the flesh.

One of the marks of gospel believers is that we continue in the things of the Lord. We may fall away at times but, the Lord always brings us back. We may fail, but we will not permanently drop out. *"The steps of a good man are ordered by the LORD: and he delights in his way. Though he fall, he shall not be utterly cast down: for the LORD upholds him with his hand"* (Psalm 37:23-24). The saints will persevere, and those who persevere are the saints.

As Grace Believers, we must be careful to avoid the opposite errors of legalism and license. Legalism says that if we are living holy lives we get favour and grace with God; however, the Bible teaches we are saved by grace alone without the addition of works (Ephesians 2:8; Titus

3:5).¹ License says, on the other hand, "I am saved by grace so it, therefore, doesn't matter how I live since grace will cover it." But this is equally untrue. I once watched a TV interview with a man in Australia who claimed to be a born-again Christian. For his livelihood, he owned and operated a brothel. A brothel!!! Even a blind man on a galloping horse could tell there's a problem here. The truth is, grace has saved us from a life of sin unto a life of good works. Titus 2:14 clearly states that Christ "... *gave himself for us, that he might redeem us from all iniquity, and purify unto himself a peculiar people, zealous of good works.*" (See also Ephesians 2:10).²

However, good works are not the reason for our salvation. Nothing must be added to the Gospel. We are saved by Grace alone, through Faith alone in Christ alone, plus nothing.

There are those who profess faith in Christ and join the church who later abandon the faith and deny Christ. A person who does this is giving evidence, not that they were saved and lost, but that they were never saved in the first place. We should note what 1 John 2:19 says,

> *"They went out from us, but they were not of us, for if they had been of us, they would have continued with us; but they went out that they might be made manifest, that none of them were of us."*

Those who are actually converted, would be miserable

---

¹ Eph 2:8 *For by grace are ye saved through faith; and that not of yourselves: it is the gift of God*:

Titus 3:5 *Not by works of righteousness which we have done, but according to his mercy he saved us, by the washing of regeneration, and renewing of the Holy Ghost;*

² Eph 2:10 *For we are his workmanship, created in Christ Jesus unto good works, which God hath before ordained that we should walk in them.*

in the world. If we ever find ourselves in love with the world, we are acting like the Lord's enemies. That's a harsh thing to say. Well, it would be if I had said it, but I didn't originate it. You'll find it in James 4:4:

> *"Do you not know that the friendship of the world is enmity with God? Whosoever, therefore, will be a friend of the world is the enemy of God."*

Many times, I've witnessed to people who say they are saved, but admit they never have a desire to assemble with the Church. They never read the Bible. They have admitted that they spend their time living hard and fast with the world. They are involved with deliberate immorality and so on and so forth, but say they are saved. Why? "Oh, I believe in once saved always saved," they say. Well so do I. I believe if a man is genuinely saved, he will always be saved; however, not everyone who says they are saved is saved.

Also, many times I have witnessed to people who said, "Yes, I'm saved. I asked Jesus into my heart and was baptized in a church," but they are not involved with the Lord in any way, dislike associating with Christians, don't read the Bible, don't pray, and never worship the Lord, but still claim to be saved. A drunk once staggered towards the great English preacher, C. H. Spurgeon. With alcohol sodden breath he slurred,

> "Mr. Spurgeon, I'm one of your converts."
> "Indeed, you must be," replied Spurgeon, "For you are certainly not one of the Lord's."

The person who says he's saved but then permanently returns to the mire of sinful living is nothing but a washed pig who never had a spiritual nature given to him. Now don't get mad at me writing this! I am merely paraphrasing what the Bible says. In 2 Peter 2:22, speaking of such people, we read,

> *"The dog is turned to his own vomit again; and the sow that was washed to her wallowing in the mire."*

Have you ever read the parable of the soils? Mark 4:3-20:

> *"Behold, there went out a sower to sow: And it came to pass, as he sowed, some fell by the wayside, and the fowls of the air came and devoured it up. And some fell on stony ground, where it had not much earth; and immediately it sprang up, because it had no depth of earth: But when the sun was up, it was scorched; and because it had no root, it withered away. And some fell among thorns, and the thorns grew up, and choked it, and it yielded no fruit. And other fell on good ground, and did yield fruit that sprang up and increased; and brought forth, some thirty, and some sixty, and some a hundred.*

In this story, there are four types of soil which represent four types of hearers. The seed is the word:

1. Some seed fell by the wayside, on hard ground, and the birds of the air ate it up. This describes people who hear the word, but it just bounces off them.

2. Then, some seed was sown in stony ground. This speaks of those who, at the start, hear the word with gladness: they were happy about getting saved, but they possessed very little spiritual soil to grow spiritual roots. They are the kind of people who only stick around for a while. It is likely that something in the Word offends them, so they quit and separate from Christians. The Word becomes an interference instead of an

intervention.

3. Other seed falls in thorny ground. These folks profess a love for Jesus and grow for a season, then are choked by the thorns, which are rooted in a love for the world. They look good at the start, but do not persevere. They get choked by the world! The drop-out rate from professed Christianity is high! In this Christian life, it's the final lap that counts, not the first.

4. But then there's the seed sown in good ground. It bears much fruit having been nurtured by the love of Christ Jesus their Saviour.

The lesson we learn is those who are truly born again will overcome the world and the devil does not touch them. Listen again to the description of real believers:

> *"For whatsoever is born of God overcomes the world: and this is the victory that overcomes the world, even our faith."*
> (1 John 5:4)

> *"We know that whosoever is born of God sins not;* (does not sin as a lifestyle) *but he that is begotten of God keeps himself, and that wicked one touches him not."* (1 John 5:18)

If a person is elected of God, they will be justified and adopted (Romans 8:29-31).[3] They cannot lose their

---

[3] Rom 8:29-31 *For whom he did foreknow, he also did predestinate to be conformed to the image of his Son, that he might be the firstborn among many brethren. Moreover whom he did predestinate, them he also called: and whom he called, them he also justified: and whom he justified, them he also glorified. What shall we then say to these things? If God be for us, who can be against us?*

salvation. Many scriptures plainly declare that all the elect already possess everlasting life and will be kept in the faith by the power of God:

> *And I give them eternal life, and they shall never perish; neither shall anyone snatch them out of My hand.* (John 10:28)

J. C. Philpot said on this subject, "This is the grand security of the saints of God; for… their inherent sinfulness and weakness are so great, Satan is so crafty and so strong, sin so powerful and deceptive, and the world so entangling and alluring, that but for the special and unceasing grace of God, they must perish, and concerning faith make sure and awful shipwreck."

I believe in the eternal security of God's elect!

Also,

> *"Who shall separate us from the love of Christ? Shall tribulation, or distress, or persecution, or famine, or nakedness, or peril, or sword? As it is written, "For Your sake we are killed all day long; we are accounted as sheep for the slaughter." Yet in all these things we are more than conquerors through Him who loved us. For I am persuaded that neither death, nor life, nor angels nor principalities nor powers nor things present nor things to come, nor height, nor depth, nor any other created thing, shall be able to separate us from the love of God in Christ Jesus our Lord."* (Romans 8:35-39)

And,

> *"Blessed be the God and Father of our Lord Jesus Christ, who according to His abundant mercy has begotten us again to a living hope through the resurrection of Jesus*

Christ from the dead, to an inheritance incorruptible and undefiled, and that does not fade away, reserved in heaven for you, who are kept by the power of God through faith for salvation ready to be revealed in the last time." (1 Peter 1:3-5)

If God has elected a person to be saved, and if God is truly sovereign, then that person cannot be lost. So, a believer's security lies not within the will and power of the believer, but in the Father's good pleasure. Scripture plainly reveals this. That is, it's all of grace! Indeed, it's Amazing Grace!

Summarizing what we have learned thus far:

1. All men are equally sinful and hopelessly lost.
2. Saving faith is not something that man acquires himself, but is a benefit bestowed on him because of Christ's sinless life and sacrifice.
3. Salvation, repentance and faith are all gifts of God.
4. If sinners were ever to be saved, God had to intervene and do the saving.
5. We come to saving faith because we are the Elect of God. In other words, God chose us unto salvation before the foundation of the world.
6. Our salvation is secure since Almighty God has declared it.[4] That is, if an individual was elected to salvation only at God's good pleasure, his salvation is sure; therefore, the essential ingredient of the believer's security lies not in his own power to persevere. His continuing in the faith depends solely on the gracious, persevering decree of God to present Christ a Bride of the Father's choosing.

Continuing our discussion:

---

[4] *"God is not a man that He should lie"* (Numbers 23:19)

When speaking of His redeemed ones, Jesus said, *"My Father who gave them to Me,"* (John 10:29). This is the starting point. The fact that we are the gift of the Father to the Son implies we were in some particular way God's possession even before we came to the Son. One cannot give something not possessed. That we are gifts of the Father to the Son is repeated many times in John's Gospel (6:37, 44, 65; 10:28, 29; 17:2, 6, 9, 11, 12, 24) and in many other places. Yet, many assert this gift fails to make us entirely secure, even though this reasoning contradicts the teaching of Christ. He said: *"This is the Father's will* (Greek "thelema,*" meaning 'intention') *who has sent Me, that of all whom He has given Me, I should lose nothing but should raise it up again at the last day"* (John 6:39). Christ Jesus cannot finally fail to save us. He is both the author and the finisher of our faith (Hebrews 12:2).[5] We are sanctified by the offering of the body of Christ once for all (Hebrews 10:10)[6] so, in the sight of God, we are perfected forever (Hebrews 10:14).[7] When Paul says nothing can separate us from the love of God which is in Christ Jesus our Lord he, as it were, "drains the English language" to make known that our security in Christ is as comprehensive as possible: Here's how he puts it:

> *"For I am persuaded, that neither death, nor life, nor angels, nor principalities, nor powers, nor things present, nor things to come, Nor height, nor depth, nor any other creature, shall be able to separate us from the love of God, which is in Christ Jesus our Lord.* (Romans 8:38-39)

---

[5] Heb 12:2 *Looking unto Jesus the author and finisher of our faith; who for the joy that was set before him endured the cross, despising the shame, and is set down at the right hand of the throne of God.*

[6] Heb 10:10 *By the which will we are sanctified through the offering of the body of Jesus Christ once for all.*

[7] Heb 10:12 *But this man, after he had offered one sacrifice for sins for ever, sat down on the right hand of God;*

It's no wonder then that we can say with absolute assurance, *"He who has begun a good work in you will perform it* [i.e., carry it through] *until the day of Jesus Christ"* (Philippians 1:6). That is, the rebirth accomplished in you by the Holy Spirit, guarantees perseverance (by the power of that same Spirit) all the way to the throne of judgement. This is a work of Amazing Grace! Note that Paul's confidence did not rest in Philippians, but in the One Who would preserve them and enable them to reach the day of Jesus Christ. As the hymn says:

> "The work which His goodness began,
> The arm of His strength will complete;
> His promise is Yea and Amen,
> And never was forfeited yet."
> —*Augustus M. Toplady*

Here's a great truth— God always finishes what He begins. In the Republic of Ireland, in County Kerry, there's a small coastal village that, some years back, had only one general handyman. His name was Dave. Dave was a skilled workman, but he rarely, if ever, completed any job he started. Eventually, the villagers dubbed him "Partially Dave."

Is God like Dave? Does He only partially complete the work he has purposed to accomplish? Should we now call Him, Partially God? Absolutely not! He is never thwarted. He always accomplishes what He purposes.

Notice that it is God who starts His work in us. Salvation always begins with God, since, if He didn't make the first move, we would never move at all! And this work He began in us will be completed. In the last day, the redeemed of Christ will understand clearly and celebrate in a glorious assembly the accomplishments wrought by the Christ of the cross. In that day, God will finish the work He began by the final perfecting of His saints, who will spend eternity with Him. That's Amazing

"AMAZING GRACE" The Most Sung but Most Disbelieved Song Ever!

Grace!
God did not save us to lose us along the way home. I like what James G. Small wrote:

> "I've found a Friend, oh, such a friend!
> He loved me ere I knew Him;
> He drew me with the cords of love, And, thus He bound me to Him.
> And round my heart still closely twine
> Those ties which naught can sever, For I am His, and He is mine,
> Forever and forever.
>
> I've found a Friend, oh, such a friend!
> He bled, He died to save me;
> And not alone the gift of life,
> But His own Self He gave me!
> Naught that I have mine own I call,
> I'll hold it for the Giver,
> My heart, my strength, my life, my all
> Are His, and His forever.
>
> I've found a Friend, oh, such a friend!
> All pow'r to Him is given,
> To guard me on my onward course,
> And bring me safe to heaven.
> Th' eternal glories gleam afar,
> To nerve my faint endeavour;
> So now to watch, to work, to war,
> And then to rest forever.
>
> I've found a Friend, oh, such a friend!
> So kind and true and tender,
> So wise a Counselor and Guide,
> So mighty a Defender!
> From Him who loves me now so well
> What pow'r my soul can sever?

Shall life or death, shall earth or hell?
No! I am His forever."

He saved us by His amazing grace and He saved us for all time and eternity. We have His precious promises to form the basis for that wonderful guarantee. For example:

1 Peter 1:5, (*Who are kept by the power of God through faith unto salvation ready to be revealed in the last time.*)

John 10:28, *And I give unto them eternal life; and they shall never perish, neither shall any man pluck them out of my hand.*

It was not our works that saved us, and it is not our works which keep us! We are saved by grace; kept by grace and secured by grace. Our salvation is about grace from beginning to end!

Look at Philippians 1:6 again: *"Being confident of this very thing, that he which hath begun a good work in you will perform it until the day of Jesus Christ."* The word *"until"* tells us that God is doing what He is doing with some end in mind. We are headed somewhere. There's a destination! In other words, God had a purpose in saving us and if we can understand that; then we can understand why we can have the blessed assurance that we are secure in our salvation.

Albert Einstein of the theory of relativity fame was a genius; however, he was also terribly absent minded. One day he was travelling on a train and the conductor came around asking for the tickets. Einstein looked in every pocket but couldn't find his. The kindly conductor said, "That's all right Professor, I know you well enough to know that you bought a ticket." Einstein, however, just kept on searching his pockets in a vain attempt to recover his ticket. "Don't worry about it Professor," said the conductor as he turned and walked away, "I know you have it somewhere." As he walked away, the conductor turned around and saw Einstein on his hands and knees looking under his seat. The conductor went back to him and assured him again that he had no need of the ticket. "But I do need it," protested Einstein, "I need to know where I'm going."

Here's where we are going:

Romans 8:29, *"For whom he did foreknow, he also did predestinate to be conformed to the image of his Son, that he might be the firstborn among many brethren."*

Ephesians 1:3-5, *"...he has chosen us in him before the foundation of the world, that we should be holy and without blame before him in love: Having predestinated us unto the adoption of children by Jesus Christ to himself, according to the good pleasure of his will."*

God redeemed, regenerated and adopted and reconciled us. We are saved by Amazing Grace. Here's the point. He did not begin our salvation to fail; He began it to finish!

Some teach that a person can be truly saved, but if he turns away from Christ, he can lose his salvation. This view is a grave error. Others teach that if a person professes faith in Christ, he is saved and, thus, eternally secure. That is only true IF HE IS ACTUALLY SAVED!

Scripture, however, teaches that salvation is entirely the work of God and not of man. The God, who is gracious enough to save, is also powerful enough to keep.

Satan loves to counterfeit the work of God. Thus, some like the seeds sown on the rocky and thorny grounds (Matthew 13), seem at first to be saved. But time proves they were not genuine, since God does not cause them to persevere.

If there is evidence that God has actually begun His work of salvation in us, then we can be confident that He will complete what He has begun.

What evidence? If a man has been saved, he will begin to love the Lord Jesus. He will begin to want to know Him, he will begin to want to hear about Him. He will begin to want to spend time with Him. He will begin to hate the darkness and the ways of the world. These things will not save him, but they are things which accompany salvation.

"Being confident of this very thing, that he which hath begun a good work in you will perform it until the day of Jesus Christ."

What is the day of Jesus Christ? —That's the Second Coming of our Lord. The Christian will not be perfected until the Lord Christ shall descend from Heaven with a shout, with the trumpet of the archangel and the voice of God. In that day, the one who brought us to the Cross will bring us to the crown!

Englishman Rowland Hill (1744-1833) was known as a great preacher, pastor and evangelist. He was a master in the craft of sermon-making, always drawing his sermon fresh from a prayerful reading of the Bible. He died in his eighty-ninth year. Shortly before he passed away, he was heard singing the following hymn as he walked through the chapel.

> "And when I die receive me, I'll cry,
> For Jesus has loved me, I cannot tell why;
> But this I can find,
> We two are so joined,
> He'll not be in heaven and leave me behind."

He was entirely right. What God begins, He finishes. Salvation is of the Lord. If salvation is, even in part, the work of man, there is the chance that it won't be finished. But if God has begun it, He will finish it.

"The Blood which, as a priest, He bears
For sinners is His own;
The incense of His prayers and tears
Perfume the holy throne.
In Him my weary soul has rest,
Though I am weak and vile;
I read my name upon His breast
And see the Father smile."
—*John Newton*

And that's the Gospel Truth!

Conclusion and Summary

———◆◇◆———

John Newton, the slave trader, turned Christian, ministered the gospel for almost sixteen years in Olney. There he became a very close associate of William Cowper, one of England's most beloved poets, with whom he published Olney Hymns in 1779. Newton shortly afterward relocated to London, where he continued his gospel ministry until his death December 21, 1807. He wrote his own epitaph, which he requested might be put upon a plain marble tablet near the vestry door of his church in London:

> **JOHN NEWTON**, Clerk,
> Once an Infidel and Libertine,
> a servant of slaves in Africa,
> by the rich mercy of our
> **LORD AND SAVIOUR JESUS CHRIST**,
> preserved, restored, pardoned,
> and appointed to preach the faith he
> had long laboured to destroy.

We are saved by Amazing Grace.

- In the first chapter, we discovered something of our wretched nature. We saw that that we were,
- Spiritually dead.
- We walked in the devil's path.
- We were children of disobedience.
- We were children of wrath.

And what made the difference? It was grace, Amazing

grace! We went on to see that,

- Salvation is entirely by grace. It is both unearned and undeserved.
- We are chosen by grace (Ephesians 1:4).[1]
- We are given to Christ by grace (John 6:37).[2]
- By grace, we are made alive together with Christ, (Ephesians 2:5).[3]
- He has glorified us by grace (Ephesians 2:6).[4]
- We are redeemed by grace (Ephesians 1:7).[5]
- We are justified by grace (Titus 3:7).[6]
- It's Grace! Grace! Grace from beginning to end.

It is clear in Scripture that God does not give one iota of credit to man regarding salvation. It is all of grace! Amazing Grace! Glorious Gospel Grace! The making alive, the undeserved favour, the adoption as children into God's family is all by grace.

- He made us accepted by grace (Ephesians 1:6).[7]

---

[1] Eph 1:4 *According as he hath chosen us in him before the foundation of the world, that we should be holy and without blame before him in love:*
[2] John 6:37 *All that the Father giveth me shall come to me; and him that cometh to me I will in no wise cast out.*
[3] Eph 2:5 *Even when we were dead in sins, hath quickened us together with Christ, (by grace ye are saved;)*
[4] Eph 2:6 *And hath raised us up together, and made us sit together in heavenly places in Christ Jesus:*
[5] Eph 1:7 *In whom we have redemption through his blood, the forgiveness of sins, according to the riches of his grace;*
[6] Titus 3:7 *That being justified by his grace, we should be made heirs according to the hope of eternal life.*
[7] Eph 1:6 *To the praise of the glory of his grace, wherein he hath made us accepted in the beloved.*

Conclusion and Summary

- We have forgiveness by grace (Ephesians 1:7).[8]
- Union with Christ and the good works that follow as God's purpose, after salvation (Ephesians 2:10),[9] are all the gift of God! It's all of grace!

It's no wonder then that Paul writes in Galatians 6:14: *"But God forbid that I should glory, save in the cross of our Lord Jesus Christ, by whom the world is crucified unto me, and I unto the world."*
To "glory" is "to boast." Paul is reminding us that we cannot boast in anything except the cross of the Lord Jesus. That's another way of saying that salvation has been accomplished by grace. All our prosperity, all our accomplishments, all our doctrinal understanding, and even our accumulated insights are nothing to glory about. We can boast only in the grace of God as revealed in the person and work of our Lord Jesus Christ!

In the Old Testament, Jesus is the coming Messiah. He is the promise of grace.

In the New Testament, He is the realized Messiah, the true Promise of Grace revealed.

Grace always brings us to Christ Jesus. He procured salvation for us. He Himself is our salvation. He Himself is the grace of God. Grace is embedded in His very name, for the name of Jesus, means salvation. Remember: *"Neither is there salvation in any other: for there is no other name*

---

[8] Eph 1:7 *In whom we have redemption through his blood, the forgiveness of sins, according to the riches of his grace;*
[9] Eph 2:10 *For we are his workmanship, created in Christ Jesus unto good works, which God hath before ordained that we should walk in them.*

under heaven given among men whereby we must be saved" (Acts 4:12).

Grace brings His elect people to Christ, and to no one else. Grace enables us to look unto Him by faith to be saved.

But what about repentance brother? Yes, what about it? Is that not important? Yes, it is! But let me ask you... from where do we get repentance? The goodness of God, exhibited in His Grace, leads us to repentance (Romans 2:4).[10] There is no other way! Praise to His Name!

It's Grace, Grace, Grace, Glorious, Gospel Grace!

So, we can say Grace is:

1. **Free Grace** - the gift of God (Ephesians 2:8-9).[11]
2. **Saving Grace** - it brings us to eternal salvation.
3. **Sovereign Grace** - not of ourselves, but by God's sovereign will. Salvation *is* not of him that wills, nor of him that runs, but of God that shows mercy (Romans 9:16).[12]
4. **Sustaining Grace** - we are kept by the power of God through faith unto salvation ready to be revealed in the last time (1 Peter 1:5).[13]

---

[10] Rom 2:4 *Or despisest thou the riches of his goodness and forbearance and longsuffering; not knowing that the goodness of God leadeth thee to repentance?*

[11] Eph 2:8-9 *For by grace are ye saved through faith; and that not of yourselves: it is the gift of God: Not of works, lest any man should boast.*

[12] Rom 9:16 *So then it is not of him that willeth, nor of him that runneth, but of God that sheweth mercy.*

[13] 1Pet 1:5 *Who are kept by the power of God through faith unto salvation ready to be revealed in the last time.*

Conclusion and Summary

The next time we sing the grand old hymn, Amazing Grace, may we sing it with gospel rejoicing in our hearts.

>Amazing Grace, how sweet the sound
>That saved a wretch like me
>I once was lost, but now am found
>Was blind, but now I see
>
>T'was grace that taught my heart to fear
>And grace, my fears relieved.
>How precious did that grace appear,
>The hour I first believed.
>
>Through many dangers, toils and snares
>I have already come
>'Tis grace that brought me safe thus far,
>And grace will lead me home
>
>When we've been there ten thousand years,
>Bright shining as the sun
>We've no less days to sing God's praise
>Than when we've first begun.

And that's the Gospel Truth!

APPENDIX I
What Does the Term "World" Mean in Scripture?

The free-will folks strenuously argue that Christ died for every individual who ever was born. According to them, when we read that Jesus died for the world, this means He died for every person without distinction. But consider the following scriptures:

Matthew 16:26, *"For what is a man profited if he gain the whole world and lose his own soul."* Are we then to understand this to mean, "What does it profit a man if he gains every individual who has ever lived?"

Luke 2:21, *"And... there went out a decree from Caesar Augustus that all the world should be taxed."* Are we to understand by this that every individual who had ever lived or even everyone alive on planet earth at that time was to be taxed? Not everyone in those days lived in the Roman Empire. (Here the word 'world' refers to the known Roman World and excludes all the people, for example, in China. It certainly does not mean every individual alive at that time).

John 12:19, *"The Pharisees said... behold the whole world is gone after him."* Again you can see this does not mean every individual alive in A.D.33. Not every individual then alive was in Jerusalem at that time.

John 14:27, *"Peace I leave with you, my peace I give unto you, not as the world giveth give I unto you."* Need I ask it? Does every individual who has ever lived give some kind of peace to us?

Acts 19:27, *"Diana... whom all Asia and the world worships."* Is that a fact? This must mean, if the free-will folks are consistent in their thinking, that they believe all the Chinese and Pygmies worshiped her. But that, of course, is nonsense. They had their own set of Deities whom they reverenced.

Acts 24:5, *"A mover of sedition among the Jews throughout the whole world."* Where was this whole world? Was Paul inciting the Jews in Japan and Mexico to sedition... or does the world in this verse mean an area around the Mediterranean?

Rom 1:8, *"Your faith is spoken of throughout the whole world."* Did every single person then alive on the planet speak of the faith of the Roman Christians? Did even every person in the Roman Empire speak of their faith? Of course not! Yet, the truth was that many people in the Empire spoke about their faith. Many people are therefore here designated as the whole world.

The point I am making is that the word world is an ambiguous term with many and varied meanings. You just cannot attribute one meaning (i.e. every individual) otherwise, it will be a screwball doctrine you come up with.

In Acts 17:24 the word 'world' stands for the whole created universe (not individuals).

In John 13:1 'world' means the earth (as in Ephesians 1:4) not individuals.

In John 12:31 it is used for this "world-system" (not individuals).

In Romans 3:19 it is used for every individual.

What Does the Term "World" Mean in Scripture?

In John 15:18 it is used for humanity minus believers (Therefore not every person who ever lived).

Romans 11:12 it is used of the Gentile world as opposed to the Jewish world (therefore not every individual).

In John 3:16, "God so loved the world" is a reference to the non-exclusive nature of this new covenant. In other words, God has burst out of the confines of Israel and is now the New Covenant God of both Jew and Gentile (the whole world). It is not a statement that Christ died for every individual.

In John. 6:33-35, "world" is used for every believer.

In John 12:47-48, it is again evident that world refers to the world of believers.

A. W. Pink writes:

> "Many people suppose they already know the simple meaning of John 3:16, and therefore they conclude that no diligent study is required of them to discover the precise teaching of this verse. Needless to say, such an attitude shuts out any further light which they otherwise might obtain on the passage. Yet, if anyone will take a concordance and read carefully the various passages in which the term "world" (as a translation of "kosmos") occurs, he will quickly perceive that to ascertain the precise meaning of, the word "world" in any given passage is not nearly so easy as is popularly supposed. The word "kosmos," and its English equivalent "world," is not used with a uniform significance in the New Testament. Very far from it. It is used in quite a

number of different ways ..."Thus it will be seen that "kosmos" (world) has at least seven clearly defined different meanings in the New Testament. It may be asked, has then God used a word thus to confuse and confound those who read the Scriptures? We answer, No! Nor has He written His Word for lazy people who are too dilatory, or too busy with the things of this world, or, like Martha, so much occupied with "serving," they have no time and no heart to "search" and "study" Holy Writ! But how is a searcher of the Scriptures to know which of the above meanings the term "world" has in any given passage? The answer is: This may be ascertained by a careful study of the context, by diligently noting what is predicated of "the world" in each passage, and by prayer fully consulting other parallel passages to the one being studied." (A. W. Pink, Appendix 3, *The Sovereignty of God*)

"...The whole world is gone after him.' Did all the world go after Christ? 'Then went all Judea, and were baptized of him in Jordan.' Was all Judea, or all Jerusalem baptized in Jordan? 'Ye are of God, little children', and 'the whole world lies in the wicked one.' Does 'the whole world' there mean everybody? If so, how was it, then, that there were some who were 'of God?' The words 'world' and 'all' are used in some seven or eight senses in Scripture, and it is very rarely that 'all' means all persons, taken individually. The words are generally used to signify that Christ has redeemed some of all sorts— some Jews, some Gentiles, some rich, some poor, and has not restricted his redemption to either Jew or Gentile." (Charles H. Spurgeon, Particular Redemption, A Sermon, 28 Feb 1858)

APPENDIX II
"All?"

Those who hold to the free-will scheme tell us that "ALL means all that's all." It's a slick statement, but is it true? Let's then consider this word all!

1 Timothy 2:1-6, *"I exhort therefore, that, first of all, supplications, prayers, intercessions, and giving of thanks, be made for all men: for kings and for all that are in authority; that we may lead a quiet and peaceable life in all godliness and honesty. For this is good and acceptable in the sight of God our Saviour who will have all men to be saved, and to come unto the knowledge of the truth. For there is one God, and one mediator between God and men, the man Christ Jesus, who gave Himself a ransom for all to be testified in due time."*

In these verses we are exhorted to pray for all men and are told that God wills that all men would be saved. Case closed says the free-will exponent!

Concerning praying for all men, we know from John 17:9 that the Lord Jesus Christ Himself deliberately refrained from doing this very thing. He said, "I pray for them (the elect): I pray not for the world but for them You have given Me." So, is Paul contradicting Jesus and telling us to pray for all men indiscriminately?

To answer that question, let's consider what we are being asked to do. The Apostle says we are to pray for ALL men. Does all mean all, that's all in this verse? If it does, that means we are to pray for every individual in the world today? The problem with that is, I don't know all the people alive on earth today and neither do you. I neither know their names nor their problems. I can't, therefore, possibly obey this command if all means all, that's all!

Also, even if I knew everyone's names and where they lived, I wouldn't have time to pray for all of them. It's hard enough to find time to pray for everyone whom I am concerned about, never mind every inhabitant of planet earth. If I set out to pray for everyone, I would, in reality, end up praying for nobody.

However, the problem is solved when we look at the phrase "all men" in the context and see that it means "for all sorts of men." I am to pray for Kings and people in authority. Without doubt, I should also pray for those whom God has brought across my path. In fact, I should not rule anyone out of my prayers because of social standing or ethnic background. I should pray for all men.

In fact, the word "all" ("pas" in the Greek) is often translated, "all kinds of," or "all manner of." Consider the following passages where "all" can mean every, or all kinds of or all manner of.

> Luke 11:42,[1] All manner of herbs
> Matthew 4:23,[2] All manner of disease
> Matthew 5:11,[3] All manner of evil

Consider also, Mark 11:32[4] tells us that all men counted that John was a prophet. But think about it, the people in Ireland didn't count him a prophet for they

---

[1] Luke 11:42 *But woe unto you, Pharisees! for ye tithe mint and rue and all manner of herbs, and pass over judgment and the love of God: these ought ye to have done, and not to leave the other undone.*
[2] Matt 4:23 *And Jesus went about all Galilee, teaching in their synagogues, and preaching the gospel of the kingdom, and healing all manner of sickness and all manner of disease among the people.*
[3] Matt 5:11 *Blessed are ye, when men shall revile you, and persecute you, and shall say all manner of evil against you falsely, for my sake.*
[4] Mark 11:32 *But if we shall say, Of men; they feared the people: for all men counted John, that he was a prophet indeed.*

"All?"

were unaware of him. So "ALL" in this passage means all who knew about John. It does not mean every individual in the world.

In John 8:2 it says of Jesus, that *"all people came to Him"* but we know the Pharisees, the Sadducees and the High Priest refused to come to Him. Therefore, the word ALL in these passages cannot possibly mean every individual in Israel and certainly not every person in the world.

In Romans 5:18, Paul wrote: *"Therefore, as by the offense of one judgment came upon all men to condemnation; even so by the righteousness of one the free gift came upon all men unto justification of life."*

Notice how in this one verse, "all" has two different meanings! All, because of Adam, are condemned— this is a case of "All means all, that's all!" But then notice that because of the free gift "all" are justified! Does all mean "all means all, that's all" in this thought? Does anybody in their right mind think this means that everybody will be justified? Will every man, without exception be justified? The Bible knows nothing of such things! If it is so that all means all that's all then Hell, in that case, will be boarded up to everyone.

Does this scripture then mean that all who were lost will be saved? We know better than that for the Bible tells a different story. We know that all people, all individuals, are lost in Adam, but not all will be saved. The truth is, all in Adam are condemned and all in Christ— everyone who is in Christ will be saved. So, the 'All' in Christ cannot possibly mean every individual in the World.

Romans 14:2 tells us how one man *"believes that he may eat all things"* whereas another eats only herbs. Does the first gentleman eat all and everything that exist? In that case he would be like Mr. Creosote, the character in Monty Python's Flying Circus who ate so much that he exploded. 'All' in this case means, rather, that he ate all kinds of things. It is obvious Paul means that some men allow themselves meat as well as herbs whereas others avoid meat.

In writing to Titus (2:11) Paul declares that *"the grace of God that brings salvation has appeared to all men."* Since all individuals are not brought to salvation this then means that grace has appeared to "to all sorts of men." This means that no class of person is excluded from the Gospel. It must be preached to the down and out and to the high and mighty. It must be preached to all out of every nation, race and tribe.

And in John 12:32, unless we assume that everyone is going to go to Heaven, the text, *"If I be lifted up from the earth, will draw all men unto Me"* means that He will draw all manner of men unto Him. If it means all individuals without exception will be drawn to Him then, according to the word of the Lord, no one will be lost.

When we read, therefore, that He wills that all men will be saved, it means He will have men of all sorts to be saved and come unto a knowledge of the truth." If He actually wills the salvation of all men, (that is, all individuals), then we must conclude His will is impotent and easily defeated.

John Nelson, a preacher in the 18th century had been a blacksmith before God saved him. And God used him in a very wonderful way to point people to Christ. One day he was talking to a self-righteous individual who said, "I don't need your Saviour. I live right, and I've done good things. I'll take my chances with the rest of the people." Mr. Nelson replied, "Well, look here my good man, if God let you into heaven, you'd bring discord there, because all the others would be singing 'worthy is the lamb that was slain to receive power and riches and wisdom and strength and honour and glory and blessing,' and you'd be singing 'worthy am I, glory to me, because I lived a consistent Christian life.'" He said, "If an angel heard you sing a song like that in heaven, why he'd throw you over the wall." And the redeemed folks will all chime in and say, 'My soul shall make her boast in the Lord, and

"All?"

nothing else.'"

There'll be nobody in heaven singing about what they have done to get there.

It's Grace! Grace! All of grace! Amazing Grace!

Our hope stands on pure Grace, Sovereign Grace, Grace unqualified! God saves us because He is good, not because we are! God saves us because He is gracious, not because He sees any goodness inherent in us! It's Grace! Grace! Grace!

Amazing Grace!

And that's the Gospel Truth

Questionnaire on Grace

---

1) In His high priestly prayer, who did the Lord Jesus pray for?
   a. Everyone in the world?
   b. Only for His people?

Answer: John 17:9

2) Which is true?
   a. Faith in Christ Jesus makes you one of His sheep.
   b. Because you are one of His sheep you eventually come to faith in Christ.

Answer: John 10:26-27

3) Why did you come to Christ Jesus? Was it…
   a. because you decided to come?
   b. because the Father gave you to Jesus Christ?

Answer: John 6:37

4) Why do some people entirely refuse to believe? Is it…
   a. because they have not had the Gospel well enough explained to them?
   b. because they are not the Lord's sheep?

Answer: John 10:26

"AMAZING GRACE" The Most Sung but Most Disbelieved Song Ever!

5) Does Jesus actually...
    a. save His people?
    b. make it possible for them to be saved?

_____

Answer: Matthew 1:21

_____

Isaiah 53:11

6) In this matter of free choice,
    a. did you choose the Lord Jesus?
    b. did He choose you?

_____

Answer: John 15:16

7) Did you become a child of God by...
    a. your free will?
    b. the free will of God?

_____

Answer: John 1:12-13

_____

Answer: Romans 9:16

8) Did you repent because...
    a. you made a decision to do so?
    b. the goodness of God led you to do so?

_____

Answer: Romans 2:4

Questionnaire on Grace

9) Did you get saving faith because…
   a. God gave it to you as a gift?
   b. you had to ability to exercise faith according to your own free will?

Answer: Ephesians 2:8

Answer: Philippians 1:29

10) Who opened your heart to the Gospel?
    a. God.
    b. You opened your own heart.

Answer: Acts 16:14

Answer: Revelation 3:7

11) Are you appointed unto eternal life because …
    a. God saw you would believe the Gospel?
    b. you believed the Gospel because you were already appointed unto eternal life?

Answer: Acts 13:48

12) Sin left man…
    a. spiritually healthy.
    b. spiritually unhealthy.
    c. spiritually dead.

Answer: Ephesians 2:1

13) God saved you because…
   a. He saw something worthwhile in you.
   b. it was His un-explainable sovereign will to do so.

Answer: Ephesians 1:5

14) Did you have any part to play in your salvation?
   a. Yes
   b. No

Answer: Ephesians 2:8-9

Answer: Romans 9:16

Miles McKee Ministries

If you profited spiritually from this book, (also available as an eBook), please spread the word.

Please also consider giving a review of this publication from whichever retailer you made your purchase.

For more of Miles McKee's writings, please visit www.milesmckee.com/books.html.

Other titles by Miles McKee include,

Jesus is God … Always Was and Always will be: Part 1

Jesus is God … Always Was and Always will be: Part 2

And that's the Gospel Truth!

Getting Into Heaven Before They Close the Door (Mini Book)

Is Divine Healing Guaranteed in the Atonement? (Mini Book)

*Amazing Grace:
The Most Sung but Most Disbelieved Ever!*

The True Believer (Mini Book)

*Smooth Stones to Slay Goliath…
Gospel Gems from Gospel Greats.*

The Gospel Truth about Assurance.

Is Jesus Enough?

About the Cover Artist

Michael Burns is a South African-born contemporary artist who splits his time between London and Ireland. After graduating from the Ulster University School of Art, he pursued a career in advertising. His work utilises colour, movement and dynamism to create striking imagery that draws the viewer towards and underlying message of personal journey and discovery.

About the Layout Designer

Jon J. Cardwell is the pastor of Calvary Baptist Church in Ninilchik, Alaska, USA. He is also the author of several books, including the devotional series, *Jesus Christ, the Bread of Life*, and the bestselling *Christ and Him Crucified*.

Miles McKee Ministries,

Ireland
India
Nepal
Myanmar
Kenya

www.milesmckee.com
miles@milesmckee.com

FERNANDO PESSOA & CO.

*Other works by
Fernando Pessoa
available in English*

PROSE
The Book of Disquietude
Always Astonished: *Selected Prose*

POETRY
Poems of Fernando Pessoa
The Surprise of Being

FERNANDO PESSOA & CO.

Selected Poems

*Edited and translated
from the Portuguese by*
RICHARD ZENITH

Grove Press/New York

For my mother and father

Translation copyright © 1998 Richard Zenith
Introduction copyright © 1998 Richard Zenith

All rights reserved. No part of this book may be reproduced in any form or by any electronic or mechanical means, including information storage and retrieval systems, without permission in writing from the publisher, except by a reviewer, who may quote brief passages in a review.

Published simultaneously in Canada
Printed in the United States of America

FIRST EDITION

Library of congress Cataloging-in-Publication Data
Pessoa, Fernando, 1888–1935.
　　Fernando Pessoa & Co. : selected poems / edited and translated from the Portuguese by Richard Zenith
　　　p.　cm.
　　ISBN 0-8021-1628-0
　　1. Pessoa, Fernando, 1888–1935—Translations into English.
　I. Zenith, Richard.　II. Title.
PQ9261.P417A288　1998
869.1'41—dc21　　　　　　　　　　　　　　　　　97-50201
　　　　　　　　　　　　　　　　　　　　　　　　　CIP

Design by Laura Hammond Hough

Grove Press
841 Broadway
New York, NY 10003

98 99 00 01 10 9 8 7 6 5 4 3 2 1

CONTENTS

xi   About the Selection and Sources
xiv   Acknowledgments
1   Introduction: The Drama and Dream of Fernando Pessoa

37   ALBERTO CAEIRO: The Unwitting Master
43   *from* THE KEEPER OF SHEEP
45   1 I've never kept sheep
48   2 My gaze is clear like a sunflower
49   5 To not think of anything is metaphysics enough
52   9 I'm a keeper of sheep
53   10 Hello, keeper of sheep
54   18 I'd rather be the dust of the road
55   20 The Tagus is more beautiful than the river that flows through my village
56   23 My gaze, blue like the sky
57   24 What we see of things are the things
58   32 Yesterday afternoon a man from the cities
60   37 Like a large blot of smudged fire
61   38 Blessed be the same sun of other lands
62   39 The mystery of things — where is it?
63   40 I see a butterfly go by
64   42 The coach came down the road, and went on
65   47 On an incredibly clear day

FERNANDO PESSOA & CO.

67 *from* THE SHEPHERD IN LOVE
69 Before I had you
70 Perhaps those who are good at seeing are poor at feeling
71 The shepherd in love lost his staff

73 *from* UNCOLLECTED POEMS
75 To see the fields and the river
76 When Spring returns
77 If I die young
79 It is night. It's very dark. In a house far away
80 The Universe is not an idea of mine
81 The child who thinks about fairies and believes in them
82 Slowly the field unrolls and shines golden
83 Yesterday the preacher of truths (his truths)
84 They spoke to me of people, and of humanity
85 I lie down in the grass
86 Dirty unknown child playing outside my door
87 You who are a mystic see a meaning in all things
88 Ah! They want a light that's better than the sun's
89 That thing over there was more there than it is
90 This morning I went out very early
91 I can also make conjectures
92 This may be the last day of my life

93 RICARDO REIS: The Sad Epicurean

99 *from* ODES
101 Others narrate with lyres or harps
102 The gods grant nothing more than life
103 Don't clap your hands before beauty
104 Ah, you believers in Christs and Marys
106 On this day when the green fields
107 Here, with no other Apollo than Apollo
108 Above the truth reign the gods

Contents

109	Let the gods
111	Lips red from wine
112	I prefer roses, my love, to the homeland
113	Follow your destiny
114	The bird alights, looking only to its alighting
115	O morning that breaks without looking at me
116	Obey the law, whether it's wrong or you are
117	I want my verses to be like jewels
118	Day after day life's the same life
119	Who delights in the mind can delight in no destiny
120	As if each kiss
121	Your dead gods tell me nothing I need
122	Fate frightens me, Lydia. Nothing is certain
123	I devote my higher mind to the ardent
124	My eyes see the fields, the fields
125	Each man is a world, and as each fountain
126	Not only wine but its oblivion I pour
127	How great a sadness and bitterness
128	Solemnly over the fertile land
129	Where there are roses we plant doubt
130	As long as I feel the full breeze in my hair
131	What we feel, not what is felt
132	I don't know if the love you give is love you have
133	Want little: you'll have everything
134	I was left in the world, all alone
135	I tell with severity. I think what I feel
136	I placidly wait for what I don't know
137	Countless lives inhabit us
139	ÁLVARO DE CAMPOS: The Jaded Sensationist
143	I study myself but can't perceive
144	Listen, Daisy. When I die, although

145	Ah, the first minutes in cafés of new cities
146	Time's Passage
169	It was on one of my voyages
170	Ah, when we set out to sea
171	But it's not just the cadaver
172	I leaned back in the deck chair and closed my eyes
173	The Tobacco Shop
180	Oporto-Style Tripe
181	A Note in the Margin
183	Deferral
185	Sometimes I meditate
186	Ah, the freshness in the face of leaving a task undone
187	At long last . . . , no doubt about it . . .
188	Pop
189	I walk in the night of the suburban street
191	Yes, I know it's all quite natural
193	Streetcar Stop
194	Birthday
196	No! All I want is freedom
197	I'd like to be able to like liking
198	Reality
200	I'm beginning to know myself. I don't exist
201	Pack your bags for Nowhere at All
202	I got off the train
203	This old anguish
205	Impassively
206	On the eve of never departing
207	Symbols? I'm sick of symbols
208	The ancients invoked the Muses
209	I don't know if the stars rule the world
210	I've been thinking about nothing at all
211	All love letters are

Contents

213 FERNANDO PESSOA-HIMSELF: The Mask Behind the Man

219 *from* SONGBOOK
221 Ocean (Morning)
222 God
223 *From* Oblique Rain
225 The wind is blowing too hard
226 The Mummy
231 The gods are happy
232 In the light-footed march of heavy time
233 Christmas
234 By the moonlight, in the distance
235 Waterfront
236 Some Music
237 I feel sorry for the stars
238 I seem to be growing calm
239 Sleep
240 I contemplate the silent pond
241 Like a uselessly full glass
242 The sun shining over the field
243 I don't know how many souls I have
244 The soul with boundaries
246 I'm sorry I don't respond
247 Autopsychography
248 I don't know how to be truly sad
249 The clouds are dark
250 Like an astonishing remnant
251 If I think for more than a moment
252 From the mountain comes a song
253 This species of madness
254 The wind in the darkness howls
255 I have ideas and reasons
256 With a smile and without haste

257	Outside where the trees
258	I hear in the night across the street
259	Almost anonymous you smile
260	This
261	The day is quiet, quiet is the wind
262	The sun rests unmoving
263	The washwoman beats the laundry
264	To travel! To change countries
265	This great wavering between
266	I have in me like a haze
267	Dreams, systems, myths, ideals
268	I divide what I know
269	The child that laughs in the street
271	*from* MESSAGE
273	Prince Henry the Navigator
274	The Stone Pillar
275	The Sea Monster
276	Epitaph of Bartolomeu Dias
277	Ferdinand Magellan
278	Portuguese Sea
279	Prayer
281	Notes to the Introduction and the Poems
289	Bibliography

ABOUT THE SELECTION AND SOURCES

From the Introduction the reader will gather a sense of how widely Pessoa's written universe stretches. This collection focuses on just one aspect of that universe: the poetry written in Portuguese. The large body of English poetry would need a collection all its own to be adequately represented (admitting, as many do not, that a poetic oeuvre can be represented by selections from it), and I preferred not to reduce the already limited space allotted to four great names in twentieth-century poetry for the sake of Pessoa's lesser work. Curious readers can consult one of the Portuguese or Brazilian editions of Pessoa's English poems, which are interesting above all for their ideas as well as for what they reveal about the poet and his art.

Except for a few signature poems, such as "The Tobacco Shop" and "Autopsychography," this volume consists largely of work never before published in English translation. In fact, many of the poems were still unpublished in Portuguese as recently as ten years ago. Where other translations exist, discrepancies are occasionally due not to different interpretations but to different source texts. I have had the advantage of working from recent, vastly improved Portuguese editions of Pessoa's works, and future translators will have the advantage of even better ones.

Pessoa's oeuvre is an editor's nightmare, perhaps more than any other produced in this century by a major Western writer. Pessoa published relatively little and left only a small percentage of the rest of his huge output—over 25,000 manuscripts have survived—in anything close to a finished state. The handwritten texts, which constitute the vast majority, tend to teeter on the brink of illegibility, requiring not just transcription but decipherment. Sometimes verses and stanzas are dispersed on a page (or in the margins around an earlier text) like the pieces of a puzzle whose correct order, if there is one, cannot with certainty be determined. To top off the confusion, Pessoa often left two, three, six, or seven textual alternates above or below a given word or phrase without crossing anything out, leaving his final decision for a later revision that all too rarely occurred.

A computer edition could perhaps fairly reflect Pessoa's ever-tentative texts by having the alternate wordings blink on and off at regularly timed intervals (an idea suggested to me by Professor K. David Jackson), but a book editor must choose which authorial variant to incorporate in the body of the text and which to relegate to the notes. Some editors give preference to Pessoa's original phrasing (provided he didn't strike it out, of course); others go with the last thing he wrote. Editors understandably want an objective methodology, a set rule to follow, but to arrive at one requires an ineluctably subjective determination: first version or last?

A translation, by its nature subjective, need not pretend to be other than what it is, and so I take whatever version—first, last, or one in between—that seems to work best. Usually, though, I prefer the first version, produced in the initial act of creation, when Pessoa was intensely immersed in the text—not always or even usually the case when he went back to tinker with it later. Ricardo Reis is an exception. The Horatian odes written in his name were so tightly woven that Pessoa could not revisit them without getting into the woof of their verse structure. I find the Pessoa-Reis variants generally better than or at least as good as the original versions.

My translations of the Reis odes are largely based on the readings presented in the critical edition made by Luiz Fagundes Duarte. For the poetry attributed to Álvaro de Campos I have relied on Teresa Rita Lopes's critical edition. Both editors have made significant improvements on earlier editions, though in a few instances I prefer the earlier readings. The original texts of the Caeiro translations can mostly be found in Maria Aliete Galhoz's edition of Pessoa's poetry; others were first published by Lopes in her *Pessoa por Conhecer*, which also

About the Selection and Sources

presents a corrected transcription of the poem whose first line is translated here as "This may be the last day of my life." I also consulted the facsimile edition of *The Keeper of Sheep* produced by Ivo Castro, who was working on a comprehensive critical edition of Caeiro's poetry as this anthology was going to press. A complete but uncritical edition of the Caeiro poetry was recently published by Teresa Sobral Cunha (*Poemas Completos de Alberto Caeiro* [Lisbon: Editorial Presença, 1994]). No critical edition exists for the Portuguese poetry signed by Pessoa himself; the originals can be found in Galhoz's edition.

ACKNOWLEDGMENTS

I am grateful to the Calouste Gulbenkian Foundation and the Instituto Camões for grants that supported my translations of Pessoa's poetry. I was greatly aided and encouraged by various Pessoa scholars, including Teresa Rita Lopes and José Blanco. Many friends helped me to interpret or render difficult passages: Jonathan Weightman, José León Acosta, Livia Apa, Manuela Correia Lopes, Manuela Rocha, Margarida Amado, and, especially, Manuela Neves. Martin Earl, after helping me to select and order the poems, read through the entire manuscript and made invaluable suggestions on the translations and on all the essay matter.

Richard Zenith

INTRODUCTION: THE DRAMA AND DREAM OF FERNANDO PESSOA

This is my morality, or metaphysics, or me: Passerby of everything, even of my own soul, belonging to nothing, desiring nothing, being nothing — abstract center of impersonal sensations, a fallen sentient mirror, reflecting the world's diversity. I don't know if I'm happy this way. Nor do I care.
                                                    The Book of Disquietude

Imagine someone pointing to his cheek with an expression of pain and saying "abracadabra!" We ask "What do you mean?" And he answers "I meant toothache."
                                                    Wittgenstein *Philosophical Investigations*

Fernando António Nogueira Pêssoa was born in Lisbon on 13 June 1888. When scarcely five years old, he lost his father. His mother remarried a year and a half later and took Fernando to Durban, South Africa, where his stepfather served as the Portuguese consul. Fernando attended English school in Durban, where he lived with his family until the age of seventeen. When he was thirteen he made a year-long visit to Portugal, returning there for good in 1905. He began studying Letters at the University of Lisbon in 1906 but dropped out after eight months. During the following years he stayed with relatives or in rented rooms, making his living by translating and drafting business letters in English and French. He began publishing criticism in 1912, creative prose in 1913, and poetry in 1914. This was also the year when the alter egos he called heteronyms — Alberto

Caeiro, Ricardo Reis, and Álvaro de Campos—came into existence. In 1915 he dropped the circumflex from his surname. Throughout the rest of his life, Pessoa contributed poems and prose pieces to magazines. He published several chapbooks of his English poems in 1918 and 1921, and a single book of Portuguese poems in 1934. He had one romantic relationship of brief duration. He died in 1935 from cirrhosis of the liver.

So goes the capsule biography of Portugal's greatest poet, who did not, however, exist. We are informed of this particular by Álvaro de Campos, one of the dramatis personae invented by Pessoa to play out his life and so save him the trouble. Campos was the dynamic, free-spirited heteronym—a bisexual dandy who studied in Glasgow, traveled to the Orient, and lived it up in London, acting out many things Pessoa dreamed of but never dared to do. Or never cared to? Whatever the case, Pessoa had no reason to regret having delegated his adventurous streak to Campos, who eventually wearied of his boisterous, footloose existence, coming home to Lisbon and to the realization that all his travels and shenanigans had been quite useless, since, as he had already discerned in an early poem, "however much I felt I never felt enough,/ And life always pained me, it was always too little, and I was unhappy." So that Campos, besides sparing his creator the bother of living, vindicated Pessoa's decision to let himself be spared.

Insofar as he was socially inept and/or uninterested, Pessoa was like many other authors, preferring to write about life instead of living it, but his renunciation went further, for the very idea of existing horrified him. Or was this horror mere poetic posturing? The question does not fit Pessoa's case, since he claimed to do nothing but pretend and posture. That claim was itself no doubt a posturing, and therefore self-fulfilling. The logic oscillates between tautology and paradox, the twin poles that governed the world according to Pessoa, who in diversifying himself was ever more the same, who wanted to be everything so as not to be anything, who disowned himself to become the universe.

Literary alter egos were almost the fashion among early twentieth-century writers. Pound had his Mauberley, Rilke his Malte Laurids Brigge, and Valéry his Monsieur Teste. But no one took the game out

Introduction

as far as Pessoa, who gave up his own life to confer quasi-real substance on the trinity of co-poets he designated as heteronyms, giving each a personal biography, psychology, politics, aesthetics, religion, and physique. Alberto Caeiro, considered the Master by the other two, was an ingenuous, unlettered man who lived in the country and had no profession. Ricardo Reis was a doctor and classicist who wrote odes in the style of Horace. Álvaro de Campos, a naval engineer, started out as an exuberant futurist with a Walt Whitmanesque voice, but over time he came to sound more like a mopey existentialist. The pithiest description and distinction of the heteronyms was made by Pessoa in a text he wrote in English: "Caeiro has one discipline: things must be felt as they are. Ricardo Reis has another kind of discipline: things must be felt, not only as they are, but also so as to fall in with a certain ideal of classic measure and rule. In Álvaro de Campos things must simply be felt."

To remind us or himself what stuff these men were made of, Pessoa gave them all his same basic build (Campos was slightly taller, Reis and Caeiro slightly shorter), his same clean-shaven face, roughly his same age, and his own status of confirmed bachelor. But the heteronyms, he cautioned, "should be considered as distinct from their author. Each one forms a drama of sorts; and together they form another drama.... The works of these three poets constitute a dramatic ensemble, with careful attention having been paid to their intellectual and personal interaction.... It is a drama in people, instead of in acts." There was also an "orthonym" who wrote poetry under the name of Fernando Pessoa and was just as much a fiction as the heteronyms, but he had nothing to do with the social entity whose middle names were António and Nogueira. The only way Pessoa could conceive of being a poet was by not being, by pretending, by achieving complete insincerity:

> The poet is a faker
> Who's so good at his act
> He even fakes the pain
> Of pain he feels in fact.

> *And those who read his words*
> *Will feel in what he wrote*
> *Neither of the pains he has*
> *But just the one they don't.*
>
> From "Autopsychography"

Poetry for Pessoa was something more than life, or at least something different from life, something capable of providing relief from our daily routine. If poets merely dish out to the reader what they really feel in their day-to-day life, then they are giving too little, according to Pessoa. "What a poor hope," wrote Pessoa in another poem, "that just hopes to exist!" The "real world" is false, in a sense akin to the word "faulty," which comes from the same Latin root. That is why the true poet must be a faker, giving not what is but what should or could be, or what cannot be except in poetry.

Pessoa was sincere in his insincerity; heteronymy was not a game he acquired or invoked along the way, it was woven into his DNA. Already as a small child he had invented his first literary playmate, the Chevalier de Pas, in whose name he wrote himself letters, perhaps in French, a language he learned from his mother. And by the time he was a teenager he had a wide circle of make-believe friends—with names such as Dr. Pancracio, Eduardo Lança, and Dr. Gaudencio Nabos—who wrote stories, poems, and humorous pieces for several "newspapers" copied out in neat columns by Fernando, in Portuguese. (Although he spent seven and a half of his formative years in the British colony of Natal, young Fernando never lost touch with the Portuguese language.) These fictitious authors were soon joined by Charles Robert Anon, Alexander Search, and other imaginary English writers. Several of these proto-heteronyms, including one Jean Seul, who wrote in French, accompanied their creator on his voyage back to Lisbon in 1905. Pessoa even had calling cards printed for Alexander Search, author of a large group of English poems under the general title "Documents of Mental Decadence."

Pessoa, in a fragmentary note only recently published, had this to say about his pathology: "The self-division of the I is a common

Introduction

phenomenon in cases of masturbation." Although it is just one of many possible glosses on Pessoa's condition, it has the virtue of revealing the extent of the poet's ruthless lucidity with respect to himself, and there is something chilling in the diagnosis when we consider that his only romantic liaison, largely epistolary, was prevented from going forward by the constant interference of Álvaro de Campos, who so exasperated the beloved, Ophelia Queiroz, that she finally declared she hated him. Pessoa, in the end, preferred to remain with Álvaro and the other literary characters he had spawned single-handedly. In a twist on Freud, we could speculate that the adult Pessoa might have been able to suppress his strange childhood urge, sublimating his inclination to self-division into a more "normal" kind of life, with marriage and the rest, but he never seems to have considered that route.

In addition to the three full-fledged heteronyms, the mature Pessoa gave birth to Bernardo Soares, a "semiheteronym" who authored the sprawling fictional diary known as *The Book of Disquietude*; António Mora, a prolific philosopher and sociologist; the Baron of Teive, an essayist; Thomas Crosse, whose critical writings in English promoted Portuguese literature in general and Alberto Caeiro's work in particular; I. I. Crosse, Thomas's brother and collaborator; Coelho Pacheco, a poet; Raphael Baldaya, astrologer; Maria José, a nineteen-year-old hunchback consumptive who wrote a desperate, unmailed love letter to a handsome metalworker who passed under her window on his way to work each day; and so on, and so on, and so on. At least seventy-two names besides Fernando Pessoa were "responsible" for the thousands of texts that were actually written and the many more that he only planned, and other names will probably turn up as scholars continue to explore the still not completely charted territory of his writings.

Or should we call those writings an expanding universe? Over the last ten years, as new texts from the archives have been transcribed and published and with many new players entering the picture, Fernando Pessoa & Co. has proved to be a larger, more complex enterprise than anyone had imagined. When Pessoa called his heteronymic venture a drama, he meant it quite literally, for his personae interacted, with him and with each other. They collaborated on publication projects, critiqued, and even translated one another. To use a trendy term, they networked. And so, in the heyday of Sensationism, his most fruitful literary theory, Pessoa invented António de Seabra to serve as one of its critics and Sher Henay to compile an English-language "Sensationist Anthology," which—had it been executed—would have featured work by Álvaro de Campos and Alberto Caeiro, the movement's two most illustrious practitioners. Another movement, Neopaganism, was ardently defended by Pessoa's philosophical persona, António Mora, who wrote at length about the importance of Alberto Caeiro and Ricardo Reis for the cause. Interaction was most intense among the main writer-characters, with Campos and Reis frequently commenting on Caeiro's poetry, usually in glowing terms, while they were rather harsher on each other's work.

All this behind-the-scenes writing activity has marginal literary value, but it does shed light on the unique genesis of Pessoa's poetry. While most poets depend on contact with the "real" world (sometimes indirectly, as through reading) for images and emotions to feed their art, Pessoa's poetry seems, in its germination, to have gained motive and momentum from his inner universe of orbiting thoughts, principles, and preoccupations, whose gravitational pulls produced moments of high tension and occasional clashes. These thoughts, principles, and preoccupations originally came from the outside, of course, and in the more purely literary realm they can be easily traced to his readings (and subsequent acceptance or rejection) of the English Romantics, French Symbolists, Poe, Walt Whitman, and Portuguese authors. Other contributions from the outside, related to the poet's family circumstances and the surroundings in which he grew up, are harder to pin down, but Pessoa and what he wrote are clearly as much a product of their time as are Shakespeare and his plays and sonnets. The difference, according to Pessoa himself, is that he created a company of Hamlets but no play for them to act in, he himself being the stage on which they extemporaneously performed.

Artists often remark that their finished art objects no longer belong to them, but Pessoa's creations were out of his hands even before

Introduction

they began. He made them, yes, but at no point were they ever his. Not even his own self belonged to him. He was so resolutely a spectator of his intimate person that he felt it as something completely extraneous. Pessoa, at his most inward, was his most impersonal.

The heteronymic conceit accentuated and in a certain way justified Pessoa's condition of self-estrangement. Each heteronym was a fresh personification of his abdication from being, a restatement of the fact that he was nothing at all, just an empty place in the universe where many roads happened to meet. He passed the time by describing for us the traffic as it went by. He assigned names to the roads in an attempt to confer, if possible, substance on his nonexistence and to give order to his self-dispersion, but they were just names. There is no essential need for the heteronyms and semi-heteronyms and the rest of the naming game, which some critics have dismissed as an author's ploy to mystify and even mythify his literary project. This may be partly true, but the names do have a practical value. They provide useful file drawers for organizing Pessoa's world, which besides poetry included fiction and drama, philosophy, social and literary criticism, political commentary, translations, linguistic theory, horoscopes, and assorted other texts on the strangest topics imaginable — a treatise on wrestling by one Carlos Otto (who also wrote epigrammatical poems), for example, or three chapters of an essay titled *Des cas d'exhibitionnisme*, in which Jean Seul, Pessoa's main French alias, describes the outward behavior and underlying psychology of those who expose their genitalia in public. Otto (and Miguel, his brother and translator) and Seul are minor characters, but a large body of English poetry was attributed to Alexander Search, while the capacious *Book of Disquietude* was credited to Bernardo Soares.

Were we to erase all the signatures from all the thousands of texts this multilingual author typed or wrote — on loose sheets, in notebooks, on stationery from the firms where he worked, on the backs of letters, on envelopes, or on whatever scrap of paper happened to be in reach — we would have an even harder puzzle to piece together or at least sort out. Like any filing system, however, heteronymy imposes an occasionally arbitrary, specious order that risks obscuring less obvious but more important affinities, and it can give rise to insurmountable problems of classification. Pessoa did not always indicate which file drawer a text belonged to, and scholars are sometimes unsure about where a particular poem or piece of prose should go. Pessoa himself was sometimes unsure. He occasionally placed a question mark after Caeiro, Reis, or whatever other fictional signature he had affixed to his latest text. Or he signed more than one name. Or he made a definite attribution and later changed his mind. The six-poem sequence titled "Oblique Rain" was variously assigned to Alberto Caeiro, Álvaro de Campos, and Bernardo Soares before it was definitively recognized by Pessoa as belonging to Pessoa. The truth is that "Oblique Rain" doesn't fit in any file, for it's quite unlike any other poetry written by Pessoa & Co.

Two paragraphs back I stated that there was "no essential need for the heteronyms," but, like most statements, that isn't completely true—in fact, not very true at all. The heteronyms were a stimulus for some of Pessoa's best poetry. Without them he might well have written the shorter Campos poems of his later years, stylistically different but thematically similar to the verses he produced under his own name, but it is doubtful that the long and loud "sensationist" poems written between 1914 and 1918—"Triumphal Ode," "Maritime Ode," "Salutation to Walt Whitman," and "Time's Passage"—would all have been realized without the futurist naval engineer's name to establish and maintain. And is it conceivable that Pessoa would have written more than two hundred Horatian-style odes without the fiction of a Ricardo Reis to keep up and—gods willing—immortalize?

If we look at other parts of the Pessoan landscape, and in particular the prose, then yes, the heteronymic attributions do often seem like nonessential I.D. tags, tacked on by an anxious author who was afraid his texts might otherwise get lost. If Pessoa had signed his own name instead of Bernardo Soares's to *The Book of Disquietude*, no one would have batted an eyelash, for the lucidly melancholy reflections of this "factless autobiography" read like they came straight from

Introduction

Pessoa's heart. Pessoa would never have admitted that, or he wouldn't have put it in those words, but he was careful never to call Bernardo Soares a heteronym. "He's a semiheteronym," explained his inventor, "because his personality, although not my own, doesn't differ from my own but is a mere mutilation of it." In fact Pessoa-himself was *Disquietude*'s first declared author, though he soon passed the pen on to one Victor Guedes, an assistant bookkeeper like Soares, who was originally assigned the task of writing short stories. At one point the Baron of Teive, lucid and melancholy but with an aristocratic point of view, was also considered for the role of author. It was only in the last and most prolific phase of the book's writing that Bernardo Soares assumed control, as it were.

Control was not Pessoa's strong point. He probably wrote on just about every day of his adult life, but in fits, as if writing were a body function (or a function of the mind, of consciousness) which he could regulate only to a limited degree. Or perhaps there is an easier explanation. Perhaps it was merely laziness that prevented him from bringing off large works. He did complete and publish "Maritime Ode," a 904–line Álvaro de Campos poem published in 1915, but the six hundred or so verses of "Time's Passage," also attributed to Campos, are spread across eight different manuscripts which his posthumous editors have tried to piece together in various ways, never convincingly. Campos's "Salutation to Walt Whitman" was left as no less than twenty pieces of an equally impossible puzzle, his "Martial Ode" as eleven such pieces, "The Departure" as fifteen. Pessoa completed and published one play, *O Marinheiro* [The Mariner], a "static drama" that takes up just ten or twelve pages, but he left over two hundred rhyming and blank-verse passages of an unfinished, hopelessly disordered and unorderable "Faust." He had big plans for complete editions of his and his heteronyms' poetry, in Portuguese and English (Pessoa translated a few Campos poems into English), but he got only a small part of his oeuvre into anything like publishable shape. If almost none of Pessoa's work appeared in book form in his lifetime, it wasn't because undiscerning publishers were rejecting the manuscripts he submitted; he simply didn't submit any. Pessoa was a discreet but well-respected literary figure, with over 150 of his poems and more than a hundred prose texts appearing in magazines during his lifetime, but some of his most stunning poems and prose pieces have only lately—half a century after his death—been lifted by specialists from the margins of prior texts and from the backs of handbills where he scribbled them one afternoon in a Lisbon café, or late at night in one of his rented rooms, or in the apartment he occupied on the Rua Coelho da Rocha during the last fifteen years of his life. More often than not he would date these texts and sign them with one of his many names, and he seems to have saved them all, but they were frequently left in an almost undecipherable scrawl, with variants and notations that throw as much doubt as light on his intentions.

Early on, when he was twenty-six years old, Pessoa wrote in a letter to a friend, "My state of mind compels me to work hard, against my will, on *The Book of Disquietude*. But it's all fragments, fragments, fragments." And in several of the many "fragments" that make up this book, the fictional author (Guedes?, Soares?, the persona called Pessoa?) complains of his inability to produce finished work. On this point *The Book of Disquietude* is eloquently self-illustrative. The more Pessoa worked on it, the more unfinished it became. It began as a collection of symbolist texts that tried to penetrate the world of dreams and the human psyche through elaborate descriptions of weather and landscape, childhood remembrances, medieval imagery, and idealized visions of sexless women. The narrative voice was impersonal and ethereal, and "disquietude" did not refer so much to human worry or anxiety as to a restlessness present in all of life. By the end of Pessoa's life, the book had become a highly intimate diary of "haphazard musings" ascribed to the existentially disquieted Bernardo Soares. Along the way, Pessoa used the forever changing, never-ending work in progress as a handy depository for prose texts that had no other home: philosophical notes, sociological commentary, aesthetic theories, aphorisms, literary criticism. Pessoa had a few hazy ideas on how to organize *The Book of Disquietude*, but no unity was possible for such an amorphous, unwieldy work that thrived on diversity and indecision, and so its skittish author just kept turning out text. It was only in 1982, after years of

Introduction

scholarly labor, that the first substantial but by no means complete edition of this astonishing nonbook saw print.

Pessoa's work flourished in the magnetic field between his attempt to impose order and his irresistible attraction to entropy. His tendency to "other himself" (to use Pessoan terminology) was no doubt partly willful. It was also a temptation he fought against. Or was it all part of the same malady? His determination to organize was as obsessive as his lust (the word is a little strong, but not too) for self-dispersion. He regularly drew up lists enumerating his literary productions, elaborated projects for the structuring of his overall output, and wrote out detailed plans for the publication of his oeuvre. But the lists were full of titles for works he never completed, the projects contradicted one another, and the publication plans came to nothing.

Pessoa's efforts to organize his ideas into something like ordered discourse met with an equal lack of success. Several volumes of his "philosophical texts" were published posthumously, but there are few interesting ideas to be culled from these one-two-three expositions of logic and metaphysics written in Portuguese and English under various names. Pessoa must have realized this, for he wrote fewer of them as time went on. Not that he didn't have anything provocative to say in this domain. Original philosophical insights—or striking reformulations and applications of ideas advanced by thinkers such as Kant, Hegel, and Nietzsche—are found in his poetry and in *The Book of Disquietude*. Pessoa was no philosopher by any stretch of the term, but like Plato and Nietzsche, he had definite ideas and no talent for arranging them into a neat system. The two named philosophers couldn't keep literature out of their writings; Pessoa's prose and poetry were "contaminated" by philosophy. Plato had his Socrates, Nietzsche his Zarathustra, and Pessoa his Caeiro, Campos, Soares, and so on.

Not by coincidence, Pessoa's production of disciplined philosophical texts took a nosedive after the emergence—in 1914—of the major heteronyms, whose launching was Pessoa's great act of philosophical praxis, or so he would have us believe. In *Ultimatum*, a futurist manifesto attributed to Álvaro de Campos and published in 1917, the Nietzschean doctrine of the Superman was promulgated as the solution to liberate Portuguese culture from emasculatory foreign influences and to clear out the literary dead wood, and this Superman was none other than the self-multiplied man, the "Synthesis-of-Humanity Man" who can say, "I am all others." Rejecting the "dogma of artistic individuality," the greatest artist "will be the one who least defines himself, the one who writes in the most genres with the most contradictions and discrepancies. No artist should have just one personality." Instead of, say, thirty or forty poets giving expression to an age, all it should take are "two poets, each with fifteen or twenty personalities." In its loud and exclamatory finale, the manifesto heralds "the scientific creation of Supermen" and, through them, "the arrival of a perfect, mathematical Humanity!"

Thus spake Álvaro de Campos, whose futuristic convictions were poetically expressed in the long Sensationist poems such as "Triumphal Ode" and "Time's Passage." Pessoa in his other incarnations (and in the later Campos poetry) was less concerned with the future of art and humanity than with his immediate intellectual distress. The problems of being and not-being, knowing and not-knowing, moral values, subjective versus objective reality, and determinism versus free will permeate the work of this "poet animated by philosophy," to use Pessoa's self-epithet. But we also find a rigor of expression which, though not resorting to linguistic analysis, is vaguely Wittgensteinian insofar as it demystifies philosophy and would sweep away those notions that cloud rather than clarify. In Caeiro, who claimed to have no philosophy, we find these lines:

> *The mystery of things? What mystery?*
> *The only mystery is that some people think about mystery.*
> *If you're in the sun and close your eyes,*
> *You begin not to know what the sun is,*
> *And you think about various warm things.*
> *But open your eyes and you see the sun.*

Introduction

This is at least reminiscent of the conclusions drawn by Wittgenstein in the *Tractatus Logico-Philosophicus*, where he states, "The right method of philosophy would be this: to say nothing except what can be said, i.e., the propositions of natural science, i.e., something that has nothing to do with philosophy."

Sometimes Pessoa does actually analyze language, as in another Caeiro poem that begins:

> *A row of trees across the way, toward the slope.* . . .
> *But what is a row of trees? There are just trees.*
> *"Row" and the plural "trees" are names, not things.*

In *The Book of Disquietude* (p. 219), Pessoa (as Bernardo Soares) often invokes clear syntax and precise terminology, as when he calls into question the notion of material possession:

> If, referring to what you eat, you were to say, "I possess this," then I would understand you. Because what you eat you obviously include in yourself, you transform it into your substance, you feel it enter into you and belong to you. But it's not in reference to what you eat that you speak of possession. What do you call possessing?

Although this kind of direct linguistic examination is relatively rare in his writing, language for Pessoa was a precision instrument, employed like a scalpel to get to the heart of the truth he did not believe in or to get to the heart of himself, which he also did not believe in. Instead of getting anywhere, therefore, the self-analysis merely accrued, filling in the void of Pessoa's unbelief, taking the place of the self he might have had if he'd been more adept at living in the world. He explains this process through his "mutilation," Bernardo Soares:

> I am, in large measure, the selfsame prose I write. I unroll myself in periods and paragraphs, I make myself punctua-

tion marks; in my unbridled allocation of images I'm like a child using newspaper to dress up as a king. . . .

I've made myself into the character of a book, a life one reads. Whatever I feel is felt (against my will) so that I can write that I felt it. Whatever I think instantly takes shape in words, mixed with images that undo it, opening it into rhythms that are something else altogether. From so much self-remodelling, I've destroyed myself. From so much self-thinking, I'm now my thoughts and not I.

. . . And so, describing myself in image after image — not without truth, but also with lies — I end up more in the images than in me, stating myself until I no longer exist, writing with my soul for ink, useful for nothing except writing.

Disquietude, pp. 113–14

At almost every point of entry into the person of Pessoa we come back to heteronymy or a variation on the theme, back to the question of literature versus life, sincerity versus insincerity. And we are stymied. Can we believe Pessoa's claim of disbelief in himself? Is his professed insincerity sincere? To wonder about these things is a bit like wondering if the statement "This statement is a lie" is true or false. But it is hard not to wonder. What are we to make of a writer who "realized that it was impossible for anyone to love me, unless the person lacked all aesthetic sensibility, in which case I would then despise him," and who consoles himself by noting, "It takes a certain intellectual courage for an individual to honestly recognize that he's nothing more than a human shred, an abortion that survived"? These citations are from a passage appropriately titled "Lucid Diary" (pp. 123–24) in *The Book of Disquietude*, which is sprinkled throughout with self-deprecation. Pessoa's or Bernardo Soares's?

What are we to make of Pessoa's fear of insanity, expressed not only in his literary writings but in letters to friends when he was still a young man? Were his letters just more literature, or had his paternal grandmother's slow but steady descent into certifiable madness inspired a genuine fear in him? What of the unfinished letter he wrote in 1919 to a French practitioner of hypnosis therapy, Hector Durville, describing himself as an *hystero-neurasthénique* and complaining that his excessive *émotivité* and *cérébralité* resulted in a total lack of will to act? Was that a fair description of his condition? Did the condition *really* bother him? Did the poet who wrote that "[t]he active life has always struck me as the least comfortable of suicides" (*Disquietude*, p. 142) really hope to become a man of action through the therapy offered by the Institut du Magnétisme et du Psychisme Expérimental?

What about the fifty love letters he wrote to his "Little Baby," Ophelia Queiroz, over a nine-month period in 1920 and a four-month period in 1929–30? Some scholars believe that the epistolary endearments, occasionally gooey to the point of embarrassment, show the poet faker at his most human and transparent; for others, it was all just another stage for Pessoa to play out life, love by mail having spared him the time commitment and emotional investment of an in-person amorous involvement. (There was, Ophelia revealed years later, an impetuous, impassioned kiss one afternoon in the office where they met, and they often took the streetcar together.)

What of Pessoa's more than passing interest in the occult? A letter in 1915 to his friend Mário de Sá-Carneiro, shortly before his young friend's death, suggests it was only for money that he translated theosophic works by C. W. Leadbeater and Madame Blavatsky into Portuguese (the volumes were published in 1916), but the same letter says he was unexpectedly overwhelmed by the "extraordinarily vast nature of this religious philosophy," by its "notion of power, of dominion, of higher and superhuman knowledge." And a letter written the following year to his Aunt Anica, who was no novice in these matters, informed her that he was becoming a "medium," experiencing phenomena such as automatic writing, astral vision, and—perhaps less surprisingly for one who preached depersonalization—the "sudden feeling of belonging to something else." He concluded that "the unknown Master" was "imposing on me this higher existence" for some likewise higher purpose, and that this would result in more inner suffering. Four years later, when he broke off with Ophelia for the first time, his letter explained that "my destiny belongs to another Law . . . and is ever more constrained to obey Masters who do not allow or forgive" any deviation. More self-dramatization?

Throughout the rest of his life Pessoa nourished his interest in things arcane and occult, writing about spiritualist beliefs and practices ranging from alchemy, Kabbala and Gnosticism to initiation rites and Rosicrucianism. His "At the Tomb of Christian Rosencreutz" seems to date from the 1930s, along with other poems of the same ilk, and the nationalistic poetry of *Mensagem* [Message], published in 1934, is infused with almost as much esoterica as patriotism. In the next and last year of his life, Pessoa drafted an autobiographical note describing himself as an anti-Catholic "gnostic Christian" faithful to "the Secret Tradition of Christianity, which has close links with the Secret Tradition in Israel (the Holy Kabbala) and with the occult essence of Freemasonry," and he published a newspaper article attacking a proposed law that would ban secret societies—namely, the Freemasons. To write such an article implied a personal risk, for Salazar was by then a firmly entrenched and intolerant dictator (the proposed law, to no one's surprise, passed unanimously), but it was the risk assumed by a bystander. Pessoa never actually joined the Freemasons, the Rosicrucians, or any other secret order. His interest in them, as in most things, seems to have been intellectual.

Astrology, on the other hand, was an occult art that Pessoa actively engaged in, producing dozens of horoscopes on himself, on his heteronyms, and on various colleagues. At one point he even toyed with the idea of hanging out a shingle to make his living as an astrologer. So skilled was he at this art that, after reading the autobiography of a well-known English magus named Aleister Crowley, alias Master Therion, he dared to inform the author that the horoscope he'd drawn up for himself and published in his book was mistaken. Crowley recognized the error, struck up a correspondence with Pessoa, and came to Lisbon in 1930 to meet the poet astrologer, who in the following year published a Portuguese version of "Hymn to Pan," a poem written by his English colleague.

Is it possible that not even Pessoa's keen interest in astrology and other occult sciences was sincere? Can we seriously suspect that he took it all with a certain grain of salt? Is it conceivable that he could expend so much ink, time, and physical and creative energy on something he didn't truly believe in or at least value highly?

Introduction

Yes: perfectly possible, conceivable, and probable. Yes, if "sincere" interest means it was somehow fundamental to his existence, affording him purpose and meaning in the way politics and religion do for their fervent adherents. Pessoa was obviously interested, even passionately interested, in the occult—the way an avid stamp collector is interested in stamps; a movie buff in David Griffith; or a diehard bowler in his bowling average, in the weight of his bowling ball, and in how it slips out of his fingers. But we cannot, with surety, say much more than that. Pessoa as Álvaro de Campos, riding a streetcar and observing a woman busily and uselessly crocheting, had this to say:

> *I also have my crochet.*
> *It dates from when I began to think.*
> *Stitch on stitch forming a whole without a whole . . .*
> *A cloth, and I don't know if it's for a garment or for nothing.*
> . . . .
> *Crochet, souls, philosophy . . .*
> *All the religions of the world . . .*
> *All that entertains us in the leisure hours of our existence. . . .*

Unless he chooses to commit suicide, a man who believes in nothing must fill his life with things he doesn't believe in, or he sees it all as crochet, about which it makes no sense to apply the notions of belief, of sincerity, or of true versus false. In a letter dated 14 January 1935, Pessoa wrote that he believed in the existence of worlds superior to our own and in higher beings with whom communication is possible "to the extent we are spiritually attuned," but the narrator of *The Book of Disquietude* specifically mentions Rosicrucianism, the Kabbala, magic, and alchemy as interests belonging to a bygone phase. "Today," he concludes, "I'm an aesthetic in my religion of myself. A cup of coffee, a cigarette and my dreams can substitute quite well for the universe and its stars" (p. 146). In another passage (p. 150), Soares speaks of his "physical revulsion" toward secret societies and occult sciences. It may be argued that Soares is not Pessoa, but Pessoa is also not Pessoa. Nor, for that matter, were his astrological texts and charts always produced under his own name. Raphael Baldaya, a subheteronym, was responsible for much of Pessoa's stargazing, which suggests that his interest in astrology, like his interest in naval engineering and shepherding, was largely if not primarily literary. Yes, Pessoa *really* wrote Crowley and *really* received him in Lisbon, but the magus astrologer who'd miscast his own horoscope turned out to be nothing but a magician actor of modest talent. Apparently inspired by the *Boca do Inferno* [Mouth of Hell], a dramatic rock formation found on the seacoast west of Lisbon, the self-styled "666 Beast" staged a mysterious disappearance down the water-eroded chasm. Pessoa, far from being disillusioned, participated in the hoax, deciphering the Kabbalistic writing of a phony suicide note and reporting to the newspapers that he had seen Crowley "or his ghost" a day after he had crossed over into Spain, according to the Portuguese border police. Pessoa enjoyed detective stories, having written a few of his own, and he did not mind being a character in the one Crowley had dreamed up. Nor did Crowley's charlatanism deter Pessoa from translating his "Hymn to Pan." If Crowley was a fake, then so much the better, according to Pessoa's artistic theory. The occult, like love and his mental health and the rest of life, was subordinated to art, whose soul was insincerity.

Interest in the occult and the equation of art to artificiality were fairly common responses to the generalized spiritual and aesthetic crisis experienced by European artists at the beginning of this century and still felt today, in Europe and far beyond. Despite his megalomania, Pessoa harbored no illusions about the unexceptional, even bourgeois etiology of his disquietude, with several long passages from his homonymously titled book describing the generation he belonged to as one that had "lost all respect for the past and all belief or hope in the future" (p. 185). With characteristic dispassion, Pessoa/Soares (p. 184) analyzes the process leading to this lostness, which was far more profound than what Hemingway's generation felt:

Introduction

Our fathers still had the believing impulse, which they transferred from Christianity to other forms of illusion. Some were champions of social equality, others were wholly enamored of beauty, still others had faith in science and its achievements, and there were some who became even more Christian, resorting to various Easts and Wests in their search for other religious forms that would entertain their otherwise hollow consciousness of merely living.

We lost all of this. We were born with none of these consolations. Each civilization follows the particular line of a religion that represents it; resorting to other religions, it loses the one it had, and ultimately loses them all.

We lost the one, and all the others with it.

And so we were left each man to himself, in the desolation of feeling ourselves live.

The upsurge in occult practices in the nineteenth century may be seen as part of the transfer of belief "from Christianity to other forms of illusion," but many European intellectuals toward the end of that century and into the twentieth began to value the occult more as a drug than as a belief, as a source of immediate sensation rather than as a system to provide long-term meaning to their existence. In Pessoa the sensation becomes merely the idea of sensation, a literary sensation, for which it makes no difference whether Crowley disappeared down the mouth of hell in actual fact or only in the suspenseful paragraphs of the newspaper.

Art, meanwhile, after centuries of service to Christianity and a short stint of duty on behalf of post-God doctrines such as Humanism and Romanticism (the two most often cited by Pessoa), had become a religion unto itself, a kind of floating currency with no more value than what faith in art might give it. Completely meaningless, since it stood in relation to nothing, art was nevertheless invoked by many—including Pessoa—to fill up the vacuum. In these circumstances, art could only be considered genuine when it was completely artificial, when it *replaced* reality instead of trying to express or explain or embody it.

Though this line of reasoning was not unique to Pessoa, in him more than in his contemporaries it led to radical action or, rather, nonaction, making him so relentlessly detached from physical life that even Álvaro de Campos, the most worldly of Pessoa's personae, "Prefers thinking about smoking opium to smoking it/ And likes looking at absinthe more than drinking it." In literature as in life, in art as in the occult, all that mattered was the gesture, not the illusory substance behind it.

Pessoa's arm's-length fascination with the occult is intimately related to what he called his "mystical" nationalism, though he might well have labeled it "mythical." The first myth, fostered by a tradition of patriotic prophetic literature, was that Portugal would be the fifth and last of the world's great empires, the fulfillment of Nebuchadnezzar's dream as interpreted by Daniel. According to most Biblical exegetes, the four earthly kingdoms described by the lion-resistant prophet correspond to the successive empires of Babylon, Media, Persia, and Greece (or Babylon, Media/Persia, Greece, and Rome), with the fifth and final kingdom—divine and indestructible—being variously understood. Transposing the interpretation forward in time and westward in geography, Pessoa associated the first four kingdoms with the empires of Greece, Rome, Christianity in the Middle Ages, and post-Renaissance Europe (or, in a variant scheme, the English colonial empire). Pessoa argued that the Fifth Empire, to be indestructible, would have to be "spiritual" rather than material, and that this could only be achieved by a small nation, since it would never even aspire to territorial domination. Pessoa marshaled other arguments—ranging from Portugal's "civilizational" vocation and its knack for getting along with other races to the supposed superiority of its language, Portuguese being "the richest and most complex of the Latin tongues"—in support of his thesis that Portugal would spearhead the Fifth Empire.

Pessoa was not a typical flag-waver. The poems of his book titled *Mensagem* celebrated the Portuguese discoveries, but he contended that his country's "first discovery was to discover the idea of discovery," and he had no use for the then still extensive Portuguese colonies,

Introduction

writing them off as a millstone around the homeland's neck, an impediment to the "cultural imperialism" he imagined would be based on Portugal's language and literature. Portugal, according to Pessoa, had not yet produced a truly great literature, and *for that very reason* was bound to generate one in the near future. Italy and France had already been cultural heavyweights; now it was Portugal's turn.

Enter Sebastianism, the companion myth and vital key to the Fifth Empire doctrine. It was a myth firmly ingrained in the Portuguese psyche, going back more than three centuries, to the year 1578, when the young and impetuous King Sebastião organized and personally led a suicidal invasion of Morocco. The predictable result was the death or capture of almost every soldier fighting under the Portuguese flag. Severely weakened and with no obvious successor to the throne, Portugal was easily dominated by Spain for the next sixty years, from 1580 to 1640. Since Sebastião's body was never actually found among the carnage left lying on the battlefield of El Ksar el Kebir, it was rumored that he still lived on some island and would return on a foggy morning to drive out the Spanish. Once Portugal regained its autonomy and was beset by other problems, such as the French invasions in the early 1800s and the country's general inability to keep pace with the rest of Europe, some people began to stake their hopes on a spiritualized, Messianic version of Sebastião to restore Portugal to its previous grandeur.

If Pessoa promoted Sebastianism, it's not because he believed in it but because he didn't. He felt that in politics, as in poetry, nothing could be accomplished without falseness and insincerity. Since "the world is run by lies," only the propagation of "a great national myth" would be able to "raise a nation's morale," he explained to an interviewer in 1926. "Fortunately," he noted, "we have the Sebastianist myth, deeply rooted in the past and in the Portuguese soul. Our work is therefore easier. We don't have to create a myth, but simply renew it."

Before concluding that Pessoa was patriotically using Sebastianism to look out for his country, we should consider how he interpreted a sixteenth-century shoemaker and street poet named Gonçalo Anes Bandarra, whose obscurely prophetic verses were a rich source text for the changing Sebastianist myth. In the visionary quatrains of this Portuguese Nostradamus, Pessoa saw not only the predicted return of Sebastião but also the specific date of that return: 1888, the year Pessoa was born. Thus all of the heteronym forger's mysticism, nationalism, and other ardent divagations came back to none other than himself, the fulfillment of the "super-Camões" whose advent he foretold in his first published prose text, a 1912 essay on "the new Portuguese poetry sociologically considered." Luís de Camões, who wrote a large body of lyric poetry as well as *The Lusiads*, the great epic about Vasco da Gama and seafaring Portugal, was almost universally regarded as his country's all-time greatest poet. Pessoa, albeit grudgingly, went along with the consensus opinion, which fit perfectly into his national-cultural-personal mythology, Camões having died in 1580, just two years after King Sebastião. The Second Coming of Sebastião, in Pessoa's scheme of cultural imperialism, was envisioned as a new and greater Camões. With God, Truth, and Humanity having lost their credibility, all there was left to believe in and hope for was individual human beings of exceptionally, inexplicably higher caliber. The literary Fifth Empire would not require a vast number of good Portuguese writers, just a handful of very gifted multifaceted ones, as described in Campos's *Ultimatum* and incarnated by Pessoa & Co.

"The Fifth Empire, *c'est moi*" could have been Pessoa's maxim, were he as ostentatious as he was megalomanic, though not even this megalomania should be taken too seriously. It was also a myth, or part of the overall myth of Pessoa, who put so much distance from all he thought or felt that probably not even he could distinguish what—if anything—was there before the mythmaking began.

His childhood? Did he not remember and miss it? Did it not belong intimately and unforgettably to who he was "deep down"? Pessoa's prose and poetry contain a number of quite specific references to childhood: to the backyard where he played ball, to his toy ships and toy dolls, to the circus where he sometimes went on Sundays, to the crib he slept in as a boy, to the house in the country

Introduction

where he and his aunts drank afternoon tea. He surely did not invent all these details, and nostalgia for childhood is a frequent motif, particularly in the poetry of Campos. And might not the fact that the heteronyms often had brothers—there was a Frederico Reis as well as a Ricardo, a Charles Search as well as an Alexander, two brothers named Guedes, three named Wyatt—be explained by Pessoa's regret over the loss of his only full brother, who died before reaching age one (Fernando was five and a half at the time)? Or did he merely regret the *idea* of a lost brother, whether his own or someone else's? Pessoa would have us believe that his self-distancing was total:

> Any nostalgia I feel is literary. I remember my childhood with tears, but they're rhythmic tears, in which prose is already being formed. . . . I feel nostalgia for scenes. Thus someone else's childhood can move me as much as my own; both are purely visual phenomena from a past I'm unable to fathom, and my perception of them is literary. They move me, yes, but because I see them, not because I remember them.
>
> *Disquietude*, p. 125

These words were penned in September of 1931. Three months later, in a letter to João Gaspar Simões, Pessoa, calling himself a futurist "in the direct sense of the word," claimed never to have felt nostalgia for his childhood or for anything else from the past. He admitted to missing certain people he once loved, but not the time in which he loved them. Any apparent hankerings for the past in his work were "literary attitudes, intensely felt by dramatic instinct, whether they are signed by Álvaro de Campos or by Fernando Pessoa."

Elsewhere in the same letter, Pessoa found fault with the excessively Freudian interpretations proffered in a book of poetry criticism just out by the still-young Gaspar Simões, who got his revenge—fulfilling what was presumably only a subconscious wish—almost twenty years later, when he wrote a biography that examined Pessoa's entire life and work through the twin lenses of frustrated Oedipal yearning and repressed homosexuality. The biographer's point of view is defensible, but his focus was far too shallow (or "deep," in the psychoanalytical sense). It's not as though Pessoa was laboring under the weight of shadowy repressions embedded in the subconscious zone of his psyche. On the contrary, he willfully, systematically frustrated his appetites and repressed his desires, denying himself so as to enrich his art. Pessoa revealed as much in another letter to his future biographer, dating from 1930 and explaining that he wrote his two long, mildly erotic poems—the heterosexual "Epithalamium" (1913) and the homosexual "Antinoüs" (1915)—to get sex out of his system. The second poem is much more convincing, which may or may not tell us something about Pessoa's sexual orientation, but who cares? The point is that he wanted it all out of his system and into his writing.

Pessoa sought to expel not only his sexual desires but his friendly affections, his religious tendencies, his aggressive feelings, his humanitarian urges, his longing for adventure, his dreams, and his regrets, and in a poem like "Time's Passage" we can find all this and more. In other Campos poems the process is inverted, the narrator taking in things from the outside and being strongly affected by them. We find him ruefully sorry to leave the man he met on a train, intensely moved by the sight of a complete stranger's cadaver, and poignantly sympathetic to the seamstress whose boyfriend left her; all were characters that Pessoa at best only grazed in real life. In both processes—expelling what he is at heart and taking to heart what doesn't belong to him—there is distance. Either way, the emotion is literary. And by investing all this in the fictional person of Álvaro de Campos, Pessoa takes detachment yet one step further.

Psychoanalysis is too poor a science to explain the case of Pessoa, who seems to have been simply, mysteriously, possessed by a demon—that of detachment. His congenital ambition was to turn all that he touched, or that touched him, into the gold of literature, but unlike King Midas he never got tired of performing this alchemical trick. Or he tired of it but could not do otherwise. He thrived on the unreal. Even the "reality" within the unreal world of his writings tends to be insubstantial, a kind of mimesis of vacancy and absence. Drama is the most lifelike genre within literature, but Pessoa's only completed play

Introduction

is a negation of action, plot, dialogue and even character. Written in 1913, *O Marinheiro* [*The Mariner*] makes no attempt to represent the real world, nor does it offer an alternative one. Discoursing in a register that is neither true dialogue nor true monologue, its three static characters vaguely long for another age, for other lands and other seas, for whatever is *other*; and then comes the "story": a hazy recollection of a dream within a dream, and the dreamer suspects that she herself may be a mere figment in a dream of the mariner she dreamed about. Nothing of substance is presented in this wispy text, only words that "seem like people." Significantly enough, it was one year after those words were written that the three major heteronyms burst onto the scene, dressed and ready to play out their author's life.

Heteronymy was the most conspicuous distancing technique employed by Pessoa; less important but almost as conspicuous was his persistent use of English. In the aforementioned letter to Gaspar Simões, Pessoa claimed not to know why he wrote "Epithalamium" and "Antinoüs" in English, which was as good as a confession that he knew exactly why. Converting his sexual drives into writing was, as he himself explained, a way to objectify them, to make them into objects outside himself. As English texts they became that much more foreign. Contrary to what some scholars have supposed, Pessoa was not *perfectly* bilingual. In his less than eight years in Durban, he mastered the English language well enough to win first prize for the essay he wrote as part of his entrance exam to the University of the Cape of Good Hope, an admirable feat (there were 900 examinees) that measured various skills besides linguistic competence. Although the prize essay does not survive, a nearly contemporaneous piece on Thomas Macaulay was published by Pessoa in the December 1904 issue of *The Durban High School Magazine*. It reveals the future poet's exceptional intellectual and critical capacities, as well as the breadth of his readings in literature, but the English itself is slightly archaic and stilted: "Therefore is it that he gives us no emotional undulations of style," begins one of the paragraphs.

Therefore was it that Pessoa's English poems, including the 35 *Sonnets* he published in 1918, might have made a hit several hundred years ago. They do not fall well on modern ears. They never have the sparkle, the music, the colloquial verve, or the quiet elegance achieved at different points in his Portuguese output. Curiously enough, the poetry attributed to Caeiro and Campos has a certain directness of style that Pessoa brought into Portuguese from English, via Walt Whitman in particular. That directness is almost always lacking in his English poetry, among which the sonnets deserve first prize for convolutedness. Take, for example, these verses from the ninth sonnet:

> *As in one sinking in a treacherous sand,*
> *Each gesture to deliver sinks the more;*
> *The struggle avails not, and to raise no hand,*
> *Though but more slowly useless, we've no power.*

We could, perhaps cruelly, see these verses as an unintentional self-parody, with the sand representing English and the last two lines referring to Pessoa's infelicitous but irresistible attempts to write poetry in that language. Though Pessoa wrote excellent English for a foreigner, it lacked the organic fiber and carnal weight of what is so aptly known as a mother tongue.

After 1916, Pessoa's creative writing was largely confined to Portuguese, though he still used English for an occasional poem and rather more extensively for his personal notes. As the years wore on, Pessoa's English deteriorated, sometimes sliding into Portuguese syntactical patterns and even exhibiting a few outright errors, but that did not daunt the poet of many masks. Not that we need to suppose that Pessoa was hiding behind his obstinate use of English. There was at least one obvious, banal reason for his jotting down notes and annotations in English—to maintain his linguistic proficiency through regular exercise, particularly since he made money by drafting letters in English and French for Portuguese firms that did business abroad. With his English poems, Pessoa hoped to gain literary recognition in Britain and perhaps elsewhere. His self-published books of English poetry did

Introduction

get reviewed by several British papers, including the *Times Literary Supplement*, and in 1920 a London journal called *The Athenaeum* even published a poem from *The Mad Fiddler*, a collection Pessoa had unsuccessfully attempted to place with an English publisher in 1917.

English had yet another attraction for Pessoa. It comprised an artificiality that became second nature, a kind of spontaneous unspontaneity. For one who eschewed the unmediated expression of emotion ("emotional undulations *of style*," he wrote at age sixteen, already subjecting feelings to aesthetics), foreign languages had the virtue of acting as a check, the linguistic strangeness automatically detaching the author from his feelings. The all too likely pitfall, into which Pessoa's English poems largely slipped, was a strained style and a radical loss of emotional power. He himself seems to have sensed this, and toward the end of his life he recognized that "my nation is the Portuguese language" (*Disquietude*, p. 151), but he continued to make forays out of that nation as part of his permanent journey away from himself. With consummate detachment, Pessoa even wrote his final words in English—"I know not what tomorrow will bring"—as if to mark an ironic or existential distance between himself and death, which is what the next day, 30 November 1935, brought.

Not even in the Portuguese poetry written under Pessoa's own name will we find a unified, integrated, "natural" voice. Removing himself from himself, Pessoa dubbed Pessoa an orthonym, a self-reflexive fiction that comprised—he wrote in a letter from 1935— "various subpersonalities," which included the pseudo-patriot who wrote *Message*, the pseudo-occultist of "Beyond God" and "The Mummy," the ephemeral Intersectionist of "Oblique Rain," and the ultra-rational Pessoa who used rhymed and metered verses to try to make sense of his scattered identity when he was not, on the contrary, doing his best to scatter it yet more. The orthonym was in a certain way the falsest poet of all, using old-style verse structures to express twentieth-century anxiety from a consistently anti-Romantic point of view. With apparent irony, Pessoa-himself employed traditional forms to highlight the utter vacuity of the traditional values that held those forms dearly. You want neat rhyme and strict meter? he seems to be saying. Here you go! Although Pessoa never explicitly stated that his use of traditional form had an ironic intention, we can infer this from his criticism of Portugal's other great poet, Luís de Camões, for not using innovative verse forms. Or perhaps Pessoa intended nothing at all; perhaps he simply enjoyed making his orthonymic verses rhyme and obey meter. And why not? When we arrive at the conclusion that everything is vacuous, that everything is equally indifferent or indifferently equal, then no one method, approach, or mode of expression is more legitimate or illegitimate than another. Anything goes, including all that has gone before.

By what to some may seem an unexpected channel, we have entered the realm of Intertextuality, in which all styles from all ages are equally valid, if not (opinions here vary) equally valuable. Bizarrely but truly, the deconstructionists' ideal is embodied in this early twentieth-century writer from a lightweight country like Portugal. Cutting across cultures, time periods, languages, and genres, Pessoa's literary production includes democratically rhyming poetry representing various traditions, free-verse styles of a kind never before used in Portuguese, the "ultra-Shakespearean Shakespeareanisms" (citing the *Times Literary Supplement*) of his English sonnets, the Zenlike verses of Alberto Caeiro, the classical odes signed by Ricardo Reis (defined by his cross-cultural creator as "a Greek Horace who writes in Portuguese"), the equally antiquitous *Inscriptions* written in English, a handful of French poems (because why not?), a few hundred witty and unpretentious folk quatrains (such a correctly uncanonical genre), some detective stories (an old favorite of the structuralists), real diaries and fictional diaries, political commentary, literary criticism, and even jokes, not to mention the poetry and prose translations that endow the oeuvre with a multicultural stamp.

In what appears to be a cynical act of self-promotion, some of today's theorists are building high-visibility careers on their "discovery" that the subject is a fiction, that there is only text born of text and leading to more text. Pessoa, acting on better faith, lived out the tex-

Introduction

tual dream, or nightmare, paying the logical price of self-effacement, and he was well aware of the limits and potentialities of his enterprise and of verbal expression in general. Consider the following observation, which many a deconstructionist could subscribe to without qualms:

> Everything stated or expressed by man is a note in the margin of a completely erased text. From what's in the note we can extract the gist of what must have been in the text, but there's always a doubt, and the possible meanings are many.
> *Disquietude*, p. 88

Some would fuss, of course, over the word "gist," but the purport of this passage is not to claim a hidden meaning or an authoritative Urtext. The point is that there are as many possible meanings as there are readers or readings. The only hidden meaning, Pessoa asserted more than once in the poetry of Alberto Caeiro, is that there *is* no hidden meaning: things are what they are, period.

Caeiro, according to his script, was interested in things themselves, in their direct apperception. Pessoa was not. To his credit, or that of his métier as a poet, he did not theorize like Derrida on whether there was any *hors-texte*, on whether writing referred to anything outside itself. With less dogma and pretense, he simply recognized his preference for the written world and his collateral lack of aptitude and taste for the "real" one. Outright aversion to everyday life is stated or implied in passage after fragmentary passage of Pessoa's "Faust," while Álvaro de Campos—in the more compact space of a poem—feels intimate horror

> *. . . that there exists a way for beings to exist,*
> *For existence to exist,*
> *For the existence of "to exist" to exist.*

These verses from late Campos—the only heteronym to evolve and grow old with the poet of masks—can be legitimately regarded as closer in spirit than Caeiro to Pessoa himself, but "Pessoa-himself" is always a slippery quantity, the heteronyms, vice-heteronyms and subheteronyms endlessly canceling each other out and leaving their creator to chart the void, or else—turning around the lens—endlessly multiplying and restating each other while Pessoa-himself drowns in the chaos, with only (and this is true either way he or we look at it) "the hope that everything is nothing and nothing, therefore, everything" (*Disquietude*, p. 301). Pessoa forever vacillated between subscribing to nothingness ("I'm nothing./ I'll always be nothing") or everythingness ("To feel everything in every way"), but it all came down to the same scattered mishmash of nothing (or everything). Even if he did not accept with bucolic equanimity the "Great Mystery" glimpsed by Caeiro on "an incredibly clear day," Pessoa certainly concurred with the truth of the vision:

> *I saw that there is no Nature,*
> *That Nature doesn't exist,*
> *That there are hills, valleys and plains,*
> *That there are trees, flowers and grass,*
> *That there are rivers and stones,*
> *But that there is no whole to which all this belongs,*
> *That a true and real ensemble*
> *Is a disease of our own ideas.*
>
> *Nature is parts without a whole.*

Yeats, in his lament that the center doesn't hold, presaged the twentieth-century collapse of Western Culture as such, with capital W and capital C. Pound, with his Cantos, was a precursor of the collage aesthetic, which attempted a kind of makeshift whole, though no longer with any hope or concern for a center of gravity. It was Fernando Pessoa, as much as any other poet of his time or before it, who prefigured—in his own person—the postmodernist experience of utter dissociation. Put more accurately, he experienced what many postmodernists only talk about: the impossibility and undesirability of a whole, and a letting go

Introduction

of all nostalgia for a consensus of thought and feeling. If Postmodernism is nothing but talk, Pessoa does not fit the bill. He did not rant against the accepted canon, nor was he a champion of equality in the arts. But if Postmodernism implies personal actions and behaviors born out of its discourse, then even before the word existed Pessoa was one of its practitioners, getting there almost on his own.

Like a Picasso of Portuguese letters, Pessoa explored one literary style after another, often as a local cultural pioneer, sometimes as a quirky revivalist. He began conservatively enough, writing English poetry influenced by his Durban high-school readings of Milton, Shakespeare, Shelley, Keats, Byron, and Browning. In 1908 or 1909 he also began writing Portuguese poetry and prose, largely according to the precepts of Symbolism, whose "post" or "neo" incarnations were to hold sway in Portugal into the 1910s and beyond, after it had already lost steam in France and elsewhere. Though it was a passing phase in Pessoa, the high-charged poetic prose of his *The Mariner* ranks with the best Symbolist work produced in Portugal and Europe in general. In 1914, a year after that play was written, Pessoa presented an aesthetic derivative of Symbolism known as *Paulismo*, which took its name from a poem whose first word was bogs (*paul* means bog) and which was loaded with the "twilight impressions" announced in the general title given to this and a companion poem, the first ones published by the adult Pessoa. The "bogging" of melancholy metaphors to express inward anguish found a great admirer in Mário de Sá-Carneiro (1890–1915), whose compressed, exquisite poetic oeuvre was much influenced by this style, but Pessoa dropped it in favor of other inventions: an equally ephemeral Intersectionism of Cubist inspiration, the more enduring Sensationism of Campos, the neoclassical style of Reis, and the tautological antipoetry of Caeiro (also categorizable as a Sensationist). It was Pessoa and his friends, including Sá-Carneiro and Almada Negreiros, who founded *Orpheu*, an avant-garde magazine far more important than its summary existence — two issues published in 1915 — would suggest, for it was the vehicle that brought Modernism to Portuguese literature. Pessoa was the creative and intellectual motor force behind this and other iconoclastic initiatives in Portugal during the teens. Abreast of the most recent artistic developments in France, England, Spain, and Italy, he was the one who heralded Futurism via the bumptious naval engineer, Álvaro de Campos. He was also probably the first writer to effectively assimilate the genius of America's Walt Whitman into European literature, relying again on the agency of Campos, whose poetry incorporated (and, for some people's money, improved on) the Whitmanian style, which also influenced Alberto Caeiro. The work of both heteronyms abandoned rhyme and fixed meters, a revolutionary move for Portuguese poetry.

Unlike with Picasso, all this inventing, innovating, reviving, and reformulating happened more or less synchronically, with the various styles and doxies overlapping each other in a time span of less than ten years. Endowed with an uncommon capacity for absorption, digestion, and organic adaptation, Pessoa hedonistically tried out all that was going in the aesthetical marketplace, creating his own house blends and reworking old recipes. Some of the isms such as *Paulismo* and Intersectionism he quickly cooked up and quickly discarded, while the rest became more or less important parts of his artistic repertoire, in which the rhetorical and the colloquial, the solemn and the humorous, the patriotic and the seditious, the absurd and the inexorably rational, the highbrow and the lowbrow could all exist together democratically, even if Pessoa was emphatically aristocratic in his sociopolitical views and in how he lived. With regard to how others lived, he was by nature and by scruple indifferent. His ballyhooing of Intersectionist and Sensationist doctrines circa 1915 was just another game; he was not concerned to convert anyone to his aesthetic standpoint.

Beyond God and beyond even the heroic stance against God, Pessoa did not even believe in art for art's sake. Art was merely for his sake, without fanfare or higher purposes. It was a means of survival, a pastime, his crochet, his solitaire. In Pessoa, the almighty I of Romantic subjectivism was reduced to "the place/ Where things are thought or felt" (from Reis's last poem), a tiny hub of consciousness whose confused mass of piecemeal percepts constituted—through memory and projection—an inflated pseudo-I, ungraspable and without sub-

Introduction

stance. Pessoa, instead of trying to maintain the illusion, celebrated the fragmentation of his own self and the shattering of the world he could only smatteringly perceive. This attitude and all that was concomitant to it—the relativizing of all truths and all standards; the recognition that no definitive statements are possible; interest in, yet skepticism toward, the "new"; a neo-Baroque taste for the "nonessential" (nothing is essential); and an awareness of the archaeological discontinuity of knowledge—all of this, which certain deconstructionists now present as the latest contributions to human thought, was not merely thought but actually lived out by Fernando Pessoa.

When we read lines from *The Book of Disquietude* such as "I'm the gap between what I am and am not, between what I dream and what life makes of me" (p. 120) and "The search for truth . . . always confers, if the searcher merits a prize, the ultimate knowledge of his nonexistence" (p. 228), we are not struck by the novelty of the ideas underlying the statements but by their absolute sincerity, or insincerity, by the complete union of statement and idea, by a sensation that feeling and thinking are one and the same activity in this writer, who elsewhere in the same *Book* aspires "to think with the emotions and to feel with the mind" (p. 79).

Nor are we often struck by novelty in the poems, whose accessibility may actually put off readers fond of linguistic acrobatics or high jinks. Yet there is something compelling in the Reis stanza that reads:

> *Reality is always*
> *More or less*
> *Than what we want.*
> *Only we are always*
> *Equal to ourselves.*

Or in the observation, taken from an orthonymic poem, that "All/ The world is a great open book/ That smiles at me in an unknown tongue." Or in this metaphor, also from a poem signed by the author's own name: "I'm the orphan of a dream/ Stranded by the outgoing tide." There is a precise dead-honestness of expression in these lines, and it is backed by the blood guarantee of Pessoa's self-sacrifice. But the metaphor is misplaced; there was no blood in this transfusion. The opposite of Faust, this troubled Portuguese soul traded in real life for the spiritual world of his writing. Perhaps most writers do this to some extent, but who has annulled himself like Pessoa? Not Joyce. Not Pound. Not even Franz Kafka. We can *see* Joyce as the brilliant conductor of his daringly dissonant narratives. We can *see* Pound hyperactively promoting literary, political, and personal causes. We can *see* Kafka suffering—as it were in his own flesh—the agony of his negative metamorphoses. With Pessoa all we can visualize is what a handful of surviving photos show: a materialized nondescriptness endowed with a mustache. Pessoa was no language master à la Joyce or Pound. He wrote careful, elegant Portuguese, inventing new locutions and recasting worn-out clichés, but his project was not to deform and reform words and syntax. His project was the universe, with himself as the raw material. He was the object clay, endlessly molded, twisted, divided, and reworked by his writing. And in this autometamorphosis there was no torment or suffering à la Kafka. As if following the recommendation of a Reis poem to "Leave pain on the altar/ As an offering to the gods," Pessoa stoically endured nonsuffering.

"If at least I could be positively crazy!" cried Álvaro de Campos in a poem from 1934, explaining his frustration in the next stanza:

> *An inmate in an insane asylum is at least someone.*
> *I'm an inmate in an asylum without an asylum.*
> *I'm consciously crazy,*
> *I'm a lucid lunatic.*

Not even in his heteronyms could Pessoa have the consolation of brooding, weeping, or going mad. What in other people would be suffering, in Pessoa was subtilized into a colorless, flavorless angst of the intellect, a chronic "bad taste in the mouth of my soul," according to a Campos poem written in July 1935, five months before the poet and his noisy universe of disquiet voices came to a sudden but unscreeching halt.

Introduction

In the Pessoan system of fictionally whirling stars, Alberto Caeiro was the one interlude of serenity, because he lived life, as it were, unconsciously, accepting objective reality at face value. The way of Caeiro was clearly not suitable for his creator, who *loved* the game of consciousness. Redirecting once more our telescope, a move that the dialectic of Nothing = Everything regularly impresses on us, we should remember that Pessoa, whose life in the real world was staid, probably felt bored by objective reality and his immediate quotidian experience. To have inner calm on top of so much outward peace might well have been an abhorrent prospect. Perhaps that is why Pessoa invented heteronyms: to stir up his life, to feel literary if not real anguish, to pretend with all this hubbub of indifferent passions, true lies, and conflicting artificialities that the world—his world or any world—mattered.

The drama of Pessoa was that there was no drama, except for the literary kind. "Real life" hardly existed for this fragmented soul, or it meant little to him. After returning from South Africa to his native Lisbon at age seventeen, he never again left Portugal and almost never even left the capital city. He traveled immensely, but it was all in his writings and his imagination. The realization of a dream will always be something less than the dream, and so the secret of successful living—according to Pessoa—is to act as little as possible, taking refuge from the world in the imagination, where everything is perfect and nothing disappoints.

Pessoa did not exactly follow his own recommendation, for he did more than dream; he wrote, and with furious dedication. He was loath, on the other hand, to realize *completely* his literary projects. He had, as has been mentioned, dozens and dozens of grandiose plans for organizing and publishing his literary output, but he never made any sustained effort to bring them off. Some of his greatest works, such as his anti-Faustian *Faust* or *The Book of Disquietude*, were left in virtual chaos as hundreds of shorter and longer passages randomly scattered across the pages and years of his adult writing life. And some of his most inspired lines occur in fragmentary poems whose pieces would no doubt yield unprecedented beauties if there were only a way to make them all fit together.

Pessoa's work stands before us today like variously sized building blocks—some rough, others exquisitely fashioned—of an impossible but marvelous monument. A master nonbuilder, Pessoa seems to have understood that by giving only partial form to the imagined work, we with our imaginations would be able to complete it. Thus he succeeded in realizing his dream in all its fullness, preserving it far beyond his own life and private pleasure. Of course, that may not have been his intention. Perhaps intention has no relevance here. Pessoa described the symptoms and development of his writing behavior, but he never explained its origin. One can find psychological motives for every behavior, and books have been written about Pessoa's, and yet the mystery remains: why did he not do something else? Why did he write? Perhaps, as he stated in letters to his aunt and his one sweetheart, he was responsible to higher powers.

I have compared Pessoa's oeuvre to a set of building blocks belonging to an unfinished monument. I could have also compared it to a set of ruins—like the temple complex of one or another acropolis, where only the gods' ghosts still wend through the columns and Apollo's lyre barely twangs in the breeze. Thinking of Pessoa's works in this way, as ruins, what I hear is not a lyre but a seemingly incongruous, wistful progression of piano chords. From one of Chopin's Preludes, Opus 28. A music critic whose name I don't remember contended that these twenty-four brief compositions were misnamed, since they sound after all more like remnants than beginnings, like works that in some mysterious, more-than-real space—as on a heavenly Olympus above the earthly one—had been realized to the point of divine perfection, after which they had fallen to the ground and broken into pieces, most of which were lost irretrievably. From the few exceedingly beautiful pieces that remain—that the higher powers have allowed to remain—we can discern something of that original glory for which we feel, as humans, a natural nostalgia.

Lisbon   Richard Zenith
April 1996

ALBERTO CAEIRO
THE UNWITTING MASTER

"The life of Caeiro cannot be told for there is nothing in it to tell." So said Ricardo Reis in the preface he drafted for his fellow heteronym's Complete Poems. But Fernando Pessoa informs us that Alberto Caeiro da Silva was born in Lisbon in 1889, lived most of his brief life with an old aunt in the country, and returned to his native city just a few months before his death, from tuberculosis, in 1915. He kept writing poems, however, until at least 1930, apparently by dictating them through Pessoa.

Álvaro de Campos left us a physical description of Caeiro— medium tall, blue eyes, fair hair, and fair skin, with a strikingly white forehead—and reported that he once loved a young lady who did not return his love. Ricardo Reis, defending his view that there was nothing in Caeiro's life worth telling, declared that this "fruitless and absurd" passion was "not an event but, so to speak, a forgetting." A forgetting of what? Perhaps his vocation as the "only poet of Nature."

Although he had no profession, Caeiro fancied himself a shepherd, with thoughts instead of sheep for his flock. His thoughts, he hastened to add in one of his poems, were sensations; his way of thinking was through his eyes and ears, hands and feet, nose and mouth. Caeiro was an unlettered man who eschewed analytical thought.

"Nature is parts without a whole." This, according to Reis, was the most telling verse written by Caeiro, who appreciated things for what they were, showing no concern to find any unifying principle. Variously described as a "pure mystic," a "reconstructor of paganism," a "Saint Francis of Assisi without faith," and an "Antichrist," Caeiro did not personally have anything against Christianity, it simply happened that his nature was antithetical to it. He felt that if God wanted us to believe in him, he would appear and say, "Look, here I am." It is possible to speculate that God is behind or in, or in some way *is*, the flowers and trees and sun and moon, but Caeiro had no interest in speculating.

> He sees things with the eyes only, not with the mind. He does not let any thoughts arise when he looks at a flower. Far from seeing sermons in stones, he never even lets himself conceive a stone as beginning a sermon. The only sermon a stone contains for him is that it exists. The only thing a stone tells him is that it has nothing at all to tell him. A state of mind may be conceived resembling this. *But it cannot be conceived in a poet.* This way of looking at a stone may be described as the totally unpoetic way of looking at it. The stupendous fact about Caeiro is that out of this sentiment, or rather, absence of sentiment, he makes poetry.
>
> From a text Pessoa wrote in English

Simple and unassuming as this poet was, the other two heteronyms considered him their Master. Ricardo Reis, in fact, never wrote a single verse until he met Caeiro, at age twenty-five. Reis, the Epicurean classicist who believed in a countless host of gods and divine powers, recognized in Caeiro not a fellow pagan but paganism itself, an innate and absolute awareness of natural forces, such that any affirmation of belief would have been superfluous, a distraction. Álvaro de Campos, on the other hand, tells us that, yes, he had written a handful of more traditional poems before meeting Caeiro in 1914, but it was only after this life-changing encounter that he began to produce his Sensationist odes in the free-verse style that was already being used by the country-bred poet. Although Campos, the worldly naval engineer, at one point chides Caeiro (along with Reis and Pessoa-himself) for *seeing* without actually *touching* reality, he acknowledged him as the Pure Sensationist and therefore as his Master. One day, when attempting to talk metaphysics with Alberto, a frustrated Álvaro finally

Alberto Caeiro

said, "Just tell me one thing. What are you to yourself?" To which the quasi shepherd answered, "I'm one of my sensations."

Caeiro was even the Master of his inventor, Fernando Pessoa. They met for the first time on March 8, 1914, and Pessoa, completely shaken up on hearing Caeiro read poems from his *The Keeper of Sheep*, immediately went home to write verses of a kind he never could have produced otherwise. For Fernando, afflicted by an "overly keen sensibility" coupled with an "overly keen mind," the direct and ingenuous poetry of Caeiro acted like a "vaccine against the stupidity of the intelligent." It is Álvaro de Campos who recounts the meeting of these two men and the consequences it had for the creator of heteronyms, but he takes care to remind us that "Fernando Pessoa, strictly speaking, doesn't exist."

from
THE KEEPER OF SHEEP

1

I've never kept sheep,
But it's as if I did.
My soul is like a shepherd.
It knows the wind and sun,
And walks hand in hand with the Seasons
Looking at what passes.
All the peace of Nature without people
Sits down at my side.
But I get sad like a sunset
In our imagination
When the cold drifts over the plain
And we feel the night come in
Like a butterfly through the window.

Yet my sadness is a comfort
For it is natural and right
And is what should fill the soul
Whenever it thinks it exists
And doesn't notice the hands picking flowers.

Like a sound of sheep bells
Beyond the curve in the road
My thoughts are content.
My only regret is that I know they're content,
Since if I did not know it
They would be content and happy
Instead of sadly content.

Thinking is a discomfort, like walking in the rain
When the wind kicks up and it seems to rain harder.

I have no ambitions and no desires.
To be a poet is not my ambition,
It's my way of being alone.

And if sometimes, in my imagination,
I desire to be a small lamb
(Or to be the whole flock
So as to be scattered across the hillside
As many happy things at the same time),
It's only because I feel what I write when the sun sets
Or when a cloud passes its hand over the light
And a silence sweeps through the grass.

When I sit down to write verses
Or I walk along roads and pathways
Jotting verses on a piece of paper in my mind,
I feel a staff in my hand
And see my own profile
On top of a low hill
Looking after my flock and seeing my ideas,
Or looking after my ideas and seeing my flock,
And smiling vaguely, like one who doesn't grasp what was said
But pretends he did.

I salute all who may read me,
Tipping my wide-brimmed hat
As soon as the coach tops the hill
And they see me at my door.
I salute them and wish them sunshine,
Or rain, if rain is needed,
And a favorite chair where they sit
At home, reading my poems
Next to an open window.

And as they read my poems, I hope
They think I'm something natural—
That old tree, for instance,
In whose shade when they were children
They sat down with a thud, tired of playing,
And wiped the sweat from their hot foreheads
With the sleeve of their striped smocks.

      8 MARCH 1914

2

My gaze is clear like a sunflower.
It is my custom to walk the roads
Looking right and left
And sometimes looking behind me,
And what I see at each moment
Is what I never saw before,
And I'm very good at noticing things.
I'm capable of having that sheer wonder
That a newborn child would have
If he realized he'd just been born.
I always feel that I've just been born
Into an endlessly new world.

I believe in the world as in a daisy,
Because I see it. But I don't think about it,
Because to think is to not understand.
The world wasn't made for us to think about it
(To think is to have eyes that aren't well)
But to look at it and to be in agreement.

I have no philosophy, I have senses.
If I speak of Nature it's not because I know what it is
But because I love it, and for that very reason,
Because those who love never know what they love
Or why they love, or what love is.

To love is eternal innocence,
And the only innocence is not to think.

8 MARCH 1914

5

To not think of anything is metaphysics enough.

What do I think of the world?
Who knows what I think of it!
If I weren't well then I'd think about it.

What's my idea about matter?
What's my opinion about causes and effects?
What are my thoughts on God and the soul
And the creation of the world?
I don't know. To think about such things would be to shut my eyes
And not think. It would be to close the curtains
Of my window (which, however, has no curtains).

The mystery of things? What mystery?
The only mystery is that some people think about mystery.
If you're in the sun and close your eyes,
You begin not to know what the sun is,
And you think about various warm things.
But open your eyes and you see the sun,
And you can no longer think about anything,
Because the light of the sun is truer than the thoughts
Of all philosophers and all poets.
The light of the sun doesn't know what it does,
And so it cannot err and is common and good.

Metaphysics? What metaphysics do those trees have?
Only that of being green and lush and of having branches
Which bear fruit in their season, and we think nothing of it.
We hardly even notice them.
But what better metaphysics than theirs,
Which consists in not knowing why they live
And in not knowing that they don't know?

"The inner makeup of things . . ."
"The inner meaning of the Universe . . ."
All of this is unreal and means absolutely nothing.
It's incredible that anyone can think about such things.
It's like thinking about reasons and objectives
When morning is breaking, and on the trunks of the trees
A faint glimmer of gold is dissolving the darkness.

To think about the inner meaning of things
Is superfluous, like thinking about health
Or carrying a glass to a spring.
The only inner meaning of things
Is that they have no inner meaning at all.

I don't believe in God because I've never seen him.
If he wanted me to believe in him,
Then surely he'd come and speak with me.
He would enter by my door
Saying, "Here I am!"

(This may sound ridiculous to those who,
Because they aren't used to looking at things,
Can't understand a man who speaks of them
In the way that looking at things teaches.)

But if God is the flowers and trees
And hills and sun and moon,
Then I believe in him,
I believe in him at every moment,
And my life is all a prayer and a mass
And a communion by way of my eyes and ears.

But if God is the flowers and trees
And hills and sun and moon,
Then why should I call him God?
I'll call him flowers and trees and hills and sun and moon.
Because if to my eyes he made himself
Sun and moon and flowers and trees and hills,
If he appears to me as trees and hills
And moon and sun and flowers,
Then he wants me to know him
As trees and hills and flowers and moon and sun.

And so I obey him.
(Do I know more about God than God knows about himself?)
I obey him by living spontaneously
As a man who opens his eyes and sees,
And I call him moon and sun and flowers and trees and hills,
And I love him without thinking of him,
And I think him by seeing and hearing,
And I am with him at every moment.

9

I'm a keeper of sheep.
The sheep are my thoughts
And each thought a sensation.
I think with my eyes and my ears
And with my hands and feet
And with my nose and mouth.

To think a flower is to see and smell it,
And to eat a fruit is to know its meaning.

That is why on a hot day
When I enjoy it so much I feel sad,
And I lie down in the grass
And close my warm eyes,
Then I feel my whole body lying down in reality,
I know the truth, and I'm happy.

10

"Hello, keeper of sheep
There on the side of the road.
What does the blowing wind say to you?"

*"That it's wind and that it blows,
And that it has blown before,
And that it will blow hereafter.
And what does it say to you?"*

"Much more than that.
It speaks to me of many other things:
Of memories and nostalgias,
And of things that never were."

*"You've never heard the wind blow.
The wind only speaks of the wind.
What you heard was a lie,
And the lie is in you."*

18

I'd rather be the dust of the road
And trampled on by the feet of the poor . . .

I'd rather be the rivers that flow
And have washerwomen along my shore . . .

I'd rather be the poplars next to the river
With only sky above and the water below . . .

I'd rather be the miller's donkey
And have him beat me and care for me . . .

Rather this than to go through life
Always looking back and feeling regret . . .

20

The Tagus is more beautiful than the river that flows through
    my village,
But the Tagus is not more beautiful than the river that flows
    through my village
Because the Tagus is not the river that flows through my village.

The Tagus has enormous ships,
And for those who see in everything that which isn't there
Its waters are still sailed
By the memory of the carracks.

The Tagus descends from Spain
And crosses Portugal to pour into the sea.
Everyone knows this.
But few know what the river of my village is called
And where it goes to
And where it comes from.
And so, because it belongs to fewer people,
The river of my village is freer and larger.

The Tagus leads to the world.
Beyond the Tagus there is America
And the fortune of those who find it.
No one ever thought about what's beyond
The river of my village.

The river of my village doesn't make one think of anything.
Whoever is next to it is simply next to it.

23

My gaze, blue like the sky,
Is calm like water in the sunlight.
It is blue and calm
Because it does not question or marvel too much.

If I questioned and marveled,
New flowers would not sprout in the meadows,
Nor would anything change in the sun to make it more beautiful.

(Even if new flowers sprouted in the meadow
And the sun changed to become more beautiful,
I would feel less flowers in the meadow
And find the sun less beautiful.
Because everything is what it is, which is how it should be,
And I accept it, and don't even give thanks,
Since that might suggest I think about it.)

24

What we see of things are the things.
Why would we see one thing when another thing is there?
Why would seeing and hearing be to delude ourselves
When seeing and hearing are seeing and hearing?

What matters is to know how to see,
To know how to see without thinking,
To know how to see when seeing
And not think when seeing
Nor see when thinking.

But this (if only we didn't have a dressed-up heart!)—
This requires deep study,
Lessons in unlearning,
And a retreat into the freedom of that convent
Where the stars—say poets—are the eternal nuns
And the flowers the contrite believers of just one day,
But where after all the stars are just stars
And the flowers just flowers,
Which is why we call them stars and flowers.

13 MARCH 1914

32

Yesterday afternoon a man from the cities
Spoke at the door of the inn.
He spoke to me as well.

He spoke of justice and the struggle for justice,
Of the workers who suffer,
Of their unending drudgery, of those who hunger,
And of the rich who only turn their backs.

And looking at me, he saw tears in my eyes
And smiled with satisfaction, convinced that I felt
The hatred he felt and the compassion
He said he felt.

(But I was scarcely listening to him.
What do I care about people
And what they suffer or suppose they suffer?
Let them be like me, and they won't suffer.
All of the world's trouble comes from us fretting over one another,
Whether it be to do good or to do evil.
Our soul and the sky and the earth are all we need.
To want more is to lose this, and to be unhappy.)

What I was thinking about
While the friend of the people spoke
(And this moved me to tears)
Was how the distant tinkling of sheep bells
As the day began to close
Did not seem like the bells of a tiny chapel
Calling to mass the flowers and streams
And simple souls like my own.

(I thank God I'm not good
But have the natural egoism of flowers
And rivers that follow their path
Unwittingly preoccupied
With only their flowering and their flowing.
That is the only mission in the world:
To exist clearly,
And to do so without thinking about it.)

And the man fell silent, looking at the sunset.
But what good is a sunset to one who hates and loves?

37

Like a large blot of smudged fire
The setting sun lingers in the clouds that remain.
I hear a faint whistle in the distance of the still evening.
It must be a distant train.

In this moment I feel a vague nostalgia
Along with a vague and placid desire
That comes and goes.

So too, sometimes, on the surface of streams,
There are bubbles of water
That appear and then pop.
And they have no meaning
But to be bubbles of water
That appear and then pop.

38

Blessed be the same sun of other lands
For making all men my brothers
Since all men, at some moment in the day, look at it as I do.
And in that pure, limpid,
And sensitive moment
They partially return
With a sigh they hardly feel
To the true and primitive Man
Who saw the sun come up and did not yet worship it.
For that is what's natural—more natural
Than worshiping the sun, then God,
And then everything else that doesn't exist.

39

The mystery of things—where is it?
Why doesn't it come out
To show us at least that it's mystery?
What do the river and the tree know about it?
And what do I, who am no more than they, know about it?

Whenever I look at things and think about what people think of them,
I laugh like a brook cleanly plashing against a rock.
For the only hidden meaning of things
Is that they have no hidden meaning.
It's the strangest thing of all,
Stranger than all poets' dreams
And all philosophers' thoughts,
That things are really what they seem to be
And there's nothing to understand.

Yes, this is what my senses learned on their own:
Things have no meaning; they exist.
Things are the only hidden meaning of things.

40

I see a butterfly go by
And for the first time in the universe I notice
That butterflies do not have color or movement,
Even as flowers do not have scent or color.
Color is what has color in the butterfly's wings,
Movement is what moves in the butterfly's movement,
Scent is what has scent in the flower's scent.
The butterfly is just a butterfly
And the flower just a flower.

7 MAY 1914

42

The coach came down the road, and went on,
And the road was no better for it, nor even any worse.
So with human action in the world at large.
We take nothing and add nothing; we pass and forget;
And the sun is on time every day.

7 MAY 1914

47

On an incredibly clear day,
The kind when you wish you'd done lots of work
So that you wouldn't have to work that day,
I saw—as if spotting a road through the trees—
What may well be the Great Secret,
That Great Mystery the false poets speak of.

I saw that there is no Nature,
That Nature doesn't exist,
That there are hills, valleys and plains,
That there are trees, flowers and grass,
That there are rivers and stones,
But that there is no whole to which all this belongs,
That a true and real ensemble
Is a disease of our own ideas.

Nature is parts without a whole.
This is perhaps the mystery they speak of.

This is what, without thinking or pausing,
I realized must be the truth
That everyone tries to find but doesn't find
And that I alone found, because I didn't try to find it.

from
THE SHEPHERD
IN LOVE

BEFORE I HAD YOU

Before I had you
I loved Nature as a calm monk loves Christ.
Now I love Nature
As a calm monk loves the Virgin Mary,
Religiously (in my manner), like before,
But in a more heartfelt and intimate way.
I see the rivers better when I walk with you
Through the fields to the rivers' banks.
When I sit next to you and watch the clouds
I see them much more clearly.
You haven't taken Nature from me,
You've changed Nature.
You've brought Nature closer.
Because you exist I see it better, though the same as before.
Because you love me I love it in the same way, but more.
Because you chose me to have you and love you
My eyes gaze at it more than at anything.
I don't regret what I was before, for I am still what I was.

6 JULY 1914

PERHAPS THOSE WHO ARE GOOD AT SEEING ARE POOR AT FEELING

Perhaps those who are good at seeing are poor at feeling
And do not enchant because they don't know how to act.
There are ways for doing all things,
And love also has its way.
Those whose way of seeing a field is by seeing the grass
Cannot have the blindness that makes a man stir feelings.
I loved, and was not loved, which I only saw in the end,
For one is not loved as one is born but as may happen.
She still has beautiful lips and hair, like before.
And I am still alone in the field, like before.
I think this and my head lifts up
As if it had been bent down,
And the divine sun dries the small tears I can't help but have.
How vast the field is and how tiny love!
I look, and I forget, as the world buries and trees lose their leaves.

Because I am feeling, I cannot speak.
I listen to my voice as if it belonged to another.
And my voice speaks of her as if this other were speaking.
Her hair is yellow-blond like wheat in bright sunlight,
And when she speaks, her mouth utters more than words.
She smiles, and her teeth gleam like the river's stones.

18 NOVEMBER 1929

THE SHEPHERD IN LOVE LOST HIS STAFF

The shepherd in love lost his staff,
And the sheep scattered over the slope.
And so lost was he in thought that he didn't even play his flute.
No one came or went. He never found his staff.
Other men, cursing him, rounded up the sheep.
He had not, after all, been loved.
When he stood up from the slope and the false truth, he saw
    everything:
The wide valleys full of the same shades of green as always,
The tall mountains in the distance, more real than any feeling,
All of reality, with the sky and air and fields that exist, they're here.
(And again the air, that he'd missed for so long, entered fresh into his
    lungs.)
And he felt the air reopen, with pain, a freedom in his chest.

10 JULY 1930

from
UNCOLLECTED POEMS

TO SEE THE FIELDS
AND THE RIVER

To see the fields and the river
It isn't enough to open the window.
To see the trees and the flowers
It isn't enough not to be blind.
It is also necessary to have no philosophy.
With philosophy there are no trees, just ideas.
There is only each one of us, like a cave.
There is only a shut window, and the whole world outside,
And a dream of what could be seen if the window were opened,
Which is never what is seen when the window is opened.

WHEN SPRING RETURNS

When Spring returns
Perhaps I will no longer be in the world.
Today I wish I could think of Spring as a person
So that I could imagine her crying for me
When she sees that she's lost her only friend.
But Spring isn't even a thing:
It's a manner of speaking.
Not even the flowers or green leaves return.
There are new flowers, new green leaves.
There are new balmy days.
Nothing returns, nothing repeats, because everything is real.

7 NOVEMBER 1915

IF I DIE YOUNG

If I die young,
Without having been able to publish a book,
Without having seen how my verses look in print,
I ask those who would protest on my account
That they not protest.
If so it will have happened, then so it should be.

Even if my verses are never published,
They will have their beauty, if they're beautiful.
But they cannot be beautiful and remain unpublished,
Because roots may be hidden in the ground
But their flowers flower in the open air for all to see.
It must be so. Nothing can prevent it.

If I die very young, take note:
I was never more than a child who played.
I was pagan like the sun and the water,
With a universal religion that only humans lack.
I was happy because I didn't ask for anything,
I didn't try to find anything,
And I didn't think there was any explanation beyond
The word explanation meaning nothing at all.

I wanted only to be in the sun or in the rain—
In the sun when there was sun
And in the rain when it was raining
(And never in what was not),
To feel warmth and cold and wind,
And to go no further.

Once I loved and thought I'd be loved back,
But I wasn't loved.
I wasn't loved for one overwhelming reason:
It wasn't meant to be.

I took consolation in the sun and the rain,
Sitting once more at the door of my house.
The fields, after all, are not as green for those who are loved
As for those who are not.
To feel is to be distracted.

                              7 NOVEMBER 1915

IT IS NIGHT. IT'S VERY DARK. IN A HOUSE FAR AWAY

It is night. It's very dark. In a house far away
A light is shining in the window.
I see it and feel human from head to toe.
Funny how the entire life of the man who lives there, whoever he is,
Attracts me with only that light seen from afar.
No doubt his life is real and he has a face, gestures, a family and
    profession,
But right now all that matters to me is the light in his window.
Although the light is only there because he turned it on,
For me it is immediate reality.
I never go beyond immediate reality.
There is nothing beyond immediate reality.
If I, from where I am, see only that light,
Then in relation to where I am there is only that light.
The man and his family are real on the other side of the window,
But I am on this side, far away.
The light went out.
What's it to me that the man continues to exist?

8 NOVEMBER 1915

THE UNIVERSE IS NOT AN IDEA OF MINE

The Universe is not an idea of mine;
My idea of the Universe is an idea of mine.
Night doesn't fall before my eyes;
My idea of night falls before my eyes.
Apart from my thinking and my having thoughts
The night concretely falls,
And the stars' shimmering exists like a weighable thing.

1 OCTOBER 1917

THE CHILD WHO THINKS ABOUT FAIRIES AND BELIEVES IN THEM

The child who thinks about fairies and believes in them
Acts like a sick god, but like a god nonetheless.
For although affirming the existence of what doesn't exist,
He knows how it is that things exist, which is by existing,
He knows that existence exists and cannot be explained,
He knows there's no reason for anything to exist,
And he knows that to exist is to occupy a point.
What he doesn't know is that thought is not a point.

1 OCTOBER 1917

SLOWLY THE FIELD UNROLLS AND SHINES GOLDEN

Slowly the field unrolls and shines golden.
The morning strays over the dips in the plain.
I'm extraneous to the scene I observe: I observe it,
It's outside me. No feeling links me to it.
This is the feeling that links me to the new morning.

29 MAY 1918

YESTERDAY THE PREACHER OF TRUTHS (HIS TRUTHS)

Yesterday the preacher of truths (his truths)
Spoke to me again.
He spoke of the suffering of the working classes
(And not of the suffering of people, who are after all the ones who
    suffer).
He spoke of the injustice of some men being rich
While others are hungry—he didn't say whether hungry for food
Or merely for someone else's dessert.
He spoke of everything that could possibly rankle him.

How happy the man must be who can contemplate the unhappiness
    of others!
How stupid if he doesn't realize that the unhappiness of others is
    theirs
And cannot be cured from the outside,
Because suffering isn't the fact of a man having no ink
Or a crate lacking metal hoops!

The existence of injustice is like the existence of death.
I would never make a move to fight
Against what is called the injustice of the world.
If I made a thousand such moves,
They would be only a thousand moves.
I accept injustice as I accept a stone not being round
And a cork tree not having sprung up as an oak or pine.

I cut the orange in two, and the two parts couldn't be equal.
To which part was I unjust—I, who am going to eat both?

THEY SPOKE TO ME OF PEOPLE, AND OF HUMANITY

They spoke to me of people, and of humanity.
But I've never seen people, or humanity.
I've seen various people, astonishingly dissimilar,
Each separated from the next by an unpeopled space.

I LIE DOWN IN THE GRASS

I lie down in the grass
And forget all I was taught.
What I was taught never made me any warmer or cooler.
What I was told exists never changed the shape of a thing.
What I was made to see never touched my eyes.
What was pointed out to me was never there: only what was there was
    there.

DIRTY UNKNOWN CHILD PLAYING OUTSIDE MY DOOR

Dirty unknown child playing outside my door,
I don't ask you if you bring me a message from symbols.
You amuse me because I've never seen you before,
And if you could be clean you'd of course be another child,
One who wouldn't even come here.
Play in the dirt, play!
I appreciate your presence with just my eyes.
To see a thing always for the first time is better than to know it,
Because to know is like never having seen for the first time,
And to never have seen for the first time is to have only heard.

This child is dirty in a way that's different from other dirty children.
Go on, play! Picking up a stone that fits in your hand,
You know it fits in your hand.
What philosophy can arrive at a greater certainty?
None. And none can come play outside my door.

12 APRIL 1919

YOU WHO ARE A MYSTIC SEE A MEANING IN ALL THINGS

You who are a mystic see a meaning in all things.
For you everything has a veiled significance.
There is something hidden in each thing you see.
What you see you always see to see something else.

I, who have eyes that are only for seeing,
See an absence of meaning in all things.
And seeing this, I love myself, since to be a thing is to mean nothing.
To be a thing is to be subject to no interpretation.

12 APRIL 1919

AH! THEY WANT A LIGHT THAT'S BETTER THAN THE SUN'S

Ah! They want a light that's better than the sun's!
They want meadows that are greener than these!
They want flowers more beautiful than these which I see!
For me this sun, these meadows and these flowers are enough.
But if they weren't enough,
What I would want is a sun more sun than the sun,
Meadows more meadows than these meadows,
Flowers more flowers than these flowers—
Everything more ideal than what it is, in the same way and same manner!

12 APRIL 1919

THAT THING OVER THERE WAS MORE THERE THAN IT IS

That thing over there was more there than it is!
Yes, sometimes I weep for the perfect body that doesn't exist.
But the perfect body is the body that's the most body of all,
And the rest is the dreams of men,
The myopia of those who see little,
And the desire to sit felt by those who don't know how to stand.
All of Christianity is a dream of chairs.
And since the soul is what doesn't appear,
The perfect soul is the one that never appears:
The soul that's made out of body,
The absolute body of things,
Existing—absolutely real—without shadows or errors,
The exact and entire coincidence of a thing with itself.

12 APRIL 1919

THIS MORNING I WENT OUT VERY EARLY

This morning I went out very early,
Because I woke up even earlier
And had nothing I wanted to do.

I didn't know which way to go,
But the wind blew hard toward one side,
And I followed in the way it pushed me.

So has my life always been, and so I would like it always to be—
I go where the wind takes me and don't need to think.

13 JUNE 1930

I CAN ALSO MAKE CONJECTURES

I can also make conjectures.
There is in each thing an animating essence.
In plants it's a tiny nymph that exists on the outside.
In animals it's a remote inner being.
In man it's the soul that lives with him and is him.
In the gods it has the same size
And fills the same space as the body
And is the same thing as the body.
For this reason it is said that the gods never die.
For this reason the gods do not have body and soul
But just body, and they are perfect.
The body is their soul,
And they have consciousness in their divine flesh.

THIS MAY BE THE LAST DAY OF MY LIFE

This may be the last day of my life.
I lifted my right hand to wave at the sun,
But I did not wave at it in farewell.
I was glad I could still see it—that's all.

RICARDO REIS
THE SAD EPICUREAN

This most elusive of Pessoa's heteronyms was born in 1887, in Oporto, and went to the Americas when already in his thirties, but his exact whereabouts and livelihood were never very clearly established. It does not seem that Ricardo Reis, a trained physician, ever practiced his profession. He was reported to be a "Latin (humanities) teacher in an important American high school," though in a letter written in 1935, Pessoa merely states that "he's been living in Brazil since 1919." Yet elsewhere among Pessoa's papers there is an address for a Dr. Ricardo Sequeira Reis in Peru.

It is fitting that Reis should be so hard to pin down, for he was not of this world. Álvaro de Campos celebrated the modern age—with its machines, bustle, and surfeit of sensations. Alberto Caeiro celebrated the natural world as it is, on the surface. But Ricardo Reis, the third in the trio of Pessoa's major heteronyms, celebrated the *spirit* of things. The atmosphere of his poetry is bucolic, but in the Greek manner, nature being appreciated as an ideal—for the spirit it embodies—rather than for its sensorial qualities.

Reis was educated by Jesuits, who no doubt taught him his Latin and perhaps fostered his religious attitude, but he was a pagan and fundamentally hostile toward Christianity. He recognized Christ as just one among many gods, all of whom were subject—like humans—to the indiscernible workings of an impersonal Fate. Far from being a means to an afterlife, the gods were a way for him to elevate this present life, spiritually and aesthetically, in answer to a primordial human need. Pessoa wrote in an English text that, whereas Caeiro only admits the external world, "Reis is less absolute; he bows down also to the primitive elements of our own nature, our primitive feelings being as real and natural to him as flowers and trees. He is therefore religious."

Ricardo's "brother" (or cousin?), Frederico Reis, summed up the neoclassical poet's philosophy in this way: "Avoiding pain wherever possible, man should seek tranquillity and calm above all else, abstaining from effort and useful activity." The best we can do, since we cannot change Fate, is to accept things as they are. The constant awareness of unrelenting Fate precluded Reis from ever being exuberant, as Campos sometimes was, or glad, as Caeiro almost always was, but it served him as a refuge, and he frequently invoked the solace of "clear seeing" in his poetry. In verses dating from 1915 he wrote that the gods could take everything from him as long as they left him his "lucid and solemn consciousness/ Of beings and of things," his "clear and useless vision of the Universe," which "fears and suffers nothing."

It was only after meeting Caeiro and hearing him read verses from *The Keeper of Sheep* that Reis came into his own and realized he was "organically" a poet. This discovery prompted Álvaro de Campos to make the following rather curious observation:

> Some physiologists claim it is possible to change sex. I don't know if it's true, because I don't know if anything is "true." But I do know that Ricardo Reis stopped being a woman and became a man, or stopped being a man and became a woman — as you like — on the day he met Caeiro.

Did Campos, with this bizarre affirmation, also mean to suggest that there was some kind of sexual discovery? Elsewhere he informs us that Reis, in an ode comparing his beloved to a flower, actually had a young man in mind, though this was only Campos's interpretation. Even if true, it may simply have been Reis's way of paying poetic homage to the Greeks, whom he so admired.

Frederico never delved into such particulars when speaking of Ricardo's "profoundly sad" poetry, which he described as "a lucid and disciplined attempt to obtain a measure of calm." Criticizing the free-verse forms of his heteronymic peers, saying that they had "no other artistic purpose than to display their sensations," Reis composed terse Horatian odes on themes reminiscent especially of the Augustan poet's second book of odes: the brevity of life, the vanity of wealth and struggle, the joy of simple pleasures, patience in time of trouble, and avoidance of extremes. Horace prided himself on introducing Greek genres, Greek meters, and Greek ambience into Latin poetry, and Ricardo Reis largely followed suit, maintaining strict blank-verse patterns and evoking the tone of Hellenistic epigrams in a conspicuously "classic" Portuguese. He did not often cite Greek people and places, but Lydia, Chloe, and Neaera, three of the Greek lovers whom Horace addresses, likewise appear in Reis's odes, though for him they were little more than ethereal companions (see Campos's theory, above). Reis was less concrete than Horace, never referring to the events of his time and the more prosaic details of daily life.

Of course, Reis himself was ethereal, almost without any time or life of his own to refer to. "I don't know, when I think or feel,/ Who it is that thinks or feels," says the poet doctor in the last poem attributed to him, just two weeks before Pessoa's death in November of 1935. And the verses continue:

> *I am merely the place*
> *Where things are thought or felt.*
>
> *I have more than just one soul.*
> *There are more I's than I myself.*

Here at last the fiction breaks down, the neoclassical veil becoming blatantly transparent, for never had Fernando Pessoa so clearly expressed the drama, the genius, and the trouble of his own uniquely multiple life.

from
ODES

OTHERS NARRATE WITH LYRES OR HARPS

Others narrate with lyres or harps;
    I tell with my thought.
For he finds nothing, who through music
    Finds only what he feels.
Words weigh more which, carefully measured,
    Say that the world exists.

THE GODS GRANT NOTHING MORE THAN LIFE

The gods grant nothing more than life,
So let us reject whatever lifts us
   To unbreathable heights,
   Eternal but flowerless.
All that we need to accept is science,
And as long as the blood in our veins still pulses
   And love does not shrivel,
   Let us go on
Like panes of glass: transparent to light,
Pattered by the sad rain trickling down,
   Warmed by the sun,
   And reflecting a little.

                                      17 JULY 1914

DON'T CLAP YOUR HANDS BEFORE BEAUTY

Don't clap your hands before beauty,
Which isn't meant to be felt too much.
   Beauty doesn't pass.
   It's the shadow of the gods.

Statues represent the gods
Because statues are calm and eternal:
   The Fates do not spin them
   A short black thread.

Jupiter thunders in accord with cold laws,
And on certain nights Diana appears,
   Divinely calm
   By the laws of her appearing.

What we call laws of how the gods act
Are merely the calm that the gods have.
   The laws are not over them:
   They're the life they desire.

AH, YOU BELIEVERS IN CHRISTS AND MARYS

Ah, you believers in Christs and Marys
Who muddle my fountain's clear waters
    Merely to tell me
    There are happier waters

Flowing in meadows with better hours—
Why speak to me of those other places
    If the waters and meadows
    In this place please me?

This reality was given by the gods,
Who made it external to make it more real.
    Can my dreams be greater
    Than the work of the gods?

Leave me with only the Reality of the moment
And my tranquil and manifest gods who live
    Not in the Uncertain
    But in fields and rivers.

Leave me this life that paganly passes
On the banks of rivers amid the soft piping
    By which the rushes
    Confess they're of Pan.

Live in your dreams and leave to me
The natural altar where I have my worship
    And the visible presence
    Of my immediate gods.

Ah, useless suitors of the better-than-life,
Leave life to the believers who are more ancient
    Than Christ and his cross
    And weeping Mary.

The queen of the fields, Ceres, consoles me,
And Apollo and Venus, and ancient Uranus,
   And thunder, because it comes
   From Jupiter's hand.

                          9 AUGUST 1914

ON THIS DAY WHEN THE GREEN FIELDS

On this day when the green fields
Are a colony goldenly ruled by Apollo,
May the sensation we have of life
   Be a dance within us.

Not randomly but with regular rhythm
May our feeling, like a nymph,
Accompany in its cadences
   The discipline of the dance.

At twilight when the fields become
An empire overwhelmed by shadows
As by a legion marching onward,
   Let us renounce the day.

And let us place on high in our memory,
Like a new god from a new land,
Whatever calm remains in us
   From the transitory day.

                          11 AUGUST 1914

HERE, WITH NO OTHER APOLLO THAN APOLLO

Here, with no other Apollo than Apollo,
Unsighing let us abandon Christ
   And the fever of seeking
   A dualistic god.

And far from Christian sensuality
May the chaste calm of ancient beauty
   Restore to us the ancient
   Feeling of life.

ABOVE THE TRUTH
REIGN THE GODS

Above the truth reign the gods.
Our science is a flawed copy
   Of the certainty with which
     They know the Universe exists.

Everything is everything,
And higher are the gods, whom science
   Cannot know, but we should
     Praise them like the flowers.

Visible to our higher sight,
They're as real as flowers are real,
   And on their calm Olympus
     They are another Nature.

16 OCTOBER 1914

LET THE GODS

    Let the gods
    Take from me
By their high and secretly wrought will
    All glory, love and wealth.

    All I ask
    Is that they leave
My lucid and solemn consciousness
    Of beings and of things.

    Love and glory
    Don't matter to me.
Wealth is a metal, glory an echo,
    And love a shadow.

    But accurate
    Attention given
To the forms and properties of objects
    Is a sure refuge.

    Its foundations
    Are all the world,
Its love is the placid Universe,
    Its wealth is life.

    Its glory is
    The supreme certainty
Of solemnly and clearly possessing
    The forms of objects.

    Other things pass
    And fear death,
But the clear and useless vision of the Universe
    Fears and suffers nothing.

   Self-sufficing,
    It desires nothing
But the pride of always seeing clearly
   Until it no longer sees.

6 JUNE 1915

LIPS RED FROM WINE

Lips red from wine,
White foreheads under roses,
Naked white forearms
Lying on the table:

May this be the picture
Wherein speechless, Lydia,
We'll forever be inscribed
In the minds of the gods.

Rather this than life
As earthly men live it,
Full of the black dust
They raise from the roads.

The gods, by their example,
Help only those
Who seek to go nowhere
But in the river of things.

29 AUGUST 1915

I PREFER ROSES, MY LOVE, TO THE HOMELAND

I prefer roses, my love, to the homeland,
   And I love magnolias
   More than fame and virtue.

As long as this passing life doesn't weary me
   And I stay the same,
   I'll let it keep passing.

What does it matter who wins or loses
   If nothing to me matters
   And the dawn still breaks,

And each year with spring the leaves appear,
   And each year with autumn
   They fall from the trees?

What do the other things which humans
   Add on to life
   Increase in my soul?

Nothing, except its desire for indifference
   And its languid trust
   In the fleeting moment.

1 JUNE 1916

FOLLOW YOUR DESTINY

Follow your destiny,
Water your plants,
Love your roses.
The rest is shadow
Of unknown trees.

Reality is always
More or less
Than what we want.
Only we are always
Equal to ourselves.

It's good to live alone,
And noble and great
Always to live simply.
Leave pain on the altar
As an offering to the gods.

See life from a distance.
Never question it.
There's nothing it can
Tell you. The answer
Lies beyond the Gods.

But quietly imitate
Olympus in your heart.
The gods are gods
Because they don't think
About what they are.

1 JULY 1916

THE BIRD ALIGHTS, LOOKING ONLY TO ITS ALIGHTING

The bird alights, looking only to its alighting,
Its desire to alight mattering more than the branch.
The river runs where it finds its repose,
    And not where it is needed.

I was never one who in love or in friendship
Preferred one sex over the other. Beauty
Attracts me in equal measure, wherever
    I find it, in season.

Thus I separate myself from distinctions
Of where and how I love or don't love,
And I don't offend the inherent innocence
    Of when people love.

Love is not in the object but in the act.
I only love something when I start loving it.
My love does not reside in it
    But in my love.

The gods who gave us this path of love
To which we have given the name beauty
Did not place it only in women
    Or only in fruit.

They also gave us the flower to pluck.
And perhaps we pluck with better love
    What we seek for the using.

O MORNING THAT BREAKS
WITHOUT LOOKING AT ME

O morning that breaks without looking at me,
O sun that shines without caring that I see you,
   It's for me that you
   Are true and real,
For it's in the foil to my desire
That I feel nature and life to be real.
   In what denies me I feel
   They exist and I am small.
And in this knowledge I become great
Even as the wave which, tossed by storms
   High into the air, returns
   With more weight to a deeper sea.

OBEY THE LAW, WHETHER IT'S WRONG OR YOU ARE

Obey the law, whether it's wrong or you are.
Man can do little against the outer life.
   Let injustice be.
   Nothing you change changes.

Your only kingdom is the mind you've been given,
And in it you're a servant to Fate and the Gods.
   The mind rules to the borders
   Of where your will pretends.

Though conquered there, at least you can boast
In your conquerors: Destiny and the great gods.
   You're not twice defeated
   By defeat and mediocrity.

So I see it. And that hasty justice
By which we try to moderate things
   I expel, like a meddling
   Servant, from the mind.

How can I, who am not even my own ruler,
Expect to rule or determine what happens
   Where my mind and body
   Are but a small part?

Let sufficiency suffice me and the rest spin
In its predestined orbit, as even the gods spin:
   Suns, centers,
   Servants of a vast flux.

                                   29 JANUARY 1921

I WANT MY VERSES
TO BE LIKE JEWELS

I want my verses to be like jewels,
Able to endure into the far future
   Untarnished by the death
   That lurks in each thing,
Verses which forget the hard and sad
Brevity of our days, taking us back
   To that ancient freedom
   We've perhaps never known.
Here in these friendly, far-removed shadows
Where history ignores us, I remember those
   Who carefully weave
   Their carefree verses.
And remembering you above all others,
I write beneath the veiled sun
   And drink, immortal Horace,
   Superfluous, to your glory.

                        5 AUGUST 1923

DAY AFTER DAY
LIFE'S THE SAME LIFE

Day after day life's the same life.
   All that happens, Lydia,
In what we are as in what we are not,
   Happens all the same.
Picked, the fruit withers; unpicked,
   It falls. Destiny is
The same, whether we seek or wait
   For it. Our lot today,
Our fate from always, and in either form
   Beyond us and invincible.

2 SEPTEMBER 1923

WHO DELIGHTS IN THE MIND CAN DELIGHT IN NO DESTINY

Who delights in the mind can delight in no destiny
Better than to know himself. To know he is nothing
   Is better than not knowing:
   Nothing inside of nothing.
If I don't have within me the power to master
The three Fates and the shapes of the future,
   May the gods at least give me
   The power of knowing it.
And since in myself I cannot create beauty,
May I enjoy it as it's given on the outside,
   Repeated in my passive eyes,
   Ponds which death will dry.

                                      22 OCTOBER 1923

AS IF EACH KISS

    As if each kiss
    Were a kiss of farewell,
Let us lovingly kiss, my Chloe.
    Perhaps already
    We're touched by the hand
Which calls to that inevitably empty boat
And binds in one sheaf
What together we were
With the alien universal sum of life.

                            17 NOVEMBER 1923

YOUR DEAD GODS TELL ME NOTHING I NEED

Your dead gods tell me nothing I need
To know. Without any love or hatred
   I dismiss the crucifix
   From my way of being.

What good to me, a Latin, are the creeds
This hanging torso of Christ would die for?
   With the sun I have fellowship
   And not with these truths.

They may be valid. But I was only given
One vision of the things that exist on earth,
   And an uncertain mind,
   And the knowledge that we die.

FATE FRIGHTENS ME, LYDIA. NOTHING IS CERTAIN

Fate frightens me, Lydia. Nothing is certain.
At any moment something could happen
   To change all that we are.
When we leave what is known, the very step
We take is strange. Grave numens guard
   The customary boundaries.
We are not gods: blind, we fear,
And prefer the meager life we know
   To novelty, the abyss.

I DEVOTE MY HIGHER MIND TO THE ARDENT

I devote my higher mind to the ardent
   Pursuit of the summit, leaving
   Verse to chance and its laws,
For when the thought is lofty and noble,
   The sentence will naturally seek it,
   And rhythm slavishly serve it.

MY EYES SEE THE FIELDS, THE FIELDS

My eyes see the fields, the fields,
The fields, Neaera, and already
I suffer the cold of the darkness
In which I will not have eyes.

I can feel, even now, the skull
I'll be when all feeling has ceased,
Unless the unknown shall assign me
Some other, unforeseeable end.

I weep less for the moment
Than for my future self,
A null and void subject
Of the universal destiny.

>   25 DECEMBER 1923

EACH MAN IS A WORLD, AND AS EACH FOUNTAIN

Each man is a world, and as each fountain
Has its own deity, might not each man
   Have a god all his own?

In the inscrutable succession of things,
Only the wise man feels he was nothing
   More than the life he left.

NOT ONLY WINE
BUT ITS OBLIVION I POUR

Not only wine but its oblivion I pour
In my cup, and I will be happy, because happiness
   Is ignorant. Who, remembering
   Or foreseeing, ever smiled?

Let us, with our thinking, obtain not the life
But the soul of animals, taking refuge
   In the impalpable destiny
   Which neither hopes nor remembers.

With mortal hand I raise the fragile cup
Of fleeting wine to my mortal mouth,
   Eyes clouded,
   Ready to stop seeing.

                                13 JUNE 1926

HOW GREAT A SADNESS AND BITTERNESS

How great a sadness and bitterness
Drowns our tiny lives in chaos!
   How often adversity
   Cruelly overwhelms us!
Happy the animal, anonymous to itself,
Which grazes in green fields and enters
   Death as if it were home;
   Or the learned man who, lost
In science, raises his futile, ascetic
Life above our own, like smoke
   Which lifts its disintegrating arms
   To the nonexistent heavens.

                      14 JUNE 1926

SOLEMNLY OVER
THE FERTILE LAND

Solemnly over the fertile land
The brief and futile white cloud passes,
And for a black instant the fields are touched
   By a cold breeze.

So too in my soul the slow thought soars
And darkens my mind, but I, like the field
That returns to itself, return to the day,
   The surface of life.

                                       31 MAY 1927

WHERE THERE ARE ROSES
WE PLANT DOUBT

Where there are roses we plant doubt.
Most of the meaning we glean is our own,
    And forever not knowing, we ponder.
Foreign to us, capacious nature
Unrolls fields, opens flowers, ripens
    Fruits, and death arrives.
I'll only be right, if anyone is right,
When death at last confounds my mind
    And I no longer see,
For we cannot find and should not find
The remote and profound explanation
    For why it is we live.

AS LONG AS I FEEL THE FULL BREEZE IN MY HAIR

As long as I feel the full breeze in my hair
And see the sun shining bright on the leaves,
   I will not ask for more.
What better thing could destiny give me
Than the sensual passing of life in moments
   Of ignorance like this?
Wise is the one who does not seek.
The seeker will find in all things
   The abyss, and doubt in himself.

                          16 JUNE 1927

WHAT WE FEEL,
NOT WHAT IS FELT

What we feel, not what is felt,
Is what we have. Winter naturally straitens.
   Like fate we accept it.
May winter wrap earth and not our minds,
As love to love, or book to book, we relish
   Our brief warm fire.

                                  8 JULY 1930

I DON'T KNOW IF THE LOVE YOU GIVE IS LOVE YOU HAVE

I don't know if the love you give is love you have
Or love you feign. You give it to me. Let that suffice.
   I can't be young by years,
   So why not by illusion?
The Gods give us little, and the little they give is false.
But if they give it, however false it be, the giving
   Is true. I accept it, and resign
   Myself to believing you.

12 SEPTEMBER 1930

WANT LITTLE: YOU'LL HAVE EVERYTHING

Want little: you'll have everything.
Want nothing: you'll be free.
The same love by which we're loved
Oppresses us with its wanting.

1 NOVEMBER 1930

I WAS LEFT IN THE WORLD, ALL ALONE

I was left in the world, all alone,
   By the Gods who ordain.
It's futile to fight them: what they've given
   I accept without question,
Like wheat that bows in the wind, raising
   Its head when the wind stops blowing.

19 NOVEMBER 1930

I TELL WITH SEVERITY. I THINK WHAT I FEEL

I tell with severity. I think what I feel.
  Words are ideas.
The purling river passes, and not its sound,
  Which is ours, not the river's.
So I wanted my verse: mine and not-mine,
  To be read by me.

16 JUNE 1932

I PLACIDLY WAIT, FOR WHAT I DON'T KNOW

I placidly wait for what I don't know—
   My future and the future of everything.
In the end there will only be silence except
   Where the waves of the sea bathe nothing.

                                  13 DECEMBER 1933

COUNTLESS LIVES
INHABIT US

Countless lives inhabit us.
I don't know, when I think or feel,
Who it is that thinks or feels.
I am merely the place
Where things are thought or felt.

I have more than just one soul.
There are more I's than I myself.
I exist, nevertheless,
Indifferent to them all.
I silence them: I speak.

The crossing urges of what
I feel or do not feel
Struggle in who I am, but I
Ignore them. They dictate nothing
To the I I know: I write.

13 NOVEMBER 1935

ÁLVARO DE CAMPOS
THE JADED SENSATIONIST

Born in Tavira, a small town in the Algarve, in 1890, Álvaro de Campos was the most substantial of Fernando Pessoa's heteronyms and the one closest to his true heart and person. The "naval engineer and Sensationist poet," as Campos often signed himself, was in many ways a larger-than-life version of his creator. Pessoa was relatively tall for a Portuguese man of his day, but Campos was slightly taller, about 5 feet 9 inches. Pessoa had some Jewish blood on his father's side, but Campos had rather more, and may actually have been Jewish. Pessoa was a heavy drinker, but it was Campos who indulged in absinthe and smoked opium. Pessoa was always well-dressed but was not a dandy like Campos, and he preferred conservative eyeglasses to his heteronym's more stylish monocle.

Álvaro de Campos was Pessoa—same basic attitudes, desires, and anxieties—but with more pizzazz and chutzpah, living out much of what his progenitor only dreamed of. When normally reserved Pessoa wanted to use strong language or announce radical ideas, Campos was usually his mouthpiece, and not only in poetry. Various manifestos, including the Futurist *Ultimatum* of 1917, were signed by the naval engineer, who also got involved in Pessoa's private life, sometimes even writing letters to Pessoa's friends. Campos was the ostensible thorn in Pessoa's one romantic relationship, saying a number of hard and disagreeable things to the beloved lady, Ophelia Queiroz, who informed Pessoa that she hated his alter ego. "I don't know why," replied Fernando. "He's rather fond of you."

Campos, whose motto was "to feel all things in all ways," was the most sexually liberated heteronym, as readily smitten by men as by women, but he was by no means a Don Juan, being too steeped in his feelings to actually *do* very much, whether socially or professionally. He studied engineering in Scotland, living there or in London when not on one of his long voyages to the Orient and other parts of the world, but he never seemed to work too hard, and when he eventually returned to Lisbon, where he'd lived as a young man, he did almost no work at all and lost interest in traveling. "The best way to travel," he wrote, "is to feel."

Campos's biography corresponds to the evolution in his poetry. Beginning as a decadent romantic, he produced several sonnets as well as a poem in rhymed quatrains justifying his use of opium. This last was written aboard a steamer in the Suez Canal. Then came his Sensationist period, in which he wrote long, exuberant poems celebrating the new machine age and life's fullness and diversity, his verses sometimes smacking of Futurism — "My body is the center of a stupendous and infinite flywheel/ Forever in frenetic motion around itself" — while at other times recalling Walt Whitman — "I feel kinship with all things, I live all in all." But despair was already lurking in between the heady affirmations. In "Time's Passage," which contains the verse just quoted, we also find: "I feel that all of what I wanted eluded what I imagined,/ That although I wanted everything, everything lacked." Or again: ". . . it would have been better not to be born,/ For no matter how interesting it is at every moment,/ Life sometimes hurts, jades, cuts, bruises, grates."

This nascent sense of futility will gradually get the upper hand, so that Campos, by the time he returns to Lisbon, is haunted by a "vague nausea, the ill-defined affliction, of feeling myself." He deplores life's ordinariness and realizes that he too is ordinary. He hates life's redundancy and comes to feel that travel itself is a dull routine. Whereas in an early poem he expressed his desire to "eat the universe" so as to incorporate and possess it, late Campos says, "If I could eat the universe to throw it up into the sink, I'd eat it." Disillusioned with real travel, real love, and real life in general, Campos travels and loves and lives in his writing, just like his creator, of whom he is finally the perfect reflection. Pessoa, however, would wonder if he himself might not be the reflection of Álvaro de Campos, the ideal poet engineer who came to him one day by seeming magic, in a dream.

I STUDY MYSELF
BUT CAN'T PERCEIVE

Lisbon, August 1913

I study myself but can't perceive.
I'm so addicted to feeling that
I lose myself if I'm distracted
From the sensations I receive.

This liquor I drink, the air I breathe,
Belong to the very way I exist:
I've never discovered how to resist
These hapless sensations I conceive.

Nor have I ever ascertained
If I *really* feel what I feel.
Am I what I seem to myself—the same?

Is the I I feel the I that's real?
Even with feelings I'm a bit of an atheist.
I don't even know if it's *I* who feels.

LISTEN, DAISY.
WHEN I DIE, ALTHOUGH

On an Orient-bound ship
December 1913

Listen, Daisy. When I die, although
You may not feel a thing, you must
Tell all my friends in London how much
My loss makes you suffer. Then go

To York, where you claim you were born
(But I don't believe a thing you claim),
To tell that poor boy who gave me
So many hours of joy (but of course

You don't know about that) that I'm dead.
Even he, whom I thought I sincerely
Loved, won't care. . . . Then go and break

The news to that strange girl Cecily,
Who believed that one day I'd be great. . . .
To hell with life and everyone in it!

AH, THE FIRST MINUTES
IN CAFÉS OF NEW CITIES

Ah, the first minutes in cafés of new cities!
The early morning arrivals at docks or at stations
Full of a tranquil and luminous silence!
The first pedestrians on the streets of a just-reached city,
And the special sound of time's passing when we travel . . .

The buses or streetcars or automobiles . . .
The novel look of streets in novel countries . . .
The peace they seem to offer for our sorrow,
The happy bustle they have for our sadness,
Their absence of monotony for our wearied heart!
The large, dependably right-angled squares,
The streets with rows of buildings that converge in the distance,
The cross streets with unexpected things of interest,
And in all of this, like something that floods without ever overflowing,
Motion, motion,
Swift-colored human thing that passes and remains . . .

The ports with their unmoving ships,
Intensely unmoving ships,
And small boats close by, waiting . . .

TIME'S PASSAGE

TO FEEL everything in every way,
To live everything from all sides,
To be the same thing in all ways possible at the same time,
To realize in oneself all humanity at all moments
In one scattered, extravagant, complete, and aloof moment.

I always want to be the thing I feel kinship with.
I always become, sooner or later,
The thing I feel kinship with, be it a stone or a yearning,
A flower or an abstract idea,
A multitude or a way of understanding God.
And I feel kinship with all things, I live all in all.
I feel kinship with superior men because they are superior,
And I feel kinship with inferior men because they are superior too,
Since to be inferior is different from being superior,
And so it is a superiority at certain moments in our seeing.
With some I feel kinship because of their character qualities,
And with others I feel kinship because they lack those qualities,
And with still others I feel kinship because I feel kinship with them,
And there are absolutely organic moments when "them" is all men.
Yes, since I'm an absolute king in my feeling of kinship,
It need only exist to have a raison d'être.
Tight against my heaving breast, in a heartfelt embrace I hold
(In the same heartfelt embrace)
The man who gives his shirt to an indigent he doesn't know,
The soldier who dies for his country without knowing what a
    country is,
And . . .
And the matricide, the fratricide, the incestuous, the child molester,
The highwayman, the freebooter, the pickpocket,
The one who lies in wait in dark alleys—
All are my preferred lover for at least a moment in life.

I kiss every whore on the lips,
I kiss every pimp on the eyes,
My passivity lies at the feet of every killer,
And my Spanish cape shields every fleeing thief.
Everything is the raison d'être of my life.

I've committed every crime,
Lived within every crime
(In vice I was not this person or that person
But the vice-in-person carried out between them,
And these are my life's most arch-triumphant times.)

I multiplied myself to feel myself,
To feel myself I had to feel everything,
I overflowed, I did nothing but spill out,
I undressed, I yielded,
And in each corner of my soul there's an altar to a different god.

The arms of every athlete have squeezed my suddenly female self,
And the mere thought made me faint in imagined muscles.

All kisses of all trysts have been placed on my lips,
All handkerchiefs of all farewells have waved in my heart,
All obscenely suggestive gestures and gazes
Pound in my sex organs and throughout all my body.
I was every ascetic, every outcast, every forgotten man,
And every pederast—absolutely every last one of them.
Black and red rendezvous in the hell of my soul's depths!

(Freddie, whom I called Baby, because you were blond, fair, and I
    loved you,
How many future empresses and dethroned princesses you were to
    me!
Mary, with whom I read Burns on days as sad as the feeling of living,
Mary, you've no idea how many honest couples and happy families
My eyes and my clasping arm and my doubting conscience have
    lived in you,
Their peaceful lives, their suburban houses with yards, their
    unexpected half-holidays . . .
Mary, I'm unhappy . . .
Freddie, I'm unhappy . . .
Oh, all of you, all, who passed by or lingered,
How many times you must have thought to think of me without
    doing it;
Ah, how little I've counted in what you are, how little, how little—
Yes, and what have I been, O my subjective universe,
O my sun, my moon, my stars, my moment,
O outer part of me lost in God's labyrinths!)

Everything passes, all in a marching file inside me,
And in me every city of the world buzzes . . .

My courthouse heart, my marketplace heart, my stock exchange
    heart, my bank counter heart,
My heart the rendezvous of all humanity,
My park bench, hostelry, boardinghouse, jail cell heart
("*Aqui estuvo Manuel antes de ser ejecutado*"),
My heart that's a club, hall, auditorium, doormat, ticket booth,
    gangway,
Bridge, turnstile, outing, march, journey, auction, fair, festival,
My service window heart,
My parcel post heart,
My letter, luggage, remittance, delivery heart,

My margin, border, summary, index heart:
Hey-ya, hey-ya, hey-ya, my bazaar of a heart.

All dawns are the dawn and are life.
All auroras shine in the same place:
Infinity . . .
Every joy of every bird comes from the same throat,
Every shiver of every leaf is from the same tree,
And everyone who gets up early to go to work
Goes from the same house to the same factory by the same road.

Roll, huge ball, anthill of consciousnesses, earth,
Roll dawned and dusked, sun-scorched and nocturnal,
Roll in abstract space, in the dimly lit night really
Roll and. . . . .

I feel in my head the speed of the earth's spinning,
And all nations and all persons spin inside me,
Centrifugal yearning, the lust to travel through space to the stars
Beats its fists against the inside of my brain,
Pokes blindfolded needles throughout my body's consciousness,
Makes me get up a thousand times to go to the Abstract,
The Undiscoverable, the There without limits,
The invisible Goal, all the points I'm not at, all at the same time.

Ah! to be neither still nor in motion,
Neither lying down nor standing up,
Neither asleep nor awake,
Neither here nor anywhere else,
To solve the equation of this prolix restlessness,
To know where to be that I could be in all parts,
To know where to lie down that I could stroll on all streets,
To know where. . . .

Whoooooooosssssssshhhhhhh
WHOOOOOOOSSSSSSSHHHHHHH
WHOOOOOOOSSSSSSSHHHHHHH
WHOOOOOOOSSSSSSSHHHHHHH

Winged cavalcade of me riding over all things,
Exploded cavalcade of me riding under all things,
Winged and exploded cavalcade of me for the sake of all things . . .
Alley-oop over the trees, alley-oop under ponds,
Alley-oop into the walls, alley-oop against tree trunks,
Alley-oop in the air, alley-oop in the wind, alley-oop on beaches,
With increasing, insistent, frenetic speed,
Alley-oop alley-oop alley-oop alley-oop . . .

Pantheistic cavalcade of me inside all things,
Energetic cavalcade of me inside all energies,
Cavalcade of me inside the coal that burns, inside the lamp that
    glows,
Inside every kind of energy,
Cavalcade of a thousand amperes,
Explosive cavalcade, exploded like a bursting bomb,
Cavalcade bursting in all directions at the same time,
Cavalcade over space, a leap over time,
Hurdling ion-electron horse, compressed solar system
Inside the driving pistons, outside the turning flywheels.

Inside the pistons I take the form of raging abstract speed,
Acting by iron and motion, come-and-go, madness, pent-up rage,
And on the rim of every flywheel I turn staggering hours,
And the entire universe creaks, sizzles, and booms in me.

Whoooosssshhhh . . .
Ever faster, the mind ever farther ahead of the body,
Ahead even of the rushing idea of the propelled body,
The mind behind ahead of the body, shadow, spark,
Hey-ya-whoooooo . . . Heyawhoooooo . . .

All energy is the same and all nature is the same . . .
The sap of tree sap is the same energy that turns
Train wheels, streetcar wheels, the diesel engine's flywheels,
And a vehicle moved by mules or gasoline is moved by the same
    thing.

Pantheistic rage of awesomely feeling
With all my senses fizzing and all my pores fuming
That everything is but one speed, one energy, one divine line
From and to itself, arrested and murmuring furies of mad speed . . .

Whoooooooosssssssshhhhhhh
WHOOOOOOOSSSSSSSHHHHHHH
WHOOOOOOOSSSSSSSHHHHHHH
WHOOOOOOOSSSSSSSHHHHHHH

Hail, hurrah, long live the hurtling unity of all things!
Hail, hurrah, long live the equality of all things soaring!
Hail, hurrah, long live that great machine the universe!
Hail, because you—trees, machines, laws—are the same,
Hail, because you—worms, pistons, abstract ideas—are the same,
The same sap fills you, the same sap transforms you,
You are the same thing, and the rest is outer and false,
The rest, the static rest that remains in eyes that stop moving,
But not in my combustion-engine nerves that run on heavy or light
    oil,
Not in my all-machine, all-gear-system nerves,

Not in my train, tram, car, steam-thresher nerves,
Ship-engine, diesel-engine, semidiesel, Campbell nerves,
100 percent steam-run, gas-run, oil-run, and electric-run nerves,
Universal machine moved by belts of all momentums!
Smash, train, against the buffer of the sidetrack!
Ram, steamer, into the pier and split open!
Dash, automobile driven by the madness of all the universe,
Over the edge of every cliff
And crash — bam! — into smithereens in the bottom of my heart!

Straight at me, all projectile objects!
Straight at me, all object directions!
Straight at me, all objects too swift to be seen!
Strike me, pierce me, pass right through me!
It's I who strike, who pierce, who pass through myself!
The rage of all impetuses closes in a me-circle!

Heya-whoooooo my train, auto, airplane desires.
Speed, force your way into all ideas,
Collide into all dreams and shatter them,
Scorch all humanitarian and useful ideals,
Crush all normal and decent and harmonious feelings,
Catch in the whirl of your heavy and dizzy flywheel
The bodies of all philosophies, the tatters of all poems,
Shredding them till only you remain, an abstract flywheel in space,
Metallic supreme lord and libido of Europe's hour.

Let's go, may the cavalcade never end, not even in God!
Let's go even if I should fall behind the cavalcade, even if I must clutch
The horse's tail and be dragged, mangled, lacerated, lost
In free fall, my body and soul behind my abstract yearning,
My giddy yearning to transcend the universe,
To leave God behind like a negligible milestone,
To leave. . . . .

My imagination hurts, I don't know how, but that's what hurts.
The sun on high inside me is sinking.
Dusk is starting to fall over the blue and in my nerves.
Let's go, cavalcade, who else will you turn me into?
I, this swift, voracious glutton of abstract energy,
Who wanted to eat, drink, claw and flay the world,
I, who could only be satisfied by trampling the universe underfoot,
Trampling, trampling, trampling until feeling nothing . . .
I feel that all of what I wanted eluded what I imagined,
That although I wanted everything, everything lacked.

Cavalcade dismantled above all summits,
Cavalcade dissolved underneath all wells,
Cavalcade flight, cavalcade arrow, cavalcade flashing thought,
Cavalcade I, cavalcade I, cavalcade universe-I.
Heyawhooooooooo . . .

My elastic being, a spring, a needle, a trembling . . .

◆

I CARRY inside my heart,
As in a chest too full to shut,
All the places where I've been,
All the ports at which I've called,
All the sights I've seen through windows and portholes
And from quarterdecks, dreaming,
And all of this, which is so much, is nothing next to what I want.

The entrance to Singapore, new day rising, all green,
The coral of the Maldives in a sweltering passage,
Macao at one in the morning . . . I wake up with a start . . .
Yhat-loh-oh-oh-oh-oh-oh-oh-oh-oh . . . Gea—. . .
And the sound reaches me from the heart of another reality . . .
The almost North African stature of Zanzibar in the sun,
Dar es Salaam (hard to clear the port),
Mahajanga, Nosy-Bé, Madagascar's lush greens,
Storms around Guardafui,
The Cape of Good Hope glowing in the morning sun,
And Cape Town with Table Mountain in the background . . .

I've visited more lands than I've set foot on,
I've seen more landscapes than I've laid eyes on,
I've experienced more sensations than all the ones I've felt,
Because however much I felt I never felt enough,
And life always pained me, it was always too little, and I was
      unhappy.

At certain times of the day I remember all this and am terrified,
I think of what will remain of these snatches of life, of this
      exaltation,
Of this winding road, of this car on the road's shoulder, of this sign,
Of this calm confusion of conflicting sensations,
Of this transfusion, of this evanescence, of this iridescent
      convergence,
Of this disquietude at the bottom of every glass,
Of this anxiety at the heart of every pleasure,
Of this satiety anticipated in every teacup's handle,
Of this tiresome card game between the Cape of Good Hope and
      the Canaries.

I don't know if life is too little or too much for me.
I don't know if I feel too much or too little, I don't know
If I lack moral scruples, a fulcrum in my mind,
Consanguinity with the mystery of things, impact
On contact, blood beneath blows, sensibility to noises,
Or if there's a simpler and happier explanation for all this.

Whatever the case, it would be better not to have been born,
For no matter how interesting it is at every moment,
Life sometimes hurts, jades, cuts, bruises, grates,
Makes us want to scream, to jump, to wallow, to walk
Out of every house and every logic and off every balcony,
And to become savage and die among trees and things forgotten,
Among collapses and hazards and the absence of tomorrows,
And all this, O life, should be something closer to what I think,
To what I think or what I feel, whatever that is.

I cross my arms on the table, I lay my head on my arms,
And I need to want to cry, but I don't know where to find the tears.
No matter how hard I try to pity myself, I don't cry,
My soul is broken under the curved finger that touches it . . .
What will become of me? What will become of me?

They ran the jester out of the palace with a whip for no reason,
They made the beggar get up from the step where he'd fallen.
They spanked the abandoned child and took away his bread,
Oh immense grief of the world, what's needed is action . . .
So decadent, so decadent, so decadent . . .
I'm only at peace when I listen to music, and not even then.
Gardens of the eighteenth century before '89,
Where are you? For I'd like to cry one way or another.

Like a balsam that only comforts because of the idea that it's a
    balsam,
The evening of today and all days, little by little, monotonously
    falls.

The lights have come on, the night is falling, life changes its face.
One way or another I have to keep on living.
My soul burns like a hand, physically.
I'm on the road of all men and they bump against me.
O house in the country, if only there were less
Than a train, a coach and the decision to leave separating me from
    you.
As it is I stay, I stay . . . I'm the one who always wants to leave
And always stays, always stays, always stays.
Until death I'll stay, even if I leave I'll stay, stay, stay . . .

Make me human, O night, make me helpful and brotherly.
Only humanitarianly can one live.
Only by loving mankind, actions, the banality of jobs,
Only in this way—alas!—only in this way can one live.
Only this way, O night, and I can never be this way!

I've seen all things, and marveled at them all,
But it was too much or too little—I'm not sure which—and I
    suffered.
I've lived every emotion, every thought, every gesture,
And remained as sad as if I'd wanted to live them and failed to.
I've loved and hated like everyone else,
But for everyone else this was normal and instinctive,
Whereas for me it was always an exception, a shock, a release valve,
    a convulsion.

Come, night, and snuff me out, come and drown me in yourself.
O beloved from Beyond, lady of infinite mourning,
Exterior grief of Earth, silent weeping of the World,
Gentle ancient mother of unexpressed emotions,
Chaste and sad older sister of incoherent ideas,
Fiancée forever waiting on our unrealized plans,
The constantly abandoned road of our destiny,
Our joyless pagan uncertainty,
Our faithless Christian weakness,
Our inert Buddhism that loves neither things nor ecstasies,
Our fever, our pallor, our weak-kneed impatience,
Our life, O mother, our lost life . . .

I'm unable to feel, to be human, to reach out
From inside my sad soul to my fellow earthly brothers.
And even were I to feel, I'm unable to be useful, practical,
    quotidian, definite,
To have a place in life, a destiny among men,
To have a vocation, a force, a will, a garden,
A reason for resting, a need for recreation,
Something that comes to me directly from nature.

So be motherly to me, O tranquil night . . .
You who remove the world from the world, you who are peace,
You who don't exist, who are only the absence of light,
You who aren't a thing, a place, an essence or a life,
Penelope who weaves darkness that tomorrow will be unraveled,
Unreal Circe of the fevered, of the anguished without cause,
Come to me, O night, reach out your hands,
And be coolness and relief, O night, on my forehead . . .

You, whose coming is so gentle you seem to be drawing away,
Whose ebb and flow of darkness, as the moon softly breathes,
Has waves of dead tenderness, the cold of vast oceans of dream,
Breezes of imagined landscapes for our inordinate anguish . . .
You, pallidly, you, faintly, you, liquidly,
Scent of death among flowers, breath of fever along riverbanks,
You, queen, you, chatelaine, you, pale lady, come . . .

◆

I TURN every corner of every street every day,
And whenever I'm thinking of one thing, I'm thinking of another.
I don't conform except by atavism,
And unless one is bedridden there's always a reason to emigrate.

From every sidewalk café of every city
Accessible to the imagination
I look at life passing by, watching without getting involved,
Belonging to it without pulling a gesture out of my pocket
And without noting down what I see to pretend later on that I
    saw it.

The definite wife of someone rides by in the yellow car,
And I'm sitting next to her although she doesn't know it.
On the sidewalk they run into each other by a planned
    coincidence,
But before they were there I was already there with them.
There's no way they can avoid finding me, no way I won't be
    everywhere.
My privilege is everything
(My soul patented, *Sans Garantie de Dieu*).

I witness everything and exhaustively.
There's no woman's jewel that's not bought by me and for me,
No thought of waiting that's not in some way mine,
No conversation that doesn't in the end have a bearing on me,
No pealing bell in Lisbon in thirty years or night at the opera
    in fifty
That hasn't been gallantly laid at my feet.

I was brought up by Imagination,
I always traveled by her hand,
And thus I always loved, hated, spoke, thought,
Having every day this window before me,
Every hour being mine in this way.

◆

BRIGHT bugle of morning on the outer edge
Of the horizon's cold half circle,
Tenuous distant bugle like hazy flags
Unfurled beyond where colors are visible . . .

Tremulous bugle, dust that hovers where the night ends,
Golden dust hovering on the edge of visibility . . .

Car that cleanly screeches, steamer that whistles,
Crane that begins to swivel in my ear,
Hacking cough announcing that the man's going out,
Light morning shiver of the joy of living,
Burst of laughter veiled in some strange way by the mist,
Seamstress destined for worse than the morning she feels,
Consumptive laborer dying of happiness in this
Inevitably vital hour
In which the contours of things are soft, friendly, and sure,
In which the walls are cool to the hand's touch, and the houses
Here and there open their white-curtained eyes . . .

Every morning is a gently waving curtain
Reviving illusions and memories in my passerby soul,
In my exiled, epidermically spirited heart,
In my tired and veiled . . . . .

. . . . . and everything proceeds
Toward the light-filled hour when shops lower their eyelids
And noise traffic pushcart train I-feel sun resounds

Vertigo of midday framed in vertigos—
Sun in the heights . . . . . of my striated vision,
Of the frozen whirl of my parched memory,
Of the faint steady glimmer of my consciousness of living.

Noise traffic train pushcart cars I-feel sun street,
Hoops crates streetcar shop street shopwindows skirt eyes
Quickly tracks pushcarts crates street crossing street
Sidewalks shopkeepers "excuse me" street
Street strolling over me strolling down the street over me
All is mirrors shops on this side in the shops on that side
The speed of the cars upside down in the tilted shopwindow
    mirrors,
The ground in the air the sun underfoot street watering flowers in
    the basket street
My past street shaking truck street I don't remember street
Me headfirst in the center of my consciousness of myself
Street unable to pinpoint just one sensation street
Street behind and ahead under my feet
Street in x in y in z in my arms
Street through my monocle in circles of a small movie projector,
Kaleidoscope in distinct iridescent curves street.

Drunk from the street and from feeling seeing hearing everything at
  once,
My temples throbbing from coming here and going there at the
  same time . . . . .

◆

I FALL full length into all of life,
And my lust for living roars within me.
No pleasures in the world can equal
The stupendous joy of one who can't tell it
Except by rolling on the ground in the grass and the daisies,
Mingling with the dirt until his suit and hair are dirty . . .
There are no verses that can grant this.
Pluck a blade of grass, bite into it, and you will understand,
You'll completely understand what I incompletely express.
I crave to be a root
Pursuing my inner sensations like a sap . . .
I'd like to have all of the senses—including
My intellect, imagination and inhibition—
On my skin's surface so that I could roll over the rough ground
More deeply within, feeling more roughness and bumps.
I'd only be satisfied if my body were my soul,
For only then would all winds, all suns and all rains
Be felt by me in the way I'd like.
This being impossible, I despair, I rage,
I wish I could gnash at my suit
And have a lion's tough claws to rip at my flesh
Until the blood would flow, flow, flow, flow . . .
I suffer because all of this is absurd,
As if I could scare somebody
With my hostile feeling toward destiny, toward God,
Which arises when we confront the Ineffable
And suddenly perceive our weakness and smallness.

♦

I'M HELD by nothing, I hold on to nothing, I belong to nothing.
All sensations seize me, and none endure.
I'm more motley than a random crowd,
I'm more varied than the spontaneous universe,
All eras have belonged to me for a moment,
All souls for a moment have had their place in me.
Current of intuitions, river of imagining me as them,
Always wave after wave,
Always the sea—now growing strange,
Always drawing away from me, indefinitely.

O wharf where I would definitively embark for Truth,
O boat with a captain and sailors, symbolically visible,
O calm waters, as of an actual river, in the twilight
In which I dream I'm possible—
Where are you in real space? When are you in real time?
I want to depart and find myself,
I want to return knowing where from,
Like one who returns home and becomes sociable again,
Like one who is still loved in his old village,
Like one who brushes against his dead childhood in each stone of each
    wall,
And spread out before him he sees the eternal fields of yesterday,
And nostalgia like a mother's lullaby wafts
In the tragedy of belonging to the past.
O native, local, and neighboring lands to the south!
O line of the horizon, hazy to my eyes,
What a tumult of approaching winds I can sense in your distance!
And how you quiver in all that I see from here!

To hell with life!
To have a profession weighs like paid freight on the shoulders,
To have duties stupefies,
To have morals stifles,
And to react against duties and rebel against morals
Lives on the street—a fool.

◆

I WALK on, nothing touches me: I'm foreign.
The women who scurry to their front doors
See only that I've walked by.
I'm always around the corner from whoever tries to see me,
Invulnerable to metals and encrustations.

O afternoon, what memories!
Just yesterday I was a child leaning over the well,
Delighted to see my face in the water down below.
Today, a man, I see my face in the deep water of the world.
And if I laugh it's only because I was once a different I:
A child delighted to see his face in the bottom of the well.

I feel them all as flesh of my own flesh.
I touch my arm and there they are:
The dead, who never leave me!
And the dead are all the people, places, and days from my past.
Sometimes amid the noise of the factory machines
A nostalgia lightly grazes my arm,
I turn around, and there in the sunlit yard of my old house
Stands the child I was, happily ignorant of what I would become.

Ah, be motherly!
Ah, be mellifluous and speechless,
O night in which I forget myself
Remembering . . .

TO FEEL everything in every way,
To hold all opinions,
To be sincere contradicting oneself every minute,
To annoy oneself with absolute open-mindedness,
And to love things just like God.

I, who am more brother to a tree than to a worker,
I, who feel the poetic pain of waves beating the shore
More than the real pain of beaten children
(Ah, but this must be a lie, poor beaten children—
And why is it that my sensations take such sudden turns?),
I, finally, who am an unending dialogue,
An unintelligible voice, dead of night in the tower,
When the bells barely sway without a hand having touched them
And it's saddening to know there's life to be lived tomorrow.
I, finally, literally I,
And I metaphorically too,
I, the poet of sensations, sent from Chance
To the irreproachable laws of Life,
I, the cigarette smoker by meet profession,
The man who smokes opium and drinks absinthe but who, in the
    end,
Prefers thinking about smoking opium to smoking it
And likes looking at absinthe more than drinking it . . .
I, this superior degenerate with no archives in the soul
And without a value-declared personality,
I, the solemn researcher of futile things,
Who could go and live in Siberia just to get bored of it
And who thinks it's fine not to feel too attached to his homeland,
For I don't have roots, I'm not a tree, and so I have no roots . . .
I, who often feel as real as a metaphor,
As a sentence written by a sick man in the book of the girl he met
    on the terrace

Or as a game of chess on the deck of an ocean liner,
I, the nursemaid who pushes baby carriages in all public gardens,
I, the policeman standing behind her on the walkway, watching,
I, the baby in the carriage who waves at his lucid unconsciousness
	with a necklace of little bells,
I, the scenery behind all this, the civic peace
Filtered through the garden's trees,
I, who wait for them all at home,
I, whomever they meet in the street,
I, whatever they don't know about themselves,
I, what you're thinking about and that makes you smile,
I, the contradictory, the fictitious, the blather, the foam,
The poster just hung up, the French girl's hips, the priest's gaze,
The place where two roads meet and the chauffeurs are sleeping
	against their cars,
The scar of the mean-looking sergeant,
The sweaty ring on the shirt collar of the sick tutor going home,
The teacup from which the little boy who died always drank,
And the handle is chipped (and all this fits in a mother's heart and
	fills it) . . .
I, the French dictation of the girl fiddling with her garter,
I, the feet that touch beneath the bridge game under the ceiling
	lamp,
I, the hidden card, the scarf's warmth, the balcony window half
	open,
The service entrance where the maid talks with her desires for her
	cousin,
That rascal José who promised to come but didn't
And we had a trick to play on him . . .
I, all this, and besides this the rest of the world . . .
So many things, the doors that open, and the reason why they open,
And the things that the hands that open the doors have already
	done . . .

I, the inborn unhappiness of all expressions,
The impossibility of expressing all feelings,
With no tombstone in the cemetery for the brother of all this,
And what seems to mean nothing always means something . . .
Yes I, the naval engineer who's as superstitious as an old farmer's wife,
Who uses a monocle so as not to look like the real idea I have of myself,
And who sometimes spends three hours getting dressed and still doesn't find it at all natural,
But I do find it metaphysical, and it vexes me if someone knocks at the door,
Not so much for interrupting my necktie but for reminding me there's life.
Yes, finally, I the addressee of sealed letters,
The chest with the worn initials,
The intonation of voices we'll never hear again—
God keeps all this in Mystery, and occasionally we feel it
And life suddenly weighs more and produces a chill more intimate than skin.
Brigida my aunt's cousin,
The general they used to talk about—a general when they were little
And life was civil war on every street corner . . .
Vive le mélodrame où Margot a pleuré!
Dry leaves fall to the ground intermittently,
But the fact is that it's always autumn in autumn,
And winter inexorably follows it,
And life has only one path, which is life.

That old man, a nobody, but he knew the last of the Romantics,
That political pamphlet from the time of the constitutional revolutions,
And the grief that all this leaves, for some unknown reason,
And the only reason to cry about it is to feel.

All lovers have kissed one another in my soul,
All vagrants have slept on me for a moment,
All the scorned have leaned for an instant on my shoulder,
All the old and infirm have crossed the street on my arm,
And there was a secret told me by every murderer.

(That woman whose smile suggests the peace I don't have,
In whose lowering of the eyes there's a Dutch landscape
With the female heads wrapped in white linen
And the daily effort of a tidy and tranquil people . . .
That woman who is the ring left on top of the dresser,
And the ribbon that's caught when the drawer is shut,
A pink ribbon, I don't like the color but I like the ribbon being
    caught,
As I don't like life but like to feel it . . .

To sleep like a spurned dog on the open road,
Definitively for the rest of the universe,
Run over by every passing vehicle . . .)

I've gone to bed with every feeling,
I've been the pimp of every emotion,
All felt sensations have bought me drinks,
I've traded glances with every motive for every act,
I've held hands with every urge to depart,
Tremendous fever of time!
Anguished furnace of emotions!
Rage, foam, the vastness that doesn't fit in my handkerchief,
The dog in heat howling in the night,
The pond from the farm going in circles around my insomnia,
The woods as they were, on our late-afternoon walks, the rose,
The indifferent tuft of hair, the moss, the pines,
The rage of not containing all this, not retaining all this,
O abstract hunger for things, impotent libido for moments,
Intellectual orgy of feeling life!

To obtain everything by divine sufficiency—
Holiday eves, permissions, useful tips,
Life's beautiful things—
Talent, virtue, impunity,
The inclination to see others home,
The status of traveler,
The convenience of boarding early so as to get a seat,
And something's always missing, a glass, a breeze, a phrase,
And the more one invents and enjoys, the more life hurts.

To be able to laugh, laugh, laugh uproariously,
To laugh like an overturned glass,
Completely crazy just from feeling,
Completely disfigured from scraping against things,
My mouth cut up from biting on things,
My fingernails bloody from clawing at things,
And then give me whatever cell you like that I may look back on life.

IT WAS ON ONE
OF MY VOYAGES

It was on one of my voyages . . .
High sea, and the moon was out . . .
The evening hubbub aboard ship had quieted.
One by one, group by group, the passengers retired.
The band was just furniture that for some reason had remained in a
      corner.
Only in the smoking lounge did a chess game silently continue.
Life droned through the open door of the engine room.
Alone . . . A naked soul face-to-face with the universe!
(O town of my birth in faraway Portugal!
Why didn't I die as a child, when all I knew was you?)

AH, WHEN WE SET OUT TO SEA

Ah, when we set out to sea,
When we shove off from land and begin to lose sight of it,
When everything starts to fill with purely ocean air,
When the coast becomes a shadowy line,
An ever hazier line as the night falls (lights hover)—
Then what joyful freedom for those who feel!
Suddenly there's no reason for existing socially,
There are no more reasons for loving, hating, doing one's duty,
There are no more laws, no human-tasting griefs . . .
There are only the Abstract Departure and the waters' movement,
The movement of pulling away, the sound
Of the waves lulling the prow,
And a large skittish peace that softly enters the soul.

Ah, to have my whole life
Unsteadily fixed in one of these moments,
To have the whole meaning of my duration on earth
Summed up in a departure from the coast where I left everything—
Loves, vexations, sorrows, alliances, duties,
The restless anguish of regrets,
The weariness caused by so much futility,
The surfeit even of imagined things,
The nausea, the lights,
The eyelids that weigh heavy over my lost life . . .

I'll go far, far away! Far away, O boat without cause,
To the prehistoric irresponsibility of the eternal waters.
Far away, forever far away, O death.
When I know faraway where and faraway why, O life . . .

BUT IT'S NOT JUST THE CADAVER

But it's not just the cadaver,
It's not just that frightful person who's no one,
That abysmal variation on the usual body,
That stranger who appears in the absence of the man we knew,
That gaping chasm between our seeing and our understanding—
It's not just the cadaver that fills the soul with dread
And plants a silence in the bottom of the heart.
The everyday external things of the one who died
Also trouble the soul, and with a more poignant dread.
Even if they belonged to an enemy,
Who can look without nostalgia at the table where this enemy sat,
At the pen with which he wrote?
Who can see without sincere anguish
The coat in whose pockets the dead beggar kept his (now forever
    absent) hands,
The now horridly tidied-up toys of the dead child,
The rifle the hunter took with him when he vanished beyond every
    hill?
All of this suddenly weighs on my foreign comprehension,
And a death-sized nostalgia terrifies my soul.

I LEANED BACK IN THE DECK CHAIR AND CLOSED MY EYES

I leaned back in the deck chair and closed my eyes,
And my destiny loomed like a cliff in my soul.
My past life mingled with that of the future,
And at some point a noise reached my ears
From the smoking lounge: the chess game must have ended.

Ah, tossed
In the feeling of the waves,
Rocked
In the comforting idea that today is still not tomorrow,
That at least right now I have no responsibilities,
That I don't have a personality as such but just feel myself here,
On this chair, like a book left by the Swedish lady . . .

Ah, sunken
In a torpor of the imagination, no doubt a bit sleepy,
Peacefully restless,
Suddenly analogous to the child I once was,
When I played at the house in the country and didn't know basic
    algebra,
Let alone the algebras with x's and y's of the emotions . . .

Ah, all of me yearns
For that moment of no importance
In my life.
All of me yearns for that as for other analogous moments —
Those in which I had no importance at all,
Those in which I grasped, without the mind, the complete
    emptiness of existence,
And there was moonlight and sea and solitude, O Álvaro.

THE TOBACCO SHOP

I'm nothing.
I'll always be nothing.
I can't want to be something.
But I have in me all the dreams of the world.

Windows of my room,
The room of one of the world's millions nobody knows
(And if they knew me, what would they know?),
You open onto the mystery of a street continually crossed by people,
A street inaccessible to any and every thought,
Real, impossibly real, certain, unknowingly certain,
With the mystery of things beneath the stones and beings,
With death making the walls damp and the hair of men white,
With Destiny driving the wagon of everything down the road of
    nothing.

Today I'm defeated, as if I'd learned the truth.
Today I'm lucid, as if I were about to die
And had no greater kinship with things
Than to say farewell, this building and this side of the street
    becoming
A row of train cars, with the whistle for departure
Blowing in my head
And my nerves jolting and bones creaking as we pull out.

Today I'm bewildered, like a man who wondered and discovered
    and forgot.
Today I'm torn between the loyalty I owe
To the outward reality of the Tobacco Shop across the street
And to the inward reality of my feeling that everything's a dream.

I failed in everything.
Since I had no ambition, perhaps I failed in nothing.
I left the education I was given,
Climbing down from the window at the back of the house.
I went to the country with big plans.
But all I found was grass and trees,
And when there were people they were just like others.
I step back from the window and sit in a chair. What should I think about?

How should I know what I'll be, I who don't know what I am?
Be what I think? But I think of being so many things!
And there are so many who think of being the same thing that we can't all be it!
Genius? At this moment
A hundred thousand brains are dreaming they're geniuses like me,
And it may be that history won't remember even one,
All of their imagined conquests amounting to so much dung.
No, I don't believe in me.
Insane asylums are full of lunatics with certainties!
Am I, who have no certainties, more right or less right?
No, not even in me . . .
In how many garrets and non-garrets of the world
Are self-convinced geniuses at this moment dreaming?
How many lofty and noble and lucid aspirations
—Yes, truly lofty and noble and lucid
And perhaps even attainable—
Will never see the true light of day or find a sympathetic ear?
The world is for those born to conquer it,
Not for those who dream they can conquer it, even if they're right.
I've done more in dreams than Napoleon.

I've held more humanities against my hypothetical breast than
    Christ.
I've secretly invented philosophies such as Kant never wrote.
But I am, and perhaps will always be, the man in the garret,
Even though I don't live in one.
I'll always be *the one who wasn't born for that*;
I'll always be merely *the one who had qualities*;
I'll always be the one who waited for a door to open in a wall
    without doors
And sang the song of the Infinite in a chicken coop
And heard the voice of God in a covered well.
Believe in me? No, not in anything.
Let Nature pour over my seething head
Its sun, its rain, and the wind that finds my hair,
And let the rest come if it will or must, or let it not come.
Cardiac slaves of the stars,
We conquered the whole world before getting out of bed,
But we woke up and it's hazy,
We got up and it's alien,
We went outside and it's the entire earth
Plus the solar system and the Milky Way and the Indefinite.

(Eat your chocolates, little girl,
Eat your chocolates!
Believe me, there's no metaphysics on earth like chocolates,
And all religions put together teach no more than the candy shop.
Eat, dirty little girl, eat!
If only I could eat chocolates with the same truth as you!
But I think and, removing the silver paper that's tinfoil,
I throw it all on the ground, as I've thrown out life.)

But at least, from my bitterness over what I'll never be,
There remains the hasty writing of these verses,
A broken gateway to the Impossible.
But at least I confer on myself a contempt without tears,
Noble at least in the sweeping gesture by which I fling
The dirty laundry that's me—with no list—into the stream of
    things,
And I stay at home, shirtless.

(O my consoler, who doesn't exist and therefore consoles,
Be you a Greek goddess, conceived as a living statue,
Or a patrician woman of Rome, impossibly noble and dire,
Or a princess of the troubadours, all charm and grace,
Or an eighteenth-century marchioness, décolleté and aloof,
Or a famous courtesan from our parents' generation,
Or something modern, I can't quite imagine what—
Whatever all of this is, whatever you are, if you can inspire, then
    inspire me!
My heart is a poured-out bucket.
In the same way invokers of spirits invoke spirits, I invoke
My own self and find nothing.
I go to the window and see the street with absolute clarity.
I see the shops, I see the sidewalks, I see the passing cars,
I see the clothed living beings who pass each other.
I see the dogs that also exist,
And all of this weighs on me like a sentence of exile,
And all of this is foreign, like everything else.)

I've lived, studied, loved, and even believed,
And today there's not a beggar I don't envy just because he isn't me.
I look at the tatters and sores and falsehood of each one,
And I think: perhaps you never lived or studied or loved or believed
(For it's possible to do all of this without having done any of it);
Perhaps you've merely existed, as when a lizard has its tail cut off
And the tail keeps on twitching, without the lizard.

I made of myself what I was no good at making,
And what I could have made of myself I didn't.
I put on the wrong costume
And was immediately taken for someone I wasn't, and I said
    nothing and was lost.
When I went to take off the mask,
It was stuck to my face.
When I got it off and saw myself in the mirror,
I had already grown old.
I was drunk and no longer knew how to wear the costume that I
    hadn't taken off.
I threw out the mask and slept in the closet
Like a dog tolerated by the management
Because it's harmless,
And I'll write down this story to prove I'm sublime.

Musical essence of my useless verses,
If only I could look at you as something I had made
Instead of always looking at the Tobacco Shop across the street,
Trampling on my consciousness of existing,
Like a rug a drunkard stumbles on
Or a doormat stolen by gypsies and it's not worth a thing.

But the Tobacco Shop Owner has come to the door and is standing
    there.
I look at him with the discomfort of a half-twisted neck
Compounded by the discomfort of a half-grasping soul.
He will die and I will die.
He'll leave his signboard, I'll leave my poems.
His sign will also eventually die, and so will my poems.
Eventually the street where the sign was will die,
And so will the language in which my poems were written.
Then the whirling planet where all of this happened will die.

On other planets of other solar systems something like people
Will continue to make things like poems and to live under things
    like signs,
Always one thing facing the other,
Always one thing as useless as the other,
Always the impossible as stupid as reality,
Always the inner mystery as true as the mystery sleeping on the
    surface.
Always this thing or always that, or neither one thing nor the other.

But a man has entered the Tobacco Shop (to buy tobacco?),
And plausible reality suddenly hits me.
I half rise from my chair—energetic, convinced, human—
And will try to write these verses in which I say the opposite.

I light up a cigarette as I think about writing them,
And in that cigarette I savor a freedom from all thought.
My eyes follow the smoke as if it were my own trail
And I enjoy, for a sensitive and fitting moment,
A liberation from all speculation
And an awareness that metaphysics is a consequence of not feeling
    very well.
Then I lean back in the chair
And keep smoking.
As long as Destiny permits, I'll keep smoking.

(If I married my washwoman's daughter
Perhaps I would be happy.)
I get up from the chair. I go to the window.

The man has come out of the Tobacco Shop (putting change into his pocket?).
Ah, I know him: it's unmetaphysical Esteves.
(The Tobacco Shop Owner has come to the door.)
As if by divine instinct, Esteves turns around and sees me.
He waves hello, I shout back "Hello, Esteves!" and the universe
Falls back into place without ideals or hopes, and the Owner of the
    Tobacco Shop smiles.

15 JANUARY 1928

OPORTO-STYLE TRIPE

One day, in a restaurant, outside of space and time,
I was served up love as a dish of cold tripe.
I politely told the missionary of the kitchen
That I preferred it hot,
Because tripe (and it was Oporto-style) is never eaten cold.

They got impatient with me.
You can never be right, not even in a restaurant.
I didn't eat it, I ordered nothing else, I paid the bill,
And I decided to take a walk down the street.

Who knows what this might mean?
I don't know, and it happened to me . . .

(I know very well that in everyone's childhood there was a garden,
Private or public, or belonging to the neighbor.
I know very well that our playing was the owner of it
And that sadness belongs to today.)

I know this many times over,
But if I asked for love, why did they bring me
Oporto-style tripe that was cold?
It's not a dish that can be eaten cold,
But they served it to me cold.
I didn't make a fuss, but it was cold.
It can never be eaten cold, but it came cold.

A NOTE IN THE MARGIN

Put time to good use!
But what's time that I should put it to use?
Put time to good use!
Not a day without a few lines . . .
Honest and first-rate work
Like that of a Virgil or Milton . . .
But to be honest or first-rate is so hard!
To be Milton or Virgil is so unlikely!

Put time to good use!
Taking from my soul the right little bits—no more and no less—
That will fit together like a jigsaw puzzle
To make a definite picture in history . . .
(And it's just as definite on the underside no one sees.)
Making my sensations into a house of cards—a miniature,
    after-dinner China . . .
Arranging my thoughts like dominoes, like against like . . .
Treating my will like a tricky billiard shot . . .
Images of games or of solitaires or of pastimes—
Images of life, images of lives, Image of Life . . .

Verbosity.
Yes, verbosity.
Put time to good use!
Not letting a minute go by without examining my conscience . . .
Not allowing a single indefinite or factitious act . . .
Not permitting any move out of line with my goals . . .
Good manners of the soul . . .
The elegance of persevering . . .

Put time to good use!
My heart is weary like a veritable beggar.
My brain's ready to go, like a bundle in a corner.
My song (verbosity!) is what it is and is sad.
Put time to good use!
Five minutes have gone by since I started writing.
Have I put them to good use or not?
If I don't know, then how will I know about other minutes?

(Lady who so often rode in the same compartment with me
On the suburban train,
Did you ever become interested in me?
Did I put time to good use by looking at you?
What was the rhythm of our silence in the moving train?
What was the understanding that we never came to?
What life was there in this? What was this to life?)

Put time to good use!
Ah, let me put nothing to use!
Neither time nor being, nor memories of time or being!
Let me be a tree leaf tickled by breezes,
The dust of a road, involuntary and alone,
The incidental runlet of the rains that are letting up,
The tracks left by wheels until new wheels come along,
The little boy's top, which is coming to a halt,
And it sways, with the same movement as the earth's,
And it quivers, with the same movement as the soul's,
And it falls, as the gods fall, onto Destiny's floor.

11 APRIL 1928

DEFERRAL

The day after tomorrow, not until the day after tomorrow . . .
I'll spend tomorrow thinking about the day after tomorrow,
And then maybe, we'll see; but not today . . .
Today is out of the question. Today I can't.
The confused persistence of my objective subjectivity,
The fatigue of my real, intermittently appearing life,
The anticipated and infinite weariness,
A multi-world weariness just to catch a streetcar,
This species of soul . . .
                    Not until the day after tomorrow . . .
Today I want to get ready,
I want to get ready to think tomorrow about the day after . . .
That will be the decisive one.
I've already planned it out; but no, today I'm not planning
    anything.
Tomorrow is the day for plans.
Tomorrow I'll sit at my desk to conquer the world,
But I'll only conquer the world the day after tomorrow . . .
I feel like crying,
I suddenly feel, deep within, like crying.
No, don't try to find out any more, it's a secret, I'm not telling.
Not until the day after tomorrow . . .

When I was a child I was amused by the Sunday circus every week.
Today I'm only amused by the Sunday circus of every week of my
    childhood.
The day after tomorrow I'll be different,
My life will triumph,
All of my real qualities of intelligence, erudition and practicality
Will be convened by an official announcement,
But by an announcement to be made tomorrow . . .
Today I want to sleep; I'll draft announcements tomorrow . . .
For today, what show is playing that would reenact my childhood?
I'll be sure to buy tickets tomorrow,
Since the day after tomorrow is when I want to go,

Not before. . .
The day after tomorrow I'll have the public image which tomorrow
    I'll rehearse.
The day after tomorrow I'll finally be what today I could never be.
The day after tomorrow, not before . . .

I feel tired the way a stray dog feels cold.
I feel very tired.
Tomorrow I'll explain it to you, or the day after tomorrow . . .
Yes, perhaps not until the day after tomorrow . . .

The future . . .
Yes, the future . . .

14 APRIL 1928

SOMETIMES I MEDITATE

Sometimes I meditate.
Sometimes I meditate deeply, more deeply, still more deeply,
And the whole mystery of things seems like an oil on the surface,
And the whole universe is a sea of faces with eyes bugging out at me.
Each thing—a corner lamppost, a stone, a tree—
Is an eye that stares at me from an inscrutable abyss,
And all the gods and ideas of the gods march through my heart.
Ah, that things exist!
Ah, that beings exist!
Ah, that there exists a way for beings to exist,
For existence to exist,
For the existence of "to exist" to exist,
For anything to exist . . .
Ah, that there can be the abstract phenomenon of being,
The existence of consciousness and reality,
Whatever these may be—
How express the horror that all of this causes me?
How tell what it's like to feel this?

29 APRIL 1928

AH, THE FRESHNESS IN THE FACE OF LEAVING A TASK UNDONE

Ah, the freshness in the face of leaving a task undone!
To be remiss is to be positively out in the country!
What a refuge it is to be completely unreliable!
I can breathe easier now that the appointments are behind me.
I missed them all, through deliberate negligence,
Having waited for the urge to go, which I knew wouldn't come.
I'm free and against organized, clothed society.
I'm naked and plunge into the water of my imagination.
It's too late to be at either of the two meetings where I should have
    been at the same time,
Deliberately at the same time . . .
No matter, I'll stay here dreaming verses and smiling in italics.
This spectator aspect of life is so amusing!
I can't even light the next cigarette . . . If it's an action,
It can wait for me, along with the others, in the nonmeeting called
    life.

                                                    17 JUNE 1929

AT LONG LAST ... NO DOUBT ABOUT IT

At long last ... no doubt about it ...
Here it is!
Madness has definitively entered my head.

My heart exploded like a two-bit bomb,
And the shock went up my spine to my head ...

Thank God that I'm crazy!
That everything I did has come back to me as garbage
And like spit in the wind has splattered all over my face!
That everything I was has gotten tangled around my feet,
Like packing cloth to pack nothing at all!
That everything I thought tickles my throat
And makes me want to vomit, although I ate nothing!
Thank God, since this, as for drunkenness,
Is a solution.

How about that, I found a solution, via my stomach!
I discovered a truth, I perceived it with my intestines!

Transcendental poetry? I've done that too!
Great lyrical raptures have already paid me a visit!
The organization of poems by general topics divided into subtopics?
That's no novelty either.
I feel like vomiting, and like vomiting my own self...
I feel a nausea such that, if I could eat the universe to throw it up
    into the sink, I'd eat it.
With a struggle, but it would be for a good purpose.
At least it would be for a purpose.
Such as I am I have no purpose and no life ...

POP

Today, feeling bored and uninspired,
Today, apathetic, short on desire,
I'll write my epitaph: "Here lies Álvaro . . ."
(The Greek Anthology has more apropos.)
What's the reason for these several rhymes?
No reason. A friend I see from time to time
Wanted to know what I'm doing these days,
And I write these verses to have something to say.
I rarely rhyme, and rhymes rarely succeed,
But sometimes to rhyme is an imperative need.
My heart goes pop like a paper sack
Filled with air and given a good smack,
And the startled stranger turns in confusion,
And I end this poem without a conclusion.

2 DECEMBER 1929

I WALK IN THE NIGHT OF THE SUBURBAN STREET

I walk in the night of the suburban street,
Returning from the conference of experts like myself.
I return alone, now a poet, without expertise or engineering,
Human unto the sound of my solitary shoes in the beginning of
    night.
In the distance the last shutters are pulled down on the last shop.
Ah, the sound of suppertime in happy homes!
I walk, and my ears peer into the homes.
My inherent exile comes alive in the darkness
Of the street which is my home, my being, and my blood.
To be a child from a well-off family,
With a nursemaid, a soft bed, and a child's slumber!
O my unprivileged heart!
My feeling of exclusion!
My bitter grief for being I!

Who made firewood out of my childhood crib?
Who made rags from the sheets I slept in as a boy?
Who tossed the lace from the shirt I wore when baptized
Into the house dust and fruit skins
Of the world's garbage cans?
Who sold me to Fate?
Who exchanged me for what I am?

I've just spoken with precision in definite circumstances.
I made concrete points, like an adding machine.
I was accurate like a scale.
I told what I knew.

Now, heading to where the streetcar turns around to go back to the city,
I walk as a metaphysical outcast by the light of streetlamps spaced far apart,
And in the shadow between two lamps I feel like not going on,
But I'll take the streetcar.
The bell at the invisible end of the cord will ring two times
When pulled by the stubby fingers of the unshaven conductor.
I'll take the streetcar.
In spite of everything—alas!—I've always taken the streetcar.
Always, always, always . . .
I've always gone back to the city.
I've always gone back, after speculations and detours.
I've always gone back, hungry for supper.
But I've never had the supper I hear behind the venetian blinds
Of happy homes on the outskirts, where people like me head back to the streetcar.
The conjugal homes of normal life!
I pay for the ticket through the slits,
And the conductor walks by me as if I were the Critique of Pure Reason . . .
I've paid my ticket. I've done my duty. I'm like everyone else.
And these are all things not even suicide can cure.

6 JANUARY 1930

YES, I KNOW IT'S ALL QUITE NATURAL

Yes, I know it's all quite natural,
But I still have a heart.
Shit and good night!
(Burst into smithereens, O heart!)
(Shit to all of humanity!)

In the house of the woman whose child was run over
All is laughter and play.
And there's a great racket of horns to commemorate.

They received compensation:
Baby equal to x.
Now they're enjoying the x,
Eating and drinking the dead baby.
Bravo! They're people!
Bravo! They're humanity!
Bravo: they're all the fathers and mothers
Who have children that can be run over!
Money can make us forget everything.
Baby equal to x.

Thus an entire house was wallpapered.
Thus the last installment on the furniture was paid.
Poor baby.
But if it hadn't been run over, how pay the bills?
Yes, it was loved.
Yes, it was cherished.
But it died.
Too bad, it died!
What a pity, it died!
But it did bring in some cash
With which to pay the bills.
Indeed it was tragic,
But the bills have been paid.

Indeed, that poor tiny body
Was crushed to a pulp,
But now, at least, no money is owed the grocer.
It's too bad, yes, but there's always a silver lining.

The baby died, but a thousand dollars exist.
Yes, a thousand dollars.
A lot can be done (poor baby) with a thousand dollars.
A lot of debts paid (precious little baby)
With a thousand dollars.
A lot put in order
(Beautiful baby that died) with a thousand dollars.
Of course it's sad
(A thousand dollars)
To have our own child run over
(A thousand dollars)
But the thought of a remodeled house
(A thousand dollars)
And of a home all fixed up
(A thousand dollars)
Can make one forget quite a lot (how we've wept!).
A thousand dollars!
As if it came straight from God
(This thousand dollars).
Poor mutilated baby!
A thousand dollars.

STREETCAR STOP

Dish me up some forgetfulness!
I want to eat the renunciation of life!
I want to kick the habit of shouting on the inside.
Enough already! I don't know what of, but enough!
Live tomorrow, you say? And what do we do with today?
Live tomorrow because today was postponed?
Did I buy a ticket for this show?
I'd roar with laughter if I could laugh.
And here's the streetcar, the one I've been waiting for.
I wish it were another one. To have to climb aboard already!
No one's forcing me, but why let it go by?
Unless I were to let all of them go by, and my own self, and life . . .
How nauseating a conscious soul is to the physical stomach!
How peacefully I'd sleep if I could be anyone else!
Now I understand why children want to be streetcar operators.
No, I don't understand anything.
Blue and gold day, human happiness, clear eyes of life . . .

                                                28 MAY 1930

BIRTHDAY

Back when they used to celebrate my birthday
I was happy and no one was dead.
In the old house even my birthday was a centuries-old tradition,
And everyone's joy, mine included, was as sure as any religion.

Back when they used to celebrate my birthday
I enjoyed the good health of understanding nothing,
Of being intelligent in my family's eyes,
And of not having the hopes that others had for me.
When I began to have hopes, I no longer knew how to hope.
When I began to look at life, it had lost all meaning for me.

Yes, that person I knew as me,
That person with a heart and family,
That person of quasi-rural evenings spent all together,
That person who was a boy they loved,
That person—my God!—whom only today I realize I was . . .
How faraway! . . .
(Not even an echo . . .)
When they used to celebrate my birthday!

The person I am today is like the damp in the hall at the back of the house
That makes the walls mildew . . .
What I am today (and the house of those who loved me trembles through my tears)—
What I am today is their having sold the house,
It's all of them having died,
It's I having survived myself like a spent match.

Back when they used to celebrate my birthday . . .
Ah, how I love, like a person, those days!
How my soul physically longs to return there,
Via a metaphysical and carnal journey,
In a duality of me to me . . .
To eat the past like the bread of hunger, with no time for butter
    between the teeth!

I see it all again, so vivid it blinds me to what's here . . .
The table with extra place settings, fancier china, more glasses,
The sideboard full of sweets and fruits, and other things in the
    shadow of the lower shelf.
Elderly aunts, different cousins, and all for my sake,
Back when they used to celebrate my birthday.

Stop it, heart!
Don't think! Leave thinking to the head!
O my God, my God, my God!
I no longer have birthdays.
I endure.
My days add up.
I'll be old when I'm old.
That's all.
If only I'd filched the goddamn past and brought it away in my
    pocket!

When they used to celebrate my birthday!

13 JUNE 1930

NO! ALL I WANT IS FREEDOM

No! All I want is freedom!
Love, glory, and wealth are prisons.
Lovely rooms? Nice furniture? Plush rugs?
Just let me out so I can be with myself.
I want to breathe the air in private.
My heart doesn't throb collectively,
And I'm unable to feel in jointly held society.
I'm only I, born only as I am, full of nothing but me.
Where do I want to sleep? In the backyard.
Without any walls, just the great conversation,
I and the universe.
And what peace, what relief to fall asleep seeing not the ghost of my wardrobe
But the black and cool splendor of all the stars in concert,
The great and infinite abyss above
Placing its breezes and solaces on the flesh-covered skull that's my face,
Where only the eyes — another sky — reveal the world of subjective being.

I told you I don't want it! Just give me freedom!
I want to be equal to myself.
Don't castrate me with ideals!
Don't put me into your straitjackets of manners!
Don't make me respectable or intelligible!
Don't make me into a living corpse!

I want to be able to throw this ball up to the moon
And hear it fall into the yard next door!
I want to lie down in the grass, thinking, Tomorrow I'll go get it . . .
Tomorrow I'll go get it from the yard next door . . .
Tomorrow I'll go get it from the yard next door . . .
Tomorrow I'll go get it from the yard
Get it from the yard
From the yard
Next door . . .

11 AUGUST 1930

I'D LIKE TO BE ABLE TO LIKE LIKING

I'd like to be able to like liking.
Just a second . . . Grab me a cigarette
From that pack lying on top of the nightstand.
Go on . . . You were saying
That in the development of metaphysics
From Kant to Hegel
Something was lost.
I agree entirely.
I really was listening.
Nondum amabam et amare amabam—St. Augustine.
What odd associations of ideas we sometimes have!
I'm tired of thinking about feeling anything else.
Thanks. Excuse me while I light up. Go on. Hegel . . .

REALITY

Yes, I often came by here twenty years ago.
Nothing has changed, as far as I can tell,
In this part of town.

Twenty years ago!
The person I was back then! Yes, I was different . . .
Twenty years ago, and the houses have no idea . . .

Twenty useless years (or maybe they weren't:
How do I know what's useful or useless?) . . .
Twenty lost years (but what would it mean to win them?) . . .

I try to reconstruct in my mind
Who and what I was when I used to come by here
Twenty years ago . . .
I don't remember. I can't remember.
The person who came by here back then
Might remember, if he still existed.
There are lots of characters from novels I know better
Than this I who came by here twenty years ago!

Yes, the mystery of time.
Yes, our knowing nothing about anything,
Yes, all of us born on a ship already at sea,
Yes, yes, all of this, or another way of saying it.

From that third-story window, still identical to what it was,
A girl who was older than I used to lean out, dressed—as I usually
    remember her—in blue.
What might she be now?
We can imagine anything about things we know nothing of.
I'm at a physical and moral standstill: I'd rather not imagine . . .

One day I walked up this road thinking happily of the future,
For God allows what doesn't exist to shine brightly.
Today, walking down this road, I don't even think happily of the
	past.
At best, I don't think at all.
I have the impression that the two figures crossed paths on this
	road, not then and not now,
But right here, their crossing undisturbed by time.
They looked indifferently at each other.
And the old I walked up the road imagining a future sunflower.
And the I of today walked down the road imagining nothing.

Perhaps this really happened . . .
Truly happened . . .
Yes, physically happened . . .

Yes, perhaps . . .

15 DECEMBER 1932

I'M BEGINNING TO KNOW MYSELF. I DON'T EXIST

I'm beginning to know myself. I don't exist.
I'm the gap between what I'd like to be and what others have made
　　me,
Or half of this gap, since there's also life . . .
That's me. Period.
Turn off the light, shut the door, and get rid of the slipper noise in the
　　hallway.
Leave me alone in my room with the vast peace of myself.
It's a shoddy universe.

PACK YOUR BAGS
FOR NOWHERE AT ALL

Pack your bags for Nowhere at All!
Set sail for the ubiquitous negation of everything
With a panoply of flags on make-believe ships—
Those miniature, multicolored ships from childhood!
Pack your bags for the Grand Departure!
And don't forget, along with your brushes and clippers,
The polychrome distance of what can't be had.
Pack your bags once and for all!
Who are you here, where you socially and uselessly exist—
And the more usefully the more uselessly,
The more truly the more falsely?
Who are you here, who are you here, who are you here?
Set sail, even without bags, for your own diverse self!
What does the inhabited world have to do with you?

          2 MAY 1933

I GOT OFF THE TRAIN

I got off the train
And said goodbye to the man I'd met.
We'd been together for eighteen hours
And had a pleasant conversation,
Fellowship in the journey,
And I was sorry to get off, sorry to leave
This chance friend whose name I never learned.
I felt my eyes water with tears . . .
Every farewell is a death.
Yes, every farewell is a death.
In the train that we call life
We are all chance events in one another's lives,
And we all feel sorry when it's time to get off.

All that is human moves me, because I'm a man.
All that is human moves me, not because I have an affinity
With human ideas or human doctrines
But because of my infinite fellowship with humanity itself.

The maid who hated to go,
Crying with nostalgia
For the house where she'd been mistreated . . .

All of this, inside my heart, is death and the world's sadness.
All of this lives, because it dies, inside my heart.

And my heart is a little larger than the entire universe.

4 JULY 1934

THIS OLD ANGUISH

This old anguish,
Which I've carried around for centuries,
Overflowed from its vessel
In tears, in wild imaginings,
In nightmarish dreams without terror,
In sudden huge emotions that make no sense.

It overflowed.
I'm at a loss to know how to live life
With this malaise that's crumpling my soul.
If at least I could be positively crazy!
But no: always this in-betweenness,
This almost,
This it might be that . . .
This.

An inmate in an insane asylum is at least someone.
I'm an inmate in an asylum without an asylum.
I'm consciously crazy,
I'm a lucid lunatic,
I'm alien to everything and equal to all:
I'm sleeping while awake with dreams that are madness
Because they're not dreams.
I'm . . .

Poor old house of my lost childhood!
Could you ever have imagined I'd so desert myself?
What happened to your boy? He went nuts.
What happened to the one who slept soundly under your provincial
    rooftop?
He went nuts.
What happened to who I was? He went nuts. Today he's who I am.

If at least I had some kind of religion.
The religion, for example, of that idol from Africa
We had at home (the one I've mentioned).
It was unsightly, it was grotesque,
But it contained the divinity of everything that's believed in.
If I could believe in some idol or other —
Jupiter, Jehovah, Humanity . . .
Any one would do,
For isn't everything merely what we think it is?

Shatter, heart of painted glass!

                                              16 JUNE 1934

IMPASSIVELY

Impassively,
Indifferently,
Distractedly,
I look at the crochet you make
With two hands.

I look at it from the top of a nonexistent hill,
Stitch after stitch forming a cloth . . .

Why are your hands and soul entertained
By this riddled thing
Through which a burnt match can be pushed?
But then again,
Why do I criticize you?

No reason.
I also have my crochet.
It dates from when I began to think.
Stitch on stitch forming a whole without a whole . . .
A cloth, and I don't know if it's for a garment or for nothing.
A soul, and I don't know if it's for feeling or living.
I watch you so intently
I stop seeing you.

Crochet, souls, philosophy . . .
All the religions of the world . . .
All that entertains us in the leisure hours of our existence . . .
A hooked needle, a loop, silence . . .

9 AUGUST 1934

ON THE EVE
OF NEVER DEPARTING

On the eve of never departing
At least there are no suitcases to pack
Or lists to draw up with things to do
(Some of which are always forgotten)
The following day, before leaving.

Nothing needs to be done
On the eve of never departing.

How relaxing not to have anything at all
To be relaxed about!
What peace of mind when there's no more reason to shrug,
Tedium (poor tedium!) having been left behind
To arrive deliberately at nothing!
What happiness it is not to need to be happy,
Like an opportunity turned inside out.

For some months now I've been living
The vegetative life of thought,
Day after day *sine linea* . . .

Yes, how relaxing . . .
Peace of mind . . .
What a relief after so many journeys—physical and mental—
To be able to look at closed suitcases as at nothing!
Doze off, soul, doze off!
Doze while you can!
Doze!

You don't have much time! Doze,
For it's the eve of never departing!

27 SEPTEMBER 1934

SYMBOLS? I'M SICK OF SYMBOLS

Symbols? I'm sick of symbols . . .
Some people tell me that everything is symbols.
They're telling me nothing.

What symbols? Dreams . . .
Let the sun be a symbol, fine . . .
Let the moon be a symbol, fine . . .
Let the earth be a symbol, fine . . .
But who notices the sun except when the rain stops
And it breaks through the clouds and points behind its back
To the blue of the sky?
And who notices the moon except to admire
Not it but the beautiful light it radiates?
And who notices the very earth we tread?
We say earth and think of fields, trees and hills,
Unwittingly diminishing it,
For the sea is also earth.

Okay, let all of this be symbols.
But what's the symbol—not the sun, not the moon, not the earth—
In this premature sunset amid the fading blue
With the sun caught in expiring tatters of clouds
And the moon already mystically present at the other end of the sky
As the last remnant of daylight
Gilds the head of the seamstress who hesitates at the corner
Where she used to linger (she lives nearby) with the boyfriend who
    left her?
Symbols? I don't want symbols.
All I want—poor frail and forlorn creature!—
Is for the boyfriend to go back to the seamstress.

18 DECEMBER 1934

THE ANCIENTS INVOKED THE MUSES

The ancients invoked the Muses.
We invoke ourselves.
I don't know if the Muses appeared
—No doubt it depended on what was invoked and how—
But I know that we don't appear.

How often I've leaned over
The well that's me
And bleated "Hey!" to hear an echo,
And I've heard no more than I've seen—
The faint dark glimmer of the water
There in the useless depths.
No echo for me . . .
Just the hint of a face, which must be mine since it can't be anyone else's.
Just an almost invisible
Luminously smudged image
There in the depths . . .
In the silence and deceptive light of the depths . . .

What a Muse!

3 JANUARY 1935

I DON'T KNOW IF THE STARS RULE THE WORLD

I don't know if the stars rule the world
Or if tarot or playing cards
Can reveal anything.
I don't know if the rolling of dice
Can lead to any conclusion.
But I also don't know
If anything is attained
By living the way most people do.

Yes, I don't know
If I should believe in this daily rising sun
Whose authenticity no one can guarantee me,
Or if it would be better (because better or more convenient)
To believe in some other sun,
One that shines even at night,
Some profound incandescence of things,
Surpassing my understanding.

For now . . .
(Let's take it slow)
For now
I have an absolutely secure grip on the stair rail,
I secure it with my hand—
This rail that doesn't belong to me
And that I lean on as I ascend . . .
Yes . . . I ascend . . .
I ascend to this:
I don't know if the stars rule the world.

            5 JANUARY 1935

I'VE BEEN THINKING ABOUT NOTHING AT ALL

I've been thinking about nothing at all,
And this central thing, which isn't anything,
Is pleasant to me like the evening air,
Fresh in contrast to the hot summer days.

I've been thinking about nothing at all, and how lucky!

To think about nothing
Is to fully possess the soul.
To think about nothing
Is to intimately live
Life's ebb and flow . . .

I've been thinking about nothing at all.
Only . . . it's as if I'd wrenched a muscle,
I feel a pain in my back, or on one side of it,
There's a bad taste in the mouth of my soul,
Because, after all,
I've been thinking about nothing,
But really, nothing,
Nothing . . .

6 JULY 1935

ALL LOVE LETTERS ARE

All love letters are
Ridiculous.
They wouldn't be love letters if they weren't
Ridiculous.

In my time I also wrote love letters
Equally, inevitably
Ridiculous.

Love letters, if there's love,
Must be
Ridiculous.

But in fact
Only those who've never written
Love letters
Are
Ridiculous.

If only I could go back
To when I wrote love letters
Without thinking how
Ridiculous.

The truth is that today
My memories
Of those love letters
Are what is
Ridiculous.

(All more-than-three-syllable words,
Along with uncountable feelings,
Are naturally
Ridiculous.)

                        21 OCTOBER 1935

FERNANDO PESSOA-HIMSELF
THE MASK BEHIND THE MAN

Fernando Pessoa the orthonym was probably born in Lisbon, in 1888, like his creator and namesake, Fernando Pessoa, who provided virtually no biographical information about his most intellectual and analytical poetic persona. From his verses we can glean that Pessoa the poet was a cigarette smoker, often sat by a window, enjoyed dreaming and daydreaming, and suffered from an acute identity problem that could cause him to lose track of whether he was the subject or the object, as when he wrote:

> *I contemplate the silent pond*
> *Whose water is stirred by a breeze.*
> *Am I thinking about everything,*
> *Or has everything forgotten me?*

Although we're told nothing very specific about his childhood, he sometimes felt nostalgia for it. At other times he felt "nostalgia for nothing at all,/ A desire for something vague." The problem for this indecisive, doubt-plagued poet was not so much that he lacked an identity but, rather, that he had too many of them. "I don't know how many souls I have," he wrote in August of 1930, because "I've changed at every moment." In another poem written on the same day, he admits that his problem is largely brought on by himself, saying, "I break my soul into pieces/ And into various persons."

This penchant for splitting his personality may have something to do — either as cause or result — with his poetic bilingualism, Pessoa having written verses in English as well as Portuguese throughout his

adult life, though the *Times Literary Supplement,* in its review of his
35 *Sonnets* (1918), commented that "Mr. Pessoa's command of English
is less remarkable than his knowledge of Elizabethan English." However antiquated his written English may have been, it was adequate to
express the poet's very immediate existential difficulty. In the eighth
sonnet he asks:

> *How many masks wear we, and undermasks,*
> *Upon our countenance of soul, and when,*
> *If for self-sport the soul itself unmasks,*
> *Knows it the last mask off and the face plain?*

Remaining on the Portuguese side of the linguistic divide, we
find that Pessoa is subdivided thematically. For besides the vaguely
nostalgic Pessoa whose verses wonder who and why he is, there is a
Pessoa who writes esoteric poems with titles such as "Beyond God,"
"The Mummy," and "Initiation." And there's the Pessoa who wrote
the national/historical poems of *Message,* the only book of Portuguese
poetry he published. And there's even a Pessoa, rarely mentioned, who
wrote several hundred traditional folk quatrains, like this one (translated into English):

> *In the dance where everyone dances*
> *There are some who don't dance, just stare.*
> *Better not to go to the dance*
> *Than to be there without being there.*
>
> 4 August 1934

Could it be that, just as there were various heteronyms, so too there
were various orthonyms—Fernando Pessoa the existentialist, Fernando
Pessoa the patriot, Fernando Pessoa the occultist, Fernando Pessoa
the rhymester—all different from one another but all having the same
name as their creator, since by definition an orthonym cannot have a
different name? (The definition belongs to Pessoa, who invented the
word.)

Fernando Pessoa-Himself

Busy as he was, producing diverse selves and diverse poetries, Pessoa hardly had time for "real" experience, but there was one crucial event in his life early on, in March of 1914, when he met Alberto Caeiro and heard him read poems from *The Keeper of Sheep*. Álvaro de Campos tells us that Pessoa, overwhelmed, went home and immediately wrote the six "intersectionist" poems that make up *Oblique Rain*. Although these poems show no evidence of Caeiro's influence, it is true that Pessoa had never written anything quite like them, nor would he ever again. Instead, he went back to his inner reflections, too immersed in "self-sport" to appreciate Nature and the world as it is on the surface, à la Caeiro. On occasion he remembered the simple yet not so simple way of the pastoral poet, as when in a poem many years later he wrote that "The sun shining over the field/ Perhaps could be the remedy," but this remained, for Pessoa-himself, a hypothetical remedy.

There's something else we find in the poetry attributed to Pessoa's orthonym: music. His creator's father, perhaps not by coincidence, was an avid devotee of this art form, working as the music critic for a Lisbon newspaper. The poems signed with the name of Fernando Pessoa—mostly short, with rhyming and metered stanzas—have a singularly musical quality, and he wanted them to be published under the general title "Songbook," but that does not mean he loved music for music's sake. In fact, he seems to have had an ulterior motive, music acting as a more effective remedy for his condition than the sun. Any kind of music would do, he wrote in the poem called "Some Music," as long as it enabled him to forget his uncertainty and "not to feel the heart."

With these scattered biographical details we can form only a fuzzy picture of this restless poet who thought too much. We can imagine him in his room next to a window, looking anxiously at the street down below without knowing what he's looking for, and when the girl from the upstairs apartment begins practicing the piano, as she does every day at that particular hour, he leans back in his chair and puffs on his cigarette, momentarily relieved. Or we can envision him in a Lisbon café or bar, where sometimes there's fado music or a blind man who plays the accordion while a little boy holds out a can, and when the fado music ends or the blind man and his boy go away, Pessoa starts to fidget, orders another drink, smokes another cigarette, pulls some paper out of his pocket, jots down verses for one of the poems that will go into his *Songbook*, recites in an undertone the rhymes he's just written, tentatively smiles, and knows another brief respite.

from
SONGBOOK

OCEAN (MORNING)

Gleaming with sunlight, soft
And enormous, the wave advances.
It rocks this way and that,
And falls as if relaxing,

So long and slow it seems
Like the sleeping blue-green breast
Of a child of the Titans
Breathing in the morning breeze.

The movement of an ocean wave
Resembles a living thing:
A snake that slithers forward
With placid turns and twists.

United, vast, and unending
In the healthy sun's tranquillity,
The ocean steadily breathes,
Drunk with the blue luminosity.

But my own sensation is devoid
Of pleasure as well as of pain:
Drunk with being estranged from me,
It tosses on the ocean's lucid wave.

                    16 NOVEMBER 1909

GOD

At times I'm the god I carry in myself,
And then I'm the god, the believer and the prayer
And the ivory image
In which this god is forgotten.

At times I'm no more than an atheist
Of this god I am when exalted.
I see in myself an entire sky,
And it's only a vast and hollow sky.

3 JUNE 1913

OBLIQUE RAIN

VI

The maestro waves his baton,
And the sad, languid music begins . . .

It reminds me of my childhood, of a day
I spent playing in my backyard, throwing a ball
Against the wall . . . On one side of the ball
Sailed a green dog, on the other side
A yellow jockey was riding a blue horse . . .

The music continues, and on the white wall of my childhood
That's suddenly between me and the maestro
The ball bounces back and forth, now a green dog,
Now a blue horse with a yellow jockey . . .

My backyard takes up the whole theater, my childhood
Is everywhere, and the ball starts to play music,
A sad hazy music that runs around my backyard
Dressed as a green dog that turns into a yellow jockey . . .
(So quickly spins the ball between me and the musicians . . .)

I throw it at my childhood, and it
Passes through the whole theater that's at my feet
Playing with a yellow jockey and a green dog
And a blue horse that pops out over the wall
Of my backyard . . . And the music throws balls
At my childhood . . . And the wall is made of baton
Movements and wildly whirling green dogs,
Blue horses and yellow jockeys . . .

The whole theater is a white wall of music
Where a green dog runs after my nostalgia
For my childhood, a blue horse with a yellow jockey . . .

And from one side to the other, from right to left,
From the trees where orchestras play music in the upper branches
To the rows of balls in the shop where I bought my ball
And the shopkeeper smiles among the memories of my childhood . . .

And the music stops like a wall that collapses,
The ball rolls over the cliff of my interrupted dreams,
And on top of a blue horse the maestro, a yellow jockey turning
    black,
Gives thanks while laying down his baton on a fleeing wall,
And he takes a bow, smiling, with a white ball on top of his head,
A white ball that rolls down his back out of sight . . .

                                                   8 MARCH 1914

THE WIND IS BLOWING TOO HARD

The wind is blowing too hard
For me to be able to rest.
I sense there's something in me
That's coming to an end.

Perhaps this thing in my soul
That thinks life is real . . .
Perhaps this thing that's calm
And makes my soul feel . . .

A hard wind is blowing.
I'm afraid of thinking.
If I let my mind go,
I'll heighten my mystery.

Wind that passes and forgets,
Dust that rises and falls . . .
Thank God I cannot know
What inside me is going on!

5 NOVEMBER 1914

THE MUMMY

I

I walked through miles of shadow
Within me, via the mind.
My dependably fickle idleness
Flourished in reverse,
And the lamps went out
In the teetering alcove.

In a flash the scene transforms
Into a soft, smooth desert
Seen not by my eyes
But by my fingers traveling
Over the alcove's velvets.
There's an oasis in the Indefinite
And, like a hint of light
Through an absence of cracks,
A caravan passes.

I suddenly forget
What space is like, and time
Instead of horizontal
Is vertical.

      The alcove
Descends I don't know where
Until I lose myself.
From my sensations
A thin smoke rises.
I no longer include me
In myself. There's no
In here and no out there.

And now the desert
Is upside down.

The notion of me moving
Has forgotten my name.

My body weighs on my soul.
I feel like a heavy drape
Hanging in the room
Where a dead person lies.

Something fell
And jingled in the infinite.

II

Cleopatra lies dead in the shade.
It rains.

The ship was dressed with the wrong flags.
It continues to rain.

Why do you gaze at the distant city?
Your soul is the distant city.
It rains a chill rain.

And as for the mother who rocks a dead child in her arms—
We all rock a dead child in our arms.
It rains, it rains.

I see the sad smile left on your weary lips
In the way your fingers won't let go of your rings.
Why does it rain?

III

Whose is the gaze
Which peers through my eyes?
When I think I'm seeing,
Who keeps seeing
While I'm thinking?
What roads are followed
Not by my sad steps
But by the reality
Of my having steps?

Sometimes in the shadows
Of my room, when
Even in my own soul
I scarcely exist,
The Universe takes on
Another meaning in me:
It's a dull stain
Of consciousness smudging
My idea of things.

If the candles are lit,
Adding to the dim light
Coming from some lamp
From somewhere outside,
I'll vaguely wish
That there never be more
In the Universe and in Life
Than the obscure moment
I'm living right now:

A fast-flowing moment
Of a river always heading
Toward forgetting to be,
A mysterious space
Among desert spaces
Whose meaning is to have none
And to be nothing to nothing.
And thus time passes
Metaphysically.

IV

My anxieties tumble
Down a flight of stairs.
My desires swing
In the middle of a vertical garden.

The Mummy's position is absolutely exact.

Music in the distance,
Far off in the distance,
So that Life will pass
And gathering forget its gathering.

V

Why do things open up passageways for me?
They're so consciously still I'm afraid to pass through them.
I'm afraid that, once behind me, they'll take off their Masks.
But there are always things behind me.
I feel their non-eyes staring at me, and I shudder.
Without moving, the walls vibrate their message to me.
Without talking, the chairs speak to me.
The designs in the tablecloth have life: each one's an abyss.
Brightly smiling with visible invisible lips,
The door consciously opens:
My hand's merely the means by which it opens.

I'm being watched, but where from?
Which things that can't see are looking at me?
Who's in everything, peering?

The edges are staring at me.
The smooth walls really smile at me.

The sensation of being nothing but my spine.

The swords.

THE GODS ARE HAPPY

The gods are happy.
They live the calm life of roots.
Fate doesn't oppress their desires,
Or it oppresses but redeems
With immortal life.
The gods are not grieved
By shadows or other beings.
And, what's more, they don't exist.

      10 JULY 1920

IN THE LIGHT-FOOTED
MARCH OF HEAVY TIME

In the light-footed march of heavy time
Always the same way of living!
The same old habit of deceiving ourselves
By believing or disbelieving!

In the nimble flight of the dying hour,
Always the same disillusion
Of the same gaze cast from the top of the tower
Across the futile plain!

Nostalgia, hope—the name changes, only
The useless soul remains
In the poverty of thinking, today, of its wealth
Yesterday or tomorrow.

Always, always, in the fickle and constant
Lapse of endless time,
The same moment returns, unavailing and far
From what in myself I want!

Day or night, always the same (even when
Different) disillusioned gaze,
Cast from the tower of the ruined church
Across the futile plain!

1 JANUARY 1921

CHRISTMAS

A God is born. Others die. The Truth
Didn't come or go. The Error changed.
Now we have a new Eternity,
Less good than what passed away.

Blind science tills the useless earth.
Irrational faith revels in its ritual.
A new god is just a word.
Don't seek or believe. Everything's hidden.

BY THE MOONLIGHT, IN THE DISTANCE

By the moonlight, in the distance,
A sailboat on the river
Sails peacefully by.
What does it reveal?

I don't know, but my being
Feels suddenly strange,
And I dream without seeing
The dreams that I have.

What anguish engulfs me?
What love can't I explain?
It's the sailboat that passes
In the night that remains.

WATERFRONT

Blessed are those to whom is waved
A handkerchief of farewell!
They're happy: they feel sorrow . . .
I suffer life without sorrow.

I grieve to the core of my thinking,
And the grief comes from thinking.
I'm the orphan of a dream
Stranded by the outgoing tide . . .

Tired of fruitless agonies,
I take a full breath and feel
(On the dock I'll never leave)
The low-tide stench of the days.

SOME MUSIC

Some music, any music at all,
As long as it cures my soul
Of this uncertainty that longs
For some kind, any kind of calm.

Some music — a guitar, fiddle,
Accordion, or hurdy-gurdy . . .
A quick, improvised melody . . .
A dream without any riddle . . .

Something that life has no part in!
Fado, bolero, the frenzy
Of the dance that just ended . . .
Anything not to feel the heart!

I FEEL SORRY FOR THE STARS

I feel sorry for the stars
Which have shined for so long,
So long, so long . . .
I feel sorry for the stars.

Is there not a weariness
Felt by things,
By all things,
Such as we feel in our limbs?

A weariness of existing,
Of being,
Just of being,
Whether sad or happy . . .

Is there not, finally,
For all things that are,
Not just death
But some other finality?
Or a higher purpose,
Some kind of pardon?

I SEEM TO BE GROWING CALM

I seem to be growing calm.
Perhaps I'm about to die.
There's a new and gentle fatigue
Around all I wanted to want.

I'm surprised to find my soul
So resigned to feeling.
Suddenly I see a river
Shining in a grove.

And they are a real presence:
The river, light, and trees.

17 MARCH 1929

SLEEP

I'm so sleepy it hurts to think.
So sleepy. Sleeping is for man
What waking is for the animals.

It's to live life unconsciously,
The way animals live on life's surface.
It's to be, unawares, my profound being.

Perhaps I'm sleepy for having touched
The spot where I feel the animal I shunned,
And sleep is a memory I found.

I CONTEMPLATE THE SILENT POND

I contemplate the silent pond
Whose water is stirred by a breeze.
Am I thinking about everything,
Or has everything forgotten me?

The pond tells me nothing.
I cannot feel the breeze.
I don't know if I'm happy,
Or even if I want to be.

O hesitant smiling ripples
In the water which is sleeping,
Why did I make my only life
A life made only of dreams?

4 AUGUST 1930

LIKE A USELESSLY FULL GLASS

Like a uselessly full glass
Which no one lifts from the table,
My unsad heart overflows
With a sorrow not its own.

It acts out sorrowful dreams
Just to have to feel them
And thus be spared the grief
It pretended to be dreading.

Fiction on a stage not of boards,
Dressed up in tissue paper,
It mimics a dance of sorrows
So that nothing will occur.

19 AUGUST 1930

THE SUN SHINING OVER THE FIELD

The sun shining over the field
Perhaps could be the remedy . . .
I dislike those who like me;
To be loved is for me a tedium.

I want only the simple kiss
Given by light when it gleams,
And the impersonal, abstract love
Of fields when their flowers bloom.

The rest is people and soul
To complicate, talk, and see.
It robs me of dreams and my calm,
And is never what it seems.

21 AUGUST 1930

I DON'T KNOW HOW MANY SOULS I HAVE

I don't know how many souls I have.
I've changed at every moment.
I always feel like a stranger.
I've never seen or found myself.
From being so much, I have only soul.
A man who has soul has no calm.
A man who sees is just what he sees.
A man who feels is not who he is.

Attentive to what I am and see,
I become them and stop being I.
Each of my dreams and each desire
Belongs to whoever had it, not me.
I am my own landscape,
I watch myself journey—
Various, mobile, and alone.
Here where I am I can't feel myself.

That's why I read, as a stranger,
My being as if it were pages.
Not knowing what will come
And forgetting what has passed,
I note in the margin of my reading
What I thought I felt.
Rereading, I wonder: "Was that me?"
God knows, because he wrote it.

24 AUGUST 1930

THE SOUL
WITH BOUNDARIES

The soul with boundaries
Is for the deaf and blind;
I want to feel everything
In every possible way.

From the summit of being conscious,
I gaze at the earth and sky,
Looking at them with innocence:
Nothing I see is mine.

But I see them so intently
And am so dispersed in them
That every thought I think
Makes me into someone else.

Since every dispersed facet
Is another sliver of being,
I break my soul into pieces
And into various persons.

And if my very own soul
I see with a varying gaze,
How can I have anything
Definite to say?

If I think I belong to me,
I'm merely self-deceived.
I'm diverse and not my own,
Like sky and land and sea.

If all things are but slivers
Of the universal intelligence,
Then let me be my parts,
Scattered and divergent.

If from myself I'm absent
And whatever I feel is distant,
How did my soul come to have
An individual existence?

I've learned to adapt my self
To the world God has made.
His mode of being is different;
My being has different modes.

Thus I imitate God,
Who, when he made what is,
Took from it the infinite
And even its unity.

    24 AUGUST 1930

I'M SORRY
I DON'T RESPOND

I'm sorry I don't respond
But it isn't, after all, my fault
That I don't correspond
To the other you loved in me.

Each of us is many persons.
To me I'm who I think I am,
But others see me differently
And are equally mistaken.

Don't dream me into someone else
But leave me alone, in peace!
If I don't want to find myself,
Should I want others to find me?

26 AUGUST 1930

AUTOPSYCHOGRAPHY

The poet is a faker
Who's so good at his act
He even fakes the pain
Of pain he feels in fact.

And those who read his words
Will feel in what he wrote
Neither of the pains he has
But just the one they don't.

And so around its track
This thing called the heart winds,
A little clockwork train
To entertain our minds.

1 APRIL 1931

I DON'T KNOW HOW
TO BE TRULY SAD

I don't know how to be truly sad
Or how to be really happy.
No, I don't know how to be.
Might sincere souls be
Like me, without knowing it?

Before the lie of emotion
And the fiction of the soul,
I cherish the calm it gives me
To see flowers without reason
Flower without a heart.

But finally there is no difference.
As flowers flower without wanting to,
Without wanting to, people think.
What in flowers is florescence
In us is consciousness.

Later, for us as for them,
When Destiny decides it is time,
The feet of the gods will come
And trample all of us under.

Fine, but until they come
Let us still flower or think.

3 APRIL 1931

THE CLOUDS ARE DARK

The clouds are dark
But toward the south
A scrap of sky
Is sadly blue.

So too in the mind,
Which has no answer,
A scrap remembers
That the heart exists.

This scrap is what
We know as the truth
Of eternal beauty
Beyond what is.

5 APRIL 1931

LIKE AN ASTONISHING REMNANT

Like an astonishing remnant
From childhood, I still retain
Half my enthusiasm — mine
Because I had it back then.

At times I'm almost ashamed
Of believing so much in what I don't
Believe. It's a kind of dream
With reality in the middle.

False beauty round a speechless
Center, the sunflower speaks,
Yellow and astonished by the black
Center which is everything.

                                18 APRIL 1931

IF I THINK FOR MORE
THAN A MOMENT

If I think for more than a moment
Of my life that's passing by,
I am — to my thinking mind —
A cadaver waiting to die.

In a little while (the longest life
Amounts to a few short years),
I, with all I've had or missed,
With my delusions and my fears,

Will cease to have visible form
Here where the sun shines down,
And — dispersed and insensible,
Or else drunk with another dawn —

I suppose I will have lost
That warm and human contact
With the passing months and years,
With earth and the dreams it contains.

The sun may gild the face
Of the days, but soundless space
Reminds us it's just a façade:
In the night all things are erased.

1 MAY 1931

FROM THE MOUNTAIN COMES A SONG

From the mountain comes a song
Saying that however much
The soul may come to have,
It will always be unhappy.

The world is not its home,
And all that the world gives it
Is given as if to someone
Who'd rather not receive.

Is that what it says? I don't know.
There's music, no voice, at the window
Where I ponder my self, alone,
Like a shining star its glow.

                                       14 NOVEMBER 1931

THIS SPECIES OF MADNESS

This species of madness
Which isn't just cleverness
And which shines in the darkness
Of my muddled intelligence

Doesn't bring me happiness.
There is always, in the city,
Either clear or cloudy skies,
But in me I don't know what there is.

THE WIND IN THE
DARKNESS HOWLS

The wind in the darkness howls,
Its sound reaching ever farther.
The substance of my thought
Is that it cannot cease.

It seems the soul has a darkness
In which blows ever harder
A madness that derives
From wanting to understand.

The wind in the darkness rages,
Unable to free itself.
I'm a prisoner to my thought
As the wind is a prisoner to air.

23 MAY 1932

I HAVE IDEAS AND REASONS

I have ideas and reasons,
Know theories in all their parts,
And never reach the heart.

WITH A SMILE AND WITHOUT HASTE

With a smile and without haste
She gracefully breezed down the road,
And I, who feel with my head,
Immediately wrote the right poem.

The poem doesn't speak of her
Or of how, grown-up but girlish,
She vanished around the corner
Of a street whose corner is eternal.

The poem speaks of the sea;
It describes the surf, and sorrow.
Rereading it makes me remember
The implacable corner, or the water.

14 AUGUST 1932

OUTSIDE WHERE
THE TREES

Outside where the trees
Are rustling to a standstill
The only thing I see
Beyond them is the ocean.

It is intensely blue,
Flashing here and there,
And in its lazy wave
There is a sleepy sighing.

But neither I nor the ocean
Sleeps on this gentle day,
And it calms while it advances,
And I don't think and I'm thinking.

14 AUGUST 1932

I HEAR IN THE NIGHT ACROSS THE STREET

I hear in the night across the street
From a faraway neighboring tavern
An old and uncertain tune that makes
Me suddenly miss what I'd never missed.

Is the tune old? The guitar is old.
I can't say about the tune, can't say . . .
I feel the blood-pain but can't see the claw.
I feel, without crying, that I've cried already.

Whose past has this music brought to me?
Not mine or anyone's, it's just the past:
All the things that have already died
To me and to everyone, in the world gone by.

It's time, time that takes the life
Which cries, and I cry in the sad night.
It's grief, the ill-defined complaint
Of all that exists, because it exists.

14 AUGUST 1932

ALMOST ANONYMOUS YOU SMILE

Almost anonymous you smile,
And the sun gilds your hair.
Why is it that, to be happy,
We cannot know we are?

        23 SEPTEMBER 1932

THIS

They say I lie or feign
In all I write. Not true.
It's simply that I feel
Via the imagination.
The heart I never use.

All I dream or live,
Whatever fails or dies,
Is no more than a covering
Over some other thing
Where true beauty lies.

That's why I base my writings
On things that are remote,
Freed from my reality,
Serious about what isn't.
Feel? That's up to the reader!

THE DAY IS QUIET,
QUIET IS THE WIND

The day is quiet, quiet is the wind,
Quiet the sun, and quiet the sky.
If only this described my thoughts!
If only this described my I!

But between myself and the quiet glories
Of this clear sky and this air without me
Dreams and memories intervene . . .
This, I know, is how I'll always be!

The world is whatever is in us.
Everything exists because I exist.
Things are because we see them.
And this is everything, everything is this!

15 AUGUST 1933

THE SUN
RESTS UNMOVING

The sun rests unmoving
Over the waving wheat.
I don't know myself.
I'm forever deceived.

If I had succeeded
In not asking who I was,
I would have forgotten
How forgotten I am.

The wheat waves in the sun,
Always aloof and equal.
How the soul here is brief
With its good and evil!

                12 SEPTEMBER 1933

THE WASHWOMAN BEATS
THE LAUNDRY

The washwoman beats the laundry
Against the stone in the tank.
She sings because she sings and is sad
For she sings because she exists:
Thus she is also happy.

If I could do in verses
What she does with laundry,
Perhaps I would lose
My surfeit of fates.

Ah, the tremendous unity
Of beating laundry in reality,
Singing songs in whole or in part
Without any thought or reason!
But who will wash my heart?

15 SEPTEMBER 1933

TO TRAVEL!
TO CHANGE COUNTRIES

To travel! To change countries!
To be forever someone else,
With a soul that has no roots,
Living only off what it sees!

To belong not even to me!
To go forward, to follow after
The absence of any goal
And any desire to achieve it!

This is what I call travel.
But there's nothing in it of me
Besides my dream of the journey.
The rest is just land and sky.

                    20 SEPTEMBER 1933

THIS GREAT WAVERING BETWEEN

This great wavering between
Believing and not quite dis-
Believing troubles the heart
Weary of knowing nothing.

Estranged from what it knows
For not knowing what it is,
The heart only has one vital
Moment, the finding of faith—

The faith that all the stars
Know, for it is the spider
Whose web they weave, and it is
The life before everything.

5 MAY 1934

I HAVE IN ME
LIKE A HAZE

I have in me like a haze,
Which holds and which is nothing,
A nostalgia for nothing at all,
The desire for something vague.

I'm wrapped by it
As by a fog, and I see
The final star shining
Above the stub in my ashtray.

I smoked my life. How uncertain
All I saw or read! All
The world is a great open book
That smiles at me in an unknown tongue.

                                      16 JULY 1934

DREAMS, SYSTEMS, MYTHS, IDEALS

Dreams, systems, myths, ideals—
Like pieces of a torn sheet of paper . . .
I stare at the water lapping the wharf,
Yielding to it as to a just fate,
Watching the shreds with eyes that reveal
Only a vain, resigned disquietude.

What consolation can they give me?
Me, who no longer cries when troubled,
And who with solitary mind and heart
Remembers shadows, just shadows, shadow?
Me, in everything, always, in vain,
Tired even of the gods that don't exist . . .

I DIVIDE WHAT I KNOW

I divide what I know.
There's what I am
And what I've forgotten.
Between the two I go.

I'm not who I have in memory
Nor who is in me now.
If I think, I self-dismember.
If I believe, there is no end.

Better than all of this
Is to listen, in the foliage,
To the soft and certain breeze
Blowing through the leaves.

                10 SEPTEMBER 1934

THE CHILD THAT LAUGHS IN THE STREET

The child that laughs in the street,
The song one hears by chance,
The absurd picture, the naked statue,
Kindness without any limit —

All this exceeds the logic
Imposed on things by reason,
And it all has something of love,
Even if this love can't speak.

                    4 OCTOBER 1934

from
MESSAGE

PRINCE HENRY
THE NAVIGATOR

God wills, man dreams, the work is born.
God willed that the earth be one,
That the sea not divide but unite it.
Anointed by Him, you unveiled the foam,

And the white crest went from island to continent,
Like dawn to the world's end,
And suddenly the entire earth
Appeared, round, from out of the blue.

The One who anointed you made you Portuguese,
A sign to us of our pact with the sea.
The Sea was won, the Empire undone.
Lord, we still must win Portugal!

THE STONE PILLAR

The labor is great and man is small.
I, Diogo Cão, a navigator,
Left this pillar by the swarthy strand
And sailed onward.

The soul is divine and the work imperfect.
This pillar is a sign to the wind and skies
That I've done my part in this venture:
The rest only God can do.

And the five shields of this coat of arms
Teach the immense and possible ocean
That the sea with limits is for Greece or Rome:
The limitless sea is Portuguese.

And the Cross on high says that what's in my soul
And gives me this fever to navigate
Will only find in God's eternal calm
The forever sought-after port.

THE SEA MONSTER

The monster that lurks at the end of the sea
On a pitch-black night rose up in flight.
It flew around the ship three times,
Round and round, hissing strange sounds,
And said, "Who has dared enter
My secret caverns with these vast
Black ceilings at the world's end?"
And the man at the helm said as he trembled:
"The King Dom João the Second!"

"Whose are these sails I brush against,
And whose these keels I see and feel?"
Asked the monster that flew round the ship.
Three times it flew, horrid and huge:
"Who comes to do what only I can do,
Living where no one ever saw me,
Dripping with the dread of the depthless sea?"
And the man at the helm, trembling, said:
"The King Dom João the Second!"

Three times he raised his hands from the helm,
Three times the helm his hands again held,
And finally, trembling three times, he said,
"This helm is manned by more than my hand:
I am a Nation that covets your sea;
And despite the monster that frightens my soul,
Flying in this darkness at the world's end,
I hold this helm, for a higher force beckons:
The King Dom João the Second!"

EPITAPH OF BARTOLOMEU DIAS

Here on this small far beach lies buried
The Captain of the End, who rounded Terror.
The sea is the same, no more to shudder!
Atlas, he lifts the world high on his shoulder.

FERDINAND MAGELLAN

A bonfire lights up the valley.
A dance shakes the entire earth.
And huge, contorted shadows
In the valley's black clearings dart
Suddenly up the slopes
Until they are lost in the dark.

What is this dance that frightens night?
The Titans, the sons of Earth,
Are dancing the death of the seaman
Who hoped to be the first to reach
His arm all the way around her body
But now is buried on a far-off beach.

They dance without knowing that the daring
Dead soul still rules the fleet,
A bodiless wrist that steers the ships
Through the rest of the end of space.
Though absent, he can still circle
The entire earth with his embrace.

He raped the earth. But they don't
Know it, and dance in the waste;
And huge contorted shadows
Leap up the slopes until
They are lost in the far horizons
Beyond the silent hills.

PORTUGUESE SEA

O salty sea, so much of whose salt
Is Portugal's tears!
The mothers who wept for us to cross you!
All the sons who prayed in vain!
All the brides who never married
For you to be ours, O sea!

Was it worth doing? Everything's worth doing
When the soul is not small.
Whoever would go beyond the Cape
Must go beyond sorrow.
God placed danger and the abyss in the sea,
But he also made it heaven's mirror.

PRAYER

Lord, night has come and the soul is wretched.
So great was the storm and the will!
All we have left, in this hostile silence,
Is nostalgia and the universal sea.

But the flame that life created in us
Still smolders if there is still life.
Cold death has hidden it in ashes;
The hand of the wind can still raise it.

Give the breath, the breeze—a yearning or curse—
To revive the flame of effort.
Make us reconquer the Distance—of the sea
Or of another frontier we can possess!

NOTES TO THE INTRODUCTION AND THE POEMS

INTRODUCTION

The opening epigraph is found on p. 125 of the Carcanet Press edition of *The Book of Disquietude*, the same translation cited throughout. The line "What a poor hope that just hopes to exist!" is from a poem signed by Pessoa and dated 2 August 1933; the Caeiro poem beginning "A row of trees across the way" is from *The Keeper of Sheep*. All other quoted verses, except those originally written in English, are taken from poems in this anthology. It is commonly accepted, but probably not true, that Pessoa died from cirrhosis of the liver; the Portuguese physician Francisco Manuel da Fonseca Ferreira makes a convincing case (see the Bibliography for the reference to his book) for death from acute pancreatitis, a malady likewise attributable to Pessoa's excessive intake of alcohol.

It was in a bibliographical note for the December 1928 issue of *Presença*, a literary magazine published in Coimbra, that Pessoa dubbed his heteronymic enterprise a "drama in people instead of in acts." The best survey of this enterprise, beginning with the literary companions of Pessoa's childhood, has been made by Teresa Rita Lopes in her *Pessoa por Conhecer*, which identifies seventy-two fictional authors invented by Pessoa and examines more closely the "behind-the-scenes writing activity" lightly touched on here. The book's second volume transcribes Pessoa's note equating the "self-division of the I" to maturbation (p. 477) as well as the French essay on exhibitionism signed by Jean Seul (pp. 202–6).

"Pessoa & Co." is a term borrowed from the writings of Jorge de Sena. In a 19 November 1914 letter addressed to Armando Cortes-Rodrigues, Pessoa wrote that he felt compelled to work, against his own will, on *The Book of Disquietude*, while in a 13 January 1935 letter to Adolfo Casais Monteiro he characterized Bernardo Soares as a mutilation of his own personality. It was in an early undated text written in English that Pessoa called himself "a poet animated by philosophy."

The quotations from Pessoa's writings on Portugal, the Fifth Empire and Sebastianism are all taken from *Sobre Portugal*. His criticism of Camões for relying on established forms such as the Petrarchan sonnet was recorded in a "Random Note" signed by Álvaro de Campos and published in November 1935. Pessoa's description of Reis as "a Greek Horace who writes in Portuguese" appears in a 1924 letter written to an Englishman and published in *Pessoa Inédito* (p. 318).

CAEIRO

The Keeper of Sheep. According to Caeiro's fictional bio-bibliography, this sequence of forty-nine poems was written in 1911–12. In fact none were written until 1914, and some much later. Pessoa determined the order of the sequence but did not establish definitive versions for all the poems, the "final" manuscript containing a number of alternate words and phrases in the margins and between the lines. Virtually every posthumous edition, therefore, presents a slightly different text, except for the twenty-four poems that Pessoa himself published in periodicals.

The Shepherd in Love. Of the eight poems that belong to this group, Pessoa wrote the first two early on, the other six much later. The fictional date for all of them would presumably be 1913 or 1914, since Caeiro dies in 1915. According to the copious notes written by Reis and Campos about their Master, the experience of being in love obscured Caeiro's "initial clarity," his pure vision of Nature, but Campos affirms that the poems produced by the pastoralist in this period were "among the great love poems of the world, because they're love poems by virtue of being about love and not by virtue of being poems. The poet loved because he loved, and not because love exists."

Uncollected Poems. Many of these poems were supposedly written after Caeiro contracted the illness that led to his death when he was just twenty-six years old. Campos writes that "in the uncollected poems there is weariness.... Caeiro is Caeiro, but a Caeiro who's sick. Not always sick, but sometimes sick. He's the same but a bit alienated. This is particularly true in the middle poems of this third part of his work."

"It is night...." Pessoa left a typed copy of this poem, at the end of which he penciled the following line, perhaps intended as another verse: "It's only he who continues to exist."

Notes to the Poems

"That thing over there. . . ." This text appears on the same autograph as the poem preceding it and might have been intended as its second stanza.

"I can also make conjectures" Titled "The Next to the Last Poem" when published by Pessoa in 1931.

"This may be the last day of my life" The autograph bears the title "Last Poem," in English, and the parenthetical remark, in Portuguese: "Dictated by the poet on the day of his death."

REIS

"Others narrate with lyres or harps." Undated, but probably written around the same time as the two odes on the front side of the autograph, dated 10 December 1931. Though far out of place chronologically, it seemed a good choice for opening the section.

"Don't clap your hands before beauty." The autograph contains two verses in the margin that could be an unfinished stanza, though they seem extraneous: "Though our sterile life may stir,/ Aeolus unleashes his winds on us."

"Follow your destiny." Pessoa may have inadvertently written "Gods" in the fourth stanza instead of the lower-case "gods" found in the third and fifth stanzas, though he often resorted to the capitalized form. A passage from *The Book of Disquietude* (p. 55), dated 6 May 1930, sheds indirect light on his usage:

> Sometimes the mere rhythm of a sentence will require the Gods and not God; other times the two words "the Gods" will impose themselves so that I must verbally change universe; still other times what will matter are the needs of an inner rhyme, a switch in meter or a burst of emotion, and polytheism or monotheism will adjust accordingly. The Gods are contingent on style.

"The bird alights. . . ." Luiz Fagundes Duarte's authoritative edition of Reis's poetry has been followed for the reading (deciphering) of the words themselves, but I prefer the arrangement of the stanzas found in Silva Bélkior's edition. Duarte's transcription reverses the order of the first two stanzas and understands the final, line-shy stanza to be not a stanza at all but a revised version of the last three lines of the stanza before it. The manuscript evidence weighs in favor of this view, but the result—as I see it—does not result. Pessoa, since he did not cross out any of the verses in question, evidently still planned to work on the ending. There can therefore be no "right" reading. Some may prefer Duarte's version of the poem, with the last of its five (instead of six) stanzas translating as:

> *The gods who gave us this path*
> *Also gave us the flower to pluck.*
> *And perhaps we pluck with better love*
> *What we seek for the using.*

"Your dead gods tell me nothing. . . ." The words "way of being" in the fourth line correspond to a blank space Pessoa meant to fill in later but did not.

"Where there are roses we plant doubt." This and the following text are published as one ode in the two critical editions that exist for the poetry attributed to Reis, but the respective editors have arranged the verses in such radically different ways that not a single verse falls in the same position. After consulting the autograph, which consists of seven stanzas scrawled in the three corners of a typewritten sheet, my own judgment is that there are two odes, not one. That they employ the same strophic model is not so strange: the typewritten text on the autograph consists of three slightly older Reis odes (including "Not only wine but its oblivion I pour" and "How great a sadness and bitterness"), with one strophic pattern common to all three. If the seven handwritten stanzas are construed as one rather than two odes, then it should probably begin—based on manuscript evidence—with the dated group of three stanzas translated and published here as a second ode (the next one).

"As long as I feel the full breeze. . . ." See preceding note.

CAMPOS

"I study myself. . . ." This is the first of three sonnets probably written in 1915 but given fictional dates in accord with Campos's "biography" and poetic evolution, as described in the introduction to this section.

"Listen, Daisy. . . ." This is the third of the three sonnets just mentioned. Pessoa published it in 1922 under the title "An Already Old Sonnet."

Notes to the Poems

"Time's Passage." Pessoa left eight fragments (plus some isolated verses not presented here) of this incomplete poem. There are virtually no clues as to how—or whether—he would have assembled them. The translation follows the transcription found in Teresa Rita Lopes's edition of Campos's poetry. The fragments have been reordered, however, according to a dramatic logic (as far as this is possible) and without regard to chronology. Five dots (. . . . .) indicates passages left incomplete by the author. Blank spaces left between stanzas, where the author may have thought to add something at a later date, are not necessarily indicated. Dates, for those fragments that have them, are given in the notes that continue.

"To feel everything in every way. . . ." Dated 22 May 1916. Numerous lacunae. The various occurrences of "Whoooosssshhhh" were written as "Ho-ho-ho-ho-ho-ho-ho" in the original. This was used to represent a "wind sound," according to a note by Pessoa.

The original contains an illegible word after the comma in the fifth line of the stanza beginning "Pantheistic cavalcade."

The name Campbell in the twelfth line of the stanza beginning "Hail, hurrah" probably refers to Sir Malcolm Campbell (1885–1948), a celebrated car and boat racer. Although he achieved his greatest fame in the 1920s and 1930s for the various land speed records he set at Daytona Beach and the Bonneville Salt Flats, Campbell was already well known in the teens. After winning gold medals in the London–Edinburgh motorcycle trials in 1906, 1907, and 1908, he took briefly to flying airplanes and then began racing automobiles at Brooklands, England.

The final verse in the penultimate stanza ends with a comma in the original. The author left blank space between this stanza and the next.

"I carry inside my heart. . . ." Dated 22 May 1916.

"I fall full length into all of life. . . ." In the eighth verse the word "blade" has been inserted where in the original the author left a blank space.

"I'm held by nothing. . . ." Dated 10 April 1923.

"I walk on, nothing touches me. . . ." Written on stationery from the firm F. Pessoa, founded in 1917.

"To feel everything in every way. . . ." Undated, but typed on the same letterhead paper used for the first fragment.

"It was on one of my voyages." Lopes's edition of Campos's poetry regards this text as the first stanza of the poem that follows.

"Sometimes I meditate." Lopes, in her edition, may well be right in considering four lines found on the reverse side of the autograph to be the poem's continuation and closure. Translating and adding these, the poem would end:

> How tell what it's like to feel this?
> What's the soul of the existence of being?
>
> Ah, the awful mystery that the tiniest thing exists,
> For it's the awful mystery of there being anything at all,
> The awful mystery of there being . . .

"Birthday." When he published this poem in a magazine, Pessoa dated it 15 October 1929, Álvaro de Campos's "birthday." According to the autograph, Pessoa actually wrote it eight months later, on his own birthday.

PESSOA-HIMSELF

"Oblique Rain." The six poems published under this title in 1915 exemplify Pessoa's Intersectionist aesthetic, which may be broadly defined as the simultaneous experience and/or expression of disparate realities or disparate facets of the same reality—a species of Cubism taken beyond the visual plane. In a text written in English, Pessoa hailed Intersectionism as a practical method for achieving the artistic aim of Sensationism: "decomposition of reality into its psychic geometrical elements." Another text, in Portuguese, explains that "the Romantics tried to *join*. The intersectionists seek to *fuse*. Wagner wanted music + painting + poetry. We want music x painting x poetry." The poem translated here records the narrator's experience of a present-day orchestral concert intersected with a childhood memory of playing ball. Pessoa's biographer, João Gaspar Simões, speculates that the "whole theater . . . at my feet" of the fifth stanza refers to the fact that Fernando the toddler lived in an apartment that looked directly down on the Teatro de São Carlos, then Lisbon's most important opera and concert hall.

"The Mummy." Published in 1917 as the first poem of "Episodes," a projected sequence that did not materialize.

"The gods are happy." Attributed by several scholars to Ricardo Reis on the basis of an early manuscript version, in which the poem has a Reis-like stro-

Notes to the Poems

phic pattern and is designated as an epigram. But whatever may have been Pessoa's original intention, his final revised version of the poem has little in common with Reis. In Portuguese the poem rhymes (extremely rare in Reis), does not keep a strict meter or strophic scheme (equally rare), and was typewritten by Pessoa without the indentations typical for Reis. The poem was not attributed by Pessoa to Reis, and there is only a partial thematic resemblance to the classicist heteronym, who believed that the gods existed. Pessoa-himself usually did not.

"I don't know how many souls I have. . . ." A virtual paraphrase of this poem is found in *The Book of Disquietude* (p. 181):

> I've created various personalities within. I constantly create personalities. Each of my dreams, as soon as it begins to be dreamed, is immediately incarnated in another person, who is then the one dreaming it, and not I.
> To create, I've destroyed myself; I've so externalized myself on the inside that I don't exist on the inside except externally. I'm the living stage where various actors act out various plays.

Message. During the more than twenty years that it was a work in progress, Pessoa called this book *Portugal*, changing the title to *Mensagem* almost as it was going to press in 1934. In a letter written in January 1935, he agreed with a literary friend that this was not an ideal publishing debut (as things turned out, it was the sole book of Pessoa's Portuguese verse to be issued in his lifetime), since it showed only the "mystical nationalist" side of him and his work. The forty-four poems employ symbols and evoke mystery to endow factual and legendary events of Portuguese history with quasi-esoteric meaning, and nostalgia for the past is used to kindle a messianic hope for Portugal's future. Of course Portugal can and sometimes patently does stand for the universe, and also for Pessoa's own personal—or impersonal—condition, as in the book's final verses: "All is scattered, nothing is whole./ O Portugal, today you are fog . . . / It's time!" The poems translated here all come from the second part, "Portuguese Sea," and were originally published, with slight differences in the titles and texts, by a Lisbon-based magazine in 1922.

"The Stone Pillar." The practice of leaving stone pillars (called *padrões*) at prominent points discovered by the Portuguese began with Diogo Cão, the first navigator to reach present-day Gabon, the Congo, and Angola. The pillars were dated, engraved with the royal Portuguese coat of arms (which has five shields), and topped by a cross. A few pillars left by other navigators are still standing on their original sites. Cão, on his first voyage (1482–83), set up one pillar at the mouth of the Zaire River and another at the Cape of Santa Maria, in Angola. He erected two more pillars on his second voyage (1485–86), when he pushed farther south without ever reaching his goal: the southernmost tip of Africa.

"The Sea Monster." A retelling of Vasco da Gama's encounter at sea with Adamastor, the giant that personified the Cape of Good Hope (originally called Cape of Storms) in the fifth canto of Luís de Camões's *The Lusiads*.

"Epitaph of Bartolomeu Dias." The first to round the Cape of Good Hope, in 1488, Dias met his death not far from there in 1500. He was part of the fleet led by Pedro Álvares Cabral that accidentally discovered Brazil, after which the India-bound voyage cut back toward the tip of Africa, where the vessel carrying Dias was shipwrecked.

"Ferdinand Magellan." After discovering and traversing the strait that bears his name, Magellan was killed in the Philippines, but one of the ships in his fleet continued westward to arrive back at Spain, where the voyage had begun.

BIBLIOGRAPHY

SOURCES FOR THE POEMS

The Pessoa Archives, reference "E3" in the archives division of the National Library in Lisbon.
Lopes, Teresa Rita. *Pessoa por Conhecer*, vol. 2. Lisbon: Editorial Estampa, 1990.
Pessoa, Fernando. *Álvaro de Campos—Livro de Versos*, ed. Teresa Rita Lopes. Lisbon: Editorial Estampa, 1993.
———. *Obra Poética*, ed. Maria Aliete Galhoz. 7th ed. Rio de Janeiro: Editora Nova Aguilar, 1977.
———. *O manuscrito de O Guardador de Rebanhos de Alberto Caeiro*, ed. Ivo Castro. Lisbon: Publicações Dom Quixote, 1986.
———. *Poemas de Álvaro de Campos*, ed. Cleonice Berardinelli. Lisbon: Imprensa Nacional–Casa da Moeda, 1990.
———. *Poemas de Ricardo Reis*, ed. Luiz Fagundes Duarte. Lisbon: Imprensa Nacional–Casa da Moeda, 1994.
———. *Poemas Ingleses*, ed. João Dionísio. Lisbon: Imprensa Nacional–Casa da Moeda, 1993.
———. *Texto Crítico das Odes de Fernando Pessoa–Ricardo Reis*, ed. Silva Bélkior. Lisbon: Imprensa Nacional–Casa da Moeda, 1988.

SOURCES FOR PESSOA'S PROSE CITED IN THE ESSAY MATTER

Lopes, Teresa Rita. *Pessoa por Conhecer*, vol. 2. Lisbon: Editorial Estampa, 1990.
Pessoa, Fernando. *The Book of Disquietude*, tr. Richard Zenith. Manchester: Carcanet Press, 1991.

———. *Cartas de Amor de Fernando Pessoa*, ed. David Mourão-Ferreira. Lisbon: Edições Ática, 1978.
———. *Escritos Íntimos, Cartas e Páginas Autobiográficas*, ed. António Quadros. Lisbon: Publicações Europa-América, 1986.
———. *Fausto: Tragédia Subjectiva*, ed. Teresa Sobral Cunha. Lisbon: Editorial Presença, 1988. A smaller selection of fragments from Pessoa's unfinished Faust can be found in *Obra Poética*.
———. *O Marinheiro*. Can be found in various editions of Pessoa's works, including *Obra Poética*.
———. *Páginas de Doutrina Estética*, ed. Jorge de Sena. Lisbon: Editorial Inquérito, 1946.
———. *Páginas de Estética e de Teoria e Crítica Literárias*, eds. Georg Rudolf Lind and Jacinto do Prado Coelho. Lisbon: Edições Ática, 1967.
———. *Páginas Íntimas e de Auto-Interpretação*, eds. Georg Rudolf Lind and Jacinto do Prado Coelho. Lisbon: Edições Ática, 1966.
———. *Pessoa Inédito*, ed. Teresa Rita Lopes. Lisbon: Livros Horizontes, 1993.
———. *Sobre Portugal: Introdução ao Problema Nacional*, eds. Maria Isabel Rocheta, Maria Paula Morão, Joel Serrão. Lisbon: Edições Ática, 1978.
———. *Textos Filosóficos*, ed. António de Pina Coelho. 2 vols. Lisbon: Edições Ática, 1968.
———. *Ultimatum e Páginas de Sociologia Política*, eds. Maria Isabel Rocheta, Maria Paula Morão, Joel Serrão. Lisbon: Edições Ática, 1978.

MAIN BIOGRAPHICAL AND CRITICAL WORKS CONSULTED

Coelho, Jacinto do Prado. *Diversidade e Unidade em Fernando Pessoa*. 10th ed. Lisbon: Editorial Verbo, 1990.
Ferreira, Francisco Manuel da Fonseca. *O Hábito de Beber no Contexto Existencial e Poético de Fernando Pessoa*. Oporto: Laboratórios Bial, 1995.
Lopes, Teresa Rita. *Pessoa por Conhecer*, vol. 1. Lisbon: Editorial Estampa, 1990.
Sena, Jorge de. *Fernando Pessoa & Cia. Heterónima*. 2nd ed. Lisbon: Edições 70, 1984.
Simões, João Gaspar. *Vida e Obra de Fernando Pessoa*. 6th ed. Lisbon: Publicações Dom Quixote, 1991.